C000160507

CLWYD COUNTY COUNCIL
LIBRARY SERVICE

WITHDRAWN
FROM STOCK

44

# THE SHOOTING GALLERY

*By the same author*

THE SENATE OF LILLIPUT
HUMMINGBIRDS AND HYENAS
LOOKING DOWN ON MRS THATCHER

# THE
# SHOOTING
# GALLERY

*by*

*Edward Pearce*

HAMISH HAMILTON

London

GWASANAETH LLYFRGELL CLWYD

RHIF
DOSBARTH
CLASS NUMBER

320.941

RHIF COPI COPY No.
2731

RHIF LLYFRWERTHWR
BOOKSELLER CODE
AS

CLWYD LIBRARY SERVICE

**HAMISH HAMILTON LTD**

Published by the Penguin Group
27 Wrights Lane, London W8 5TZ, England
Viking Penguin Inc., 40 West 23rd Street, New York, New York 10010, USA
Penguin Books Australia Ltd, Ringwood, Victoria, Australia
Penguin Books Canada Ltd, 2801 John Street, Markham, Ontario, Canada L3R 1B4
Penguin Books (NZ) Ltd, 182–190 Wairau Road, Auckland 10, New Zealand

Penguin Books Ltd, Registered Offices: Harmondsworth, Middlesex, England

First published in Great Britain by Hamish Hamilton Ltd 1989

Copyright © Edward Pearce, 1989

10 9 8 7 6 5 4 3 2 1

All rights reserved. Without limiting the rights under copyright reserved above, no part of this publication may be reproduced, stored in or introduced into a retrieval system, or transmitted, in any form or by any means (electronic, mechanical, photocopying, recording or otherwise), without the prior written permission of both the copyright owner and the above publisher of this book

Filmset in Linotron Times
at The Spartan Press Ltd, Lymington, Hants
Printed in Great Britain

A CIP catalogue record for this book is available from the British Library

ISBN 0–241–12508–1

*For my mother*

# CONTENTS

# INTRODUCTION

For better or worse, any knowledge of Parliament I may have derives not from the Parliamentary Lobby, an institution drawn increasingly slim and haggard upon the rack of the politically motivated briefing, but from the Gallery. The Chamber of the Commons has many to disparage it, especially at a time when the Commons, in the present era of secure majorities and peremptory unamendable government, looks like the oldest conference centre in Britain.

For me it remains, even in bleak times, the wind tunnel of politics, the place where talent is tested. It is, in its judgement of men, the most sophisticated electoral filter anywhere available. For despite Mr Benn, politics is indeed about personalities in all their triviality and not about destiny or historical necessity. For that reason I value and write about political personalities. Those described here include obvious leading figures like Kenneth Baker and Robin Cook, but the book also concerns itself with conspicuous rebels and professional outsiders and especially with rising talents, seen a little or a long way off.

Deliberately, it makes no attempt to be comprehensive. For no single reason neither Nigel Lawson nor John Smith, both perversely admired, are here: perhaps because inclusion of the one would have enforced the presence of the other, but simply their status is clear and well enough established to compel no analysis. *A fortiori*, Margaret Thatcher and Neil Kinnock, both of whom I should like to write essays about, having been the subject of oceanic publicity do not desperately need further comment.

What I do offer is a scatter of interesting politicians, the great majority of them with the bulk of their political lives still to be fulfilled, people half known and worth knowing more about. However, many figures unlisted as chapters have a lively existence here, flitting in and out of the careers of characters discussed. Despite the aggressive title, not all these essays are compositions for firing squad and small orchestra. I have written with some admiration about potential leaders of their parties, with affection about trouble-makers, with derision for the too gruesomely aspiring and with a combination of amusement and amazement about yet other Parliamentarians.

Categorically, these are not potted biographies, they are essays about people. The reader who wants to know that the Honourable Member's father was called Ernest, that he was educated at Charterhouse, is a non-executive director of the Baal and Mammon Corporation, keeps Borzoi dogs and is a Wagnerian, will have to consult the standard references.

These essays are assessments and analyses, attempts to understand the people examined. The detailed facts are drawn upon but not recited. Above all, this is a subjective book, a view from the Gallery which says what it can about some of those noticed, liked and disliked, and it says why.

# CHAPTER 1

## *Paddy Ashdown*

Many things can be exceptional about a man without his being in himself remotely remarkable. This would be a cruel judgement to make on Paddy Ashdown but it is a temptation.

In fact nothing about the man I still compulsively think of as the Liberal leader justifies any but the most interim opinion. In banking terms Ashdown is unsecured, though in his own naval terminology he is not necessarily a loose cannon. We do not, except by speculation, have a firm or fixed view of the man. Life for the moment is all learning curve and the accompanying mistakes.

The exceptional thing about him is of course the office he holds, so suddenly and after an unprecedentedly short time in the House. He entered Parliament in 1983 at the same time as Tony Blair and Michael Howard. It is the measure of the political reserves in parties that Blair should be a new member of the Shadow Cabinet, considered an exceptional reward for brilliance, and Howard a Minister of State albeit an important one. Both are intellectually heavier metal than Ashdown, but Ashdown is leading his party.

His rise has its tragic side. It occurred in the aftermath of the long evisceration of the post-election dispute between the friends and enemies of David Owen. He is the replacement for an exhausted David Steel and, in at least one man's eyes, the usurper of the rightful place of Alan Beith. He is leader by reason of the rank and file, more influential inside the SLD than the Parliamentary party. In that group the high point of his esteem would be a sort of animated indifference.

For, above all else, this selection was predicated by the existence of David Owen. The Liberals and their successor party are united in one thing: their loathing of the Plymouth registrar. But, equally, they are fascinated by the Byronic flash of the man, what to Liberals and to the followers of Lord Jenkins is the meretricious daub of primitive colour which makes Owen striking. Accordingly, being men of instinct as well as principle, they sought a meretricious daub of personality of their own.

This of course was simple death to the long-standing Liberal crown prince. Alan Beith had been in Parliament since 1974, a year ahead of Ashdown's decision to join the Liberal party! He is intellectually substantial having been a lecturer, not at a polytechnic nor in the WEA, but at a university. He knows, if not like Mr Toad all there is to be knowed, rather more than most Liberal MPs and certainly more than the new Member for Yeovil.

But Mr Beith is dull. He *talks* like a university lecturer, he has glasses which he looks over and notes which he quotes from. The idea of his climbing hand over hand in the rigging of a sailing ship is as imaginable as it would be useful to the leader of a small party of moderate reform within the limits of the constitution. Not even the fact that, as his contribution to originality and irrelevance, he speaks Welsh and Danish did him much good. Ashdown speaks Malay and Dayak as well as having a degree in Chinese!

Now David Steel as Liberal leader, despite some serious mistakes, had been a good professional politician and, apart from insisting on riding horses around the boundaries of his border constituency, was without serious eccentricity or glamour. He was a politician's politician, ill at ease with upbeat rhetoric. Ashdown in his first month was promising to conquer both major parties.

In choosing the man they did, the battered SLD were copying Owen, abandoning sober caution and declaring themselves desperate. To give up Steel for Ashdown is like surrendering an annuity to take up roulette.

His career has a notable element of high-risk games of chance about it. The ways up for most politicians are secure enough. There are standard forms of employment: banking for the Tories, education for the camp of progress. Trade unionism abides if diminished, but ex-soldiers are not the bristling cohort they were.

Ashdown had in the early part of his life a career which could be called brilliant. Highly creditable service, so far as can be discerned, in the Special Boat Service, a force of élite garotters, managed to incorporate a service-sponsored university course in Hong Kong. The degree (in Chinese) was a First, something which tends to stop the phrase 'lightweight' as it leaves the tongue. In 1972, at the age of thirty-one, he left the Marines for a diplomatic posting; within two years he was First Secretary to the UK Mission to the UN at Geneva. By the end of the decade he was selling sheepskin coats in the West of England, having made what he himself called 'a crazy, irresponsible and naïve decision' to put everything into a Liberal candidacy for a seat in which the Liberals at that time came third.

If Paddy Ashdown sometimes sounds like a naïve impossibilist in his very Irish promise to fight (and beat) all the other parties, the sequential events of his career make such grandiloquence seem quite restrained. Anyone who can go from Marine officer to fast-lane diplomat, to salesman, to unemployed, to salesman again, to MP, to party leader will view the rules of inching caution differently.

There is about Ashdown something so mercurial and uncertain that one is wise to avoid either dismissal or exaltation. Obviously he is very intelligent and as obviously naïve and inexpert at the political game. He has been a member of a political party for only fourteen years and in the Commons for six. He has a gift of personality and positively inspirational traits or he would not have swung around a seat which apart from being situated in the hopeful West was nowhere identified as a serious Liberal prospect. Fools sometimes win seats freakishly but usually in by-elections; the notably dim Bill Pitt comes to mind. But fools do not turn safe Tory seats around across seven years (first selected 1976) to take them at the second general election. Not even dazzling personalities do that. There has to be a phenomenal measure of application, single-purposed ambition and a real organisational talent. As gifted, amusing and endearing a personality as Richard Holme remains perennially baulked short of the line in impercipient Cheltenham.

In another personality the lunch-despising, road-training iron-stomached Ashdown could, with his fierce purpose, be a very great pain. As it is, he has the full quota of obsessiveness which marks the true serious politician. But he is not remotely dislikeable. Not to onlookers that is. His ratings in the Parliamentary party are low, but that may involve resentment at the disturbance of a grouping which is distinctly cosy and whose collective blood courses slow and thin. But the Ashdown style to meet and talk with is disarming. Perhaps there are meretricious aspects to the charm. He *is* Irish, born between the confessions, diligent with the Prods, cute with the Micks. 'Paddy' is a nickname, real name Jeremy for heaven's sake, acquired at Bedford School when he had an accent to lose. There is a touch perhaps of the Phineas Finns, though Trollope's Irish adventurer always comes over as a middle-aged bore in training. The clever, amusing Irishman comes from nowhere, blazes in the sky, takes huge risks, making resentful enemies who hope he will be a passing phenomenon, but also delighting and charming people by avoiding the stolid norm of English politics. It is one of life's pleasing ironies that during the early troubles Captain Ashdown should have been involved in the arrest of just such a man, John Hume of Derry. The instinct to gamble has something to do with life in England being slightly unreal, a handful of casino chips to be used enterprisingly.

Ashdown's intellectual course rather reflects the instability of the rest of his career. Zimri-like, he has seemed everything by turns and nothing long. His years of hard work in Somerset meant that he came to Parliament already very well known to the national Liberal party. The Liberal conference of that year was remarkable for the immediate take-up of Ashdown paper by the activist market. There was the unforgettable mimeographed sheet put out by the forgotten if unforgettable Young Liberals, marking the cards of all the MPs (they truly hated Stephen Ross, the Whip). Of Paddy Ashdown it remarked prophetically, 'Megastar'.

It was of course not remotely far-sighted. The Young Liberals, a witless collection of Trotskyite rejects and junior bores, were taken with a single fact. Ashdown could pass with the light behind him for a unilateralist, though he was quite sharp enough to keep his views blurred and ambiguous. This, in a party kept up to the realistic anti-neutralist mark by just such sensible men as Stephen Ross, was a joy to them. To have something like the correct, idealistic line expressed by someone youthful and attractive constituted an instant condition of megastardom. I have recollections a year or so later of Mr Ashdown at an international conference chastely locked in earnest conversation with the then chairman of CND, the nice and dedicated Mrs Ruddock, who looked like Father D'Arcy securing a well-connected soul for the faith. Yet, by the time we went to Harrogate a couple of years later, another very prominent Liberal remarked with only the permissible measure of malice: 'We are *Major* Ashdown now and all this talk about a soft line on defence is totally wrong; we are *dedicated* to nukes.' You could credit the creation of Paddy Climbdown to opportunism – a swift run-in with the disarmers making for heavy exposure, the conversion rendering him a more valuable catch for the Alliance establishment. More realistically, there is an innocent explanation. The existence of the Alliance meant exposure to the SDP element. And the SDP, however much they hated one another (an old tradition brought from the Labour party), were clear and united about one thing: our nukes good, no nukes bad. Exposure on this topic to Owen or Jenkins would have constituted a rapid education out of innocent optimism.

It is in Ashdown's style to say things which have to be retracted later. His position on deals with other parties has gone through a sea-change in the time it would take to cross a small pond. In politics he starts with a general strategy and no detailed tactics. He believes sincerely enough in the party god but looks on its theology as a supermarket.

It has been argued that his response to the Richmond by-election and the disconcertingly good performance of the SDP candidate Michael Potter was that of a soldier: we are enfiladed, make a retreat, orderly or otherwise. That his sudden conversion to talks with the Owen faction went counter to his advisers and party and looked more than a little ridiculous didn't alter the fact that getting out of the suicide pact, of fighting every seat against one another to the joy of the Conservatives, was something to be commended. Given the obsessive inter-party hatreds of two factions (based more upon personality and vicarious identification with élite participants in vendetta), Ashdown is as relaxed as he is because of being less identified with the ancient enmity than the older hands. There is no Owen-Ashdown quarrel to compete with the modest Owen-Steel tiff and the towering Owen-Jenkins hate match. The course of good sense might involve disregarding the preoccupations of colleagues, a course of therapeutic betrayal worth entertaining.

However, the subject must not be given credit for getting things right by error. His charge into instant conciliation after Richmond was the right thing far too quickly and too public. Like many Ashdown moves, it was amateurish, accepting a defeat as a defeat with inexcusable candour instead of laying a finger to the side of the nose in the approved, mystifying way of the regulars on late-night postmortems. Ashdown will succeed, if he does succeed, only with the electorate. His standing with the Commons is not big. Kenneth Baker for the Conservatives left the usual bland civility of his public style to savage him for his performance as a pertinacious but fuzzy member of the committee on the Education bill. A majority of his own party would have preferred someone else. A successful parade before a Jenkins houseparty at East Hendred (civil service style) in order to be pronounced satisfactory is no substitute for real support. Mr Beith sits in a prolonged resentful sulk with Mr Alexander Carlile appointing himself unofficial censor. All of this can of course be put down to the inherent childishness of the Liberals. There is something pathetic about that party whatever its name. If Ashdown is an amateur precipitately chosen, what sort of party is so bald of talent, so crashingly ill-equipped for serious political conflict that Ashdown remained the best choice? He is leader because Steel is worn down by the petty quarrels, because MacLennan made a major strategic blunder, because Jenkins lost his seat, because Williams couldn't get in at another, because Owen has fought his peers to a standstill and because Beith is as exciting as a naked lettuce.

Fortunately for him, he has a clean slate with the voters. He has also a manner perfectly adjusted to wooing a mass audience. The silly boyish charm which elevated the slight talents and idle character of John Kennedy to irrational heights of secular sainthood are there, along with the inexperience. And if Ashdown is not altogether a proper professional politician that is no slight recommendation to an electorate familiar with the real thing.

The leader of the SLD has come an impressive way. He has a team of speechwriters and advisers, in Richard Holme and Tom MacNally, which has put in enough man hours at the vote-face of professional politics and which has a healthy aversion to flashy gestures. More than most leaders, Ashdown will be responsive to those around him. He has chosen quite well and he is shrewdly aware of his own limitations, even more so of the things he doesn't know. No one should underestimate his ability to work and learn. The example of his candidacy and its hopeless prospects should not be ignored. Ashdown is totally serious about ambition and oddly humble about his own deficiencies. Humility can come before a rise.

In the Commons he is neither scoring a brilliant success nor coming unglued. His attack on Lord Chalfont, hysterical appointment to the IBA and a sub-contracting spook, reduced Mrs Thatcher to a satisfactorily juddering rage. His stand on the Hong Kong Chinese and citizenship was splendidly big-minded. He is soft-spoken in debate, unusually gentle and, if anything, his Parliamentary manner is slowly improving. The idea that in some way the SLD have chosen a duffer should be violently resisted. Naïve sometimes, rash absolutely, a gambler, and too ready to concede the naked condition of those without clothes, he is a defiance of conventional politics. But he is very intelligent, attractive, uncluttered by the ancient obsessions of his party. What doesn't work is likely to be junked and he is no part of the coffee-morning-to-sort-out-the-galaxy tradition of Liberalism.

Making prophecies about third-party politics is a dubious undertaking, especially with Labour trembling at the margins of renewal, and Ashdown's high-IQ cackhandedness could lead anywhere. But, if pressed, I would incline to optimism about him.

A man who can survive guerrilla war in Sarawak must have a chance even with the Liberals.

# CHAPTER 2

# Diane Abbott

How easy it is to agree with the left in their contempt for 'tokenism', the putting forward of one or more nominated representatives of minority groups to prove good humour by quotient.

It is a failing of editors that they expect black and female representation in all collections of notables without reference to how interesting or useful are the blacks and women concerned. Having see in a York cakeshop gingerbread men nervously retailed as 'ginger persons', I feel slightly persecuted by the ubiquity of cringing, to-the-letter *égalité*.

However, the beauty of Miss Diane Abbott is that she combines both fashionable conditions, allowing two statutory requirements to be met with the minimum of inconvenience. And indeed she makes a very tolerable ginger person. She is also a quite interesting anachronism. At thirty-six Miss Abbott is an ambulating lexicon of the student clichés of the sixties and the municipal baby-Trot activism of the seventies.

Another feature of Diane Abbott is outstanding failure. Along with George Galloway and Ken Livingstone, she is someone from whom great if controversial impact had been expected. In the case of all three, the contribution has been that of a battery conclusively and irretrievably flat. She is accused by her constituency, Hackney, of laziness. Notoriously, left-wing Labour constituency parties make extravagant attacks upon their own members. For my part, I have never noticed any indications of slackness or laziness on the side of Miss Abbott. Her ineffectiveness as a Member has never seemed to derive from lack of earnest application.

But perhaps what they really mean is that they expected her to be a force in politics, someone they would be reading about regularly in the press. Away from established frontbench positions, that is not lightly achieved except by the 'characters' of Parliament, the professionally outrageous, the good-for-a-quote toilers at the trivia-face of the school of the late Sir Gerald Nabarro.

There may be some shared insensibility between Sir Gerald, who once referred to a gentleman from the New Commonwealth as 'a buck nigger' and Miss Abbott who denounced Britain as one of the most fundamentally racist nations on earth. There is a shared silliness here which should delight the news agencies looking for weekend padding. But she has never been willing to strive at the publicity trade. Abbott in Parliament has been a few tantrums, one or two resentful self-pitying speeches and not much more.

She is of course a victim three times over, of her race, of her sex and of her boring preoccupation with both conditions. 'Look at me, I'm a black woman' is an interesting topic for features editors anxious for easy obvious copy. But it evades the need in public figures to be inherently and personally interesting and to stay interesting after early characteristics have lost their shine. Being black and a woman if you are otherwise tiresome and boring quickly comes to look like a double side-order of gimmick.

Far and away the most useful thing Abbott could do would be to take her colour and sex lightly and develop other interests. Theoretically she should be capable of something. She had decent academic attainment: four 'A' levels and ten 'O' levels and a degree from Cambridge. But frankly it doesn't show. The speeches are sloppy and shapeless, the words chosen are heavy with jargon when they are not tedious with cliché. She is unlucky in her choice of male acquaintance. Friendship with the most lamentable, humourless and uncharming of all Trot hurdy-gurdy grinders – the open-necked, bearded, word-pulping, fist-clenching failed atrocity, Jeremy Corbyn – did nothing for her.

She has been exploited and encouraged to exploit herself, treating black skin and a different hormone structure as virgin seams of limitless self-comfort, a means of being permanently the object of sympathy while violently rejecting it, a state of continuing autistic revolution, very gratifying, though with diminishing returns even to the exponent, and for everyone else useless egotistical frothblowing! It is spoiled selfishness masquerading as a high tone.

The ideal black MP will be someone capable of good to high personal achievements in the ordinary legitimate ambitions of politics, able to work hard at subjects with no racial connotation; a hard grasp of transport economics suggests itself, as do housing conditions. He will not talk overtly about race but will maintain his fidelities; he will be listened to and regarded in mainstream politics neither more nor less than a high-achieving, hard working white politician; and it will not matter or be better if he is she.

Despite a few lingering spots of old-style rhetoric from his municipal adventure playground days, Paul Boateng is showing every prospect of being very much like this. My Conservative friends assure me that John Taylor, a barrister from the Midlands, will be in every way as good in that interest (and if the Tories don't wish to validate Miss Abbott's view of 'racist Britain' they will help him to a seat with great urgency).

But the whole point of such activity is that it integrates minorities into being part of and as good as the rest of us. There is quite enough bad racial feeling around but hypocrisy, that essentially benign influence, will have none of it; and where hypocrisy leads sincere conviction follows the fashion. In the seeing-off of racial prejudice, hypocrisy is joined by capitalism (which has better ways of measuring things) and by ambition. It isn't necessary for Malcolm Rifkind to talk about his Jewishness, though some anti-Semitic feeling still skulks around. His first-rate abilities and wholly agreeable personality, together with his rapid acceleration to high and rising positions, make their own point.

It will not do to argue how much further back Caribbean-rooted people are on the winding staircase. Despite the example of Disraeli, a Christian from the age of thirteen, Jewish MPs used to be few and in a less kindly age somewhat sniffed at. Twenty-five years ago there were only two Jewish Tories in the House – Keith Joseph and Henry D'Avigdor

Goldsmid, both baronets! The ascent was not quick, indeed it was something of a Smilesian affair, patient merit battling its way up. And it is not an accident that Mrs Thatcher regularly runs a Cabinet one-fifth Jewish, just as she will welcome black Conservative MPs with pleasure. Ultimately it is the rigorous meritocrat, the work-ethic believer in the rewards of striving, who most deeply rejects racial assumptions.

Diane Abbott, who shares with Thatcher only the tendency to run people over with high-speed discourse and the perfect absence of any sense of humour, will never understand this, though she has on paper, at least, the talent to do real and substantial things for black self-respect. The exercise is too slow and gradual, involves too much tedious application to the steady joggery of political business. And sadly Miss Abbott isn't at present grown-up enough for the real task. She has taken the soft option, the public orphan spot under the lights, and, however benign her intentions, she has left herself a futile rant which does nothing for real deprived black people at the bottom of the sheer-sloped social well in Brixton or Hackney.

To be of any use to them she has to think about someone other than the self she so noisily cherishes. Were she to shut up, grow up, put her head down and shed the childish leftism which talks about instituting 'our own machinery of class rule', Diane Abbott could become useful and worthwhile. She could win respect for black people. At present she frankly retards them, preaching the sort of millennium which is the preoccupation of those without real expectations. Patience for the little increments has been beyond her.

Miss Abbott has time to change, time to become useful. At thirty-six, she can be excused the hungover adolescence of her views, views deriving from fatuous but manipulative people like Jeremy Corbyn. She doesn't have to be a public orphan, an attention-demanding statutory black woman. And, especially, she doesn't have to be as self-defeatingly angry. The comfortable chippiness which rejects all improvement as meliorism, and all goodwill as a front, was after all a characteristic correct mood for downtrodden proletarians among old hard Marxists. A legion of rising manual workers on Norman Tebbit's social – if not necessarily political – wavelength have made a nonsense of this. It will be a poor and sad thing for black people in Britain, who indeed face every sort of travail, to become a sort of quarry for post-Marxists deprived of proletarians.

The problems of the poorest, least fulfilled part of the population with the heaviest unemployment and fewest realistic expectations should very deeply concern us. But the kin of such people, acting as their spokesmen, must look at the question of counter-productivity. Otherwise they fulfil the very stereotypes which constitute racist expectations and become happy with their own unhappiness – the most sterile and melancholy of all human conditions. It will be a pleasure then to praise Diane Abbott – when she deserves it.

# CHAPTER 3

## Kenneth Baker

Politicians, unlike footballers, are long maturing and often at their best after a heavy marination in events. Starting early as a bright, over-keen face in a by-election, Kenneth Baker has become almost effortlessly senior and respected. We are watching him now in the key period of his life and in the job which will matter most. He is, without messing about, a potential Prime Minister – not one of this Prime Minister's choosing, but if he can avoid gratuitous self-injury she seems bent upon his inadvertent advancement.

It is a secret denied to none that Mrs Thatcher has wanted the next Prime Minister to be Mr Cecil Parkinson. It is no more controversial to say that under no imaginable circumstances will the Parliamentary Conservative party advance Mr Parkinson into the Prime Ministership. As the Mikado observes about the execution of Nanki-Poo, 'It's very unfair but there you are.' Mr Parkinson, the only credible right-winger near the top, is esteemed by the lady to a degree not attempted by his colleagues.

The implications of this for Baker are enormous. The jumping-off post is the Treasury. It is the house next door; there is ample opportunity for special relationships with the Premier, and it is, beyond the dreams of Defence and Agriculture, on camera. It has been part of the charm of Nigel Lawson for his colleagues that despite conceit, contempt for lesser minds and an interesting trade deficit, he is delightfully and candidly free of all ambition to succeed Mrs Thatcher. Given that, of those occupying the other senior posts, Mr Hurd is not now running in the race and Sir Geoffrey has at most twelve months of papability left before seniority embraces him for ever, Baker, born in 1934 and long occupying the high-profile office of Education Secretary before taking up the chairmanship, is entitled to smile quietly.

The ability of Mr Baker to get exactly the right job at the right time is a delicious asset, a form of luck which may imply a lot about his future. Yet his mere survival under a leader whose gift for tolerance and forgiveness is hardly up to Plantagenet standards is remarkable enough. Baker was not merely a protégé of Edward Heath, he was on the record saying bitter things about Margaret Thatcher after her accession, which he early regarded as a Gothic interlude. Cheekiness was pushed as far as the address responding to the Queen's speech when he spoke of 'treading the narrow path between sycophancy and rebellion'. To revert to Gilbert for a moment, nothing better than a chippy-chippy chopper and a big black block might have been expected.

But the early Thatcher was unsure of her survival, her place in the cosmos or indeed herself, and jobs were offered (they had to be) to people who were not remotely one of us. It was Baker's great wisdom to identify a hole in the market, high technology, and effectively to volunteer himself into it. The glory of high technology is that no one, with the exception of the more obscurantist trade unionists, is actually against it. If a promising politician should grow learned and concerned – if that is the expression – about integrated circuits, no one will resent the fact. The field of embittered political controversy about integrated circuits is limited.

By sending Mrs Thatcher a memorandum and demonstrating himself very proficient in high technology, Baker succeeded in taking the heat off. It took him rather longer than his merits deserved to make the Cabinet but less long than expected from so evident a non-Thatcherite. For a time he was run in tandem with Norman Tebbit as joint Minister of State in Trade.

They make an instructive comparison, in that neither has any quarterings on his escutcheon; both owe advancement to the application of simple intelligence, but Tebbit, despite the wit and style, was always stalked by resentments and indeed restored to the Commons a tradition of unarmed combat not seen since before Baldwin began the long process of soothing it. Baker, by contrast, could have been ADC to Baldwin. His instinct is to rub along with Labour opponents; he had an excellent relationship with his immediate opponent, Jack Straw – another cerebral, courteous politician. The only recent visible display of active dislike for an opponent from Baker was that sudden mugging of Mr Ashdown, leader of the SLD. Behind that lay a certain contempt for what he saw as Ashdown's opportunistic garnering of ideas from advisers as he went along without – in Baker's view – actually understanding them. But the basic Baker approach to politics is that it is both profitable and pleasant to be nice to people.

Part of the interesting distinction from Norman Tebbit is that, though both are of an age and though both lack social connnection, there is a generation of embourgeoisment between them. Baker's grandfather was a docker (and a strike leader like Mr Speaker Weatherill's father) but his father was a civil servant and Baker, starting at grammar school in Lancashire, managed to finish by way of St Paul's and Magdalen, Oxford; Tebbit's father was a shop assistant and he himself left school at sixteen. If Baker is more good-natured, he has more to be good-natured about.

Even in politics he is blessed with splendid luck. Quite the best thing to happen to him was the rise of Kenneth Livingstone. Nowadays, with Mr Livingstone shuffling along the cluttered margins of politics with his 'Homeless' placard and his plastic ice-cream box for contributions, the public forgets that he was once the terror of the earth. The status of Livingstone in the mid-eighties was of the sharp axehead of a menacing and dynamic left which commanded London borough and constituency politics and would, in due course, command the earth.

He had driven out the elected Leader of the GLC, Andrew Mackintosh, in a mid-morning *putsch*, he had introduced an expensive but popular pricing régime on to the Underground, he had instituted a brilliant political advertising campaign on the buses (and the rates), he was best buddies with Sinn Fein but greeted the Queen at the opening of the Thames Barrage with the sort of flair not seen since Walter Raleigh. He was also taking on and spitting out Conservative politicians like apple pips in any debate on the future of the GLC. One of those so expectorated was the Environment Secretary, Patrick Jenkin, a man of club-footed ineptitude yoked with unwise ambition.

But it was Margaret Thatcher who was truly exalting Mr Livingstone. It was her undemocratic impulse to reduce London local government to the condition of Carthage which, as it were, put Livingstone in the right. There were plenty of Conservatives (in the GLC itself and more import- ant in the House of Lords) who took affront at the destruction of a well-liked institution merely because it was in leftwing opposition hands. It was they who would actually vote down the GLC abolition bill first time round while the wretched Jenkin sat on the steps of the throne, like Charles I trying to get Parliament to obey him (and with a very similar life expectancy to that monarch).

The defeat of the bill was combined with a series of encounters on TV and other public platforms between Livingstone and Tory politicians, in which he took them elegantly apart. Having grossly underrated him, the Tories, for whom panic and arrogance uneasily rotate, elevated the People's Kenneth into a sort of monster. The bandit Mamone, described by Norman Douglas in his *Old Calabria* wearing at his belt a number of dripping hearts extracted from interlocutors with no further need for them, upon one of which he would occasionally, as with a lemon, give a pull, exactly described the Conservative view of Kenneth Living- stone.

It was the great glory of Baker that he was appointed as nominal deputy (still Minister of State) to Jenkin, now in the terminal ward of politics. One thing was certain and could be guaranteed. No House of Lords will throw out a piece of legislation, not even one directed at a cull of the population, if it is introduced a second time. Their Lordships, a self- conscious if cherished anachronism, are into the art of the possible deeper than Fabius Cunctator. *They* knew, Baker

knew, probably even Jenkin knew (though that is speculation) that they would pass the second GLC Bill. The glory
came to Baker rather in the way of a TV dinner, foil-
wrapped and wanting only heating in a moderate oven.

What was not guaranteed – and the point at which Baker
came off the chorus line and into the cast – was that he
would go into public debate with Livingstone and emerge
not just uneviscerated but marginally ahead on points.
Baker is an intelligent and pleasant debater, not easily
flustered, not given to the exaggerated rhetoric which Livingstone had enjoyed puncturing. He was aware by then of
the weakness of the charge of extravagance if aimed at the
bizarre sidelines of the Greater London Council. Lesbian
day centres are not popular but they are peanuts to the rates
bill. And though Livingstone is good in debate he is, in
the manner of Grendel, not actually invincible. Baker's
strength is that, unusually for the Tories, he understands
and likes words. He is not one of those accountants who
have taken up politics; he is a proper, old-fashioned, literate, articulate politician. There aren't very many in his
party. Even so, in the climate of the time it was notably
brave to take on the demon king and skilful to come out
even or better.

Now we know that the Livingstone reputation for dreadful
menace was merely so much kindling used by Mrs Thatcher
in her purpose of putting local government generally, and
the London sort in particular, to the stake. She has already
ruled twice as long as Mary Stuart, but to the left and the
municipalities it seems longer. The role of Baker was to do
her bidding and destroy what she wanted destroyed. It was a
conflict between hard right and hard left into which the
ambitious soft right – like our protagonist – were necessarily
sucked. He who serves an autocrat will emerge a henchman.

The irony of the politics of the last ten years is almost
encapsulated in the GLC debate. Was the left immensely
powerful and was it put to rout by heroes? Or was it never
more than a lath-and-plaster prop, a *paravento* past reason
hated and past reason feared? And, if one reputation for

invincibility was so frail, how many lines of bricks sustain the great ones of the present?

Nevertheless, from this encounter Baker emerged as a major political force, a dragon slayer. He did so through a combination of courage and luck which attaches only to generals who win wars. His luck was to hold at the Department of Education. Whereas at Environment he had inherited a *chie-en-lit* from a disastrous Minister, he took over from Keith Joseph a historically dismal state of affairs which that excellent mind had identified and focused but not assaulted. Again he came in at a happy moment.

The reputation of the teachers' unions as a producers' ring had been fearsomely outmatched only by the miners and farmers in getting their own way and sitting on Ministers' heads. But if you apply tight money long enough to a salaried profession it is possible to obtain submission almost as readily as flight from that sort of employment. In a better world, reform of education would have been won much earlier and with the profession happier and better paid than it is. A victory among the debris of morale is what is possible.

As Education Secretary, Baker will be remembered for facing up to issues. (For a soft-spoken literary sort of chap he is, in his quiet way, remarkably combative.) He will be on record as the bringer-in of a central curricular requirement hard-core education as it were, and for an opting-out scheme less his own than the wish of the Prime Minister and her henchman, Professor Brian Griffiths, a professor of sorts in a university of sorts and a chum of God's, who supplies the hard ideology. It will be a very long time before any judgement can be formed on the wisdom of this application of the market. But politically everything is working fairly smoothly – the teaching profession is under assault in the middle of a buyers' market. This is not a state of affairs enjoyed by producers.

Baker has adapted and survived and in the process has sometimes done things which his own temperament would have guided him against. The abolition of the ILEA for example was pure Thatcher. That organisation, in its high irresponsible, leftwing days, had made enough enemies, but in the hands of the rational, conciliatory Neil Fletcher it was finding its way. Destruction actually handed more power to the very leftwing boroughs and *their* education committees which most upset the Tories. But to work for Thatcher is sometimes to become the prisoner of liquid rage. Ministers must temper the wind to their own necks.

The immediate pressure came from Tebbit and Heseltine, but there was not much doubt who was looking on and taking sides. If one praises this Secretary of State for being a proper realistic, cynical, genial politician, there is no point in expecting heroic stands against the lady when she is in her Arthur Scargill mood. But Baker is also the most literate and cultivated figure in a government in which accountantly virtues are esteemed, words treated as potential subversives and culture as a dubious abstraction with links to society (which is known not to exist). Baker is an unaffected, old-fashioned bookman, a reader, cherisher and collector of the things and, with his anthologies, something of a trainee Palgrave. His great triumph, the core curriculum, has nothing to do with the divisions of wet and dry. It is part of a general revulsion in favour of old-fashioned solid education, of an exasperation at producers' education and its unlettered consequences.

Interestingly, Jack Straw, Labour's Education spokesman, was highly discriminating in his opposition. The sense that things were bad and that a tightening and hardening of education had to come was formidable. Baker was able at Education to do things which went down well with the generality of his party. And of course he had gorgeous enemies. When Brent Education Commitee began the persecution of a conscientious and blameless teacher, Mrs Maureen McGoldrick – extremely popular with black children and parents – as 'a racist' (an instance of ethno-McCarthyism at its ranting worst), it was Ken Baker's pleasant duty to protect her. There is, incidentally, something near enough to tragic in the way genuine bigots on the London councils have worked hand in hand with the prejudices of the Prime Minister against reasonable local educa-

tion administration. Between her prejudices and their parodistic inclinations useful functions come out burnt.

The claim which Baker has on us is that he represents adult
politics: not intolerant nor inclined to confuse enemies and
opponents. He represents good-tempered civil politics without a message from God – Church of England conservatism
rather than the Muggletonian certitudes now in command.
Most of the charges made against him – 'I have seen the future
and it smirks' and various comparisons to cats and quantities
of cream – set standards for a politician higher than can be
altogether expected. If he smiles a little to himself it is the
smile of someone who in many ways has no business to have
lasted so well or come so far. He is also reflecting on a run of
luck, which Napoleon considered the first requirement of a
good general, and one of the few things he has in common
with the lady.

Whether he will become leader of the Tory party and Prime
Minister, posts so lately linked in the constitution, depends
on the manner of her going and its date. Mrs Thatcher would
like to leave a party entirely reconstructed in her name and
ways. The new intake preponderates with dull, shrill,
modestly talented backbenchers, devoted to her colours.
The 1988 defeat, organised by two 1922 Committee Whips –
Michael Mates and Jill Knight, who had stepped out of line
on one major piece of legislation each – may suggest that a
rightwing majority already exists, though that is very dubious.

If Mrs Thatcher goes with the flag flying at full mast and no
duns on the doorstep, she is likely to nominate a successor
and she will never nominate Kenneth Baker. There is, in fact,
no wholly adequate, wholly rightwing successor in sight
unless the gifted Mr Major can persuade voters that he stands
rather closer to her perception of the universe than I think he
does.

A Baker succession (though no one will say this) depends
upon something going wrong. It hardly matters what: the
economy, an opposition reconstruction of its act which in fact
seems to be happening, or that souring of the cream which
affected the last years of Gloriana. Baker can do something

by way of concession, technocratic neutrality and cool self-adjustment, but it will never be enough. The hard men of the right will be out to stop him. What he really needs is a rather bad election result.

He represents normality, a tempered, one-nation view of the world. Previously excluded liberal Tories like Chris Patten would be big in a Baker government, though he is quite shrewd enough to know that the right will always require sweetening and assuagement. But there *are* factions and only a fool would deny that he is the nominee, however discreet, of one of them, and that his accession to power would mean very significant change.

Given the servility of so many Tories to every twitch the Americans make, Baker may actually benefit from the example of George Bush. Bush with his country-club circle, his humanity and good nature is not what the US right wanted, not what they wanted at all. Within the limits of possibility and exertion, Bush will be a civilising influence upon Americans. The Tories may feel that to show their loyalty they need to make a similar sacrifice. Civilisation may come back into fashion here. Interestingly, Baker was very helpful to an enquiring Mrs Bush when she called at his department. Barbara Bush now speaks highly of him.

The difference of course is that where America has managed for eight years without a President, Britain has been governed, bossed, commanded and hit on the head by Prime Ministerial power distilled three times over into what might be called central command politics. Normality for us would be the restoration of Cabinet government under a Prime Minister. We know that turkeys do not vote for Christmas, but how do the vegetables feel?

# CHAPTER 4

# Alan Clark

Alan Clark is exceptional among politicians for his status as a full-dress individual as remote from general-issue Ministers as could be asked.

An aristocrat, an aesthete, a writer with an elegant and biting style, he is a loyal supporter of Mrs Thatcher – 'I *adore* Margaret Thatcher' – yet the Etonian drawl conveys the cool favour of his esteem; he is light years from sycophancy. On paper we ought not to like him: he does have a tinge of racial contempt mixed with his impudent insouciance. The bit about Bongoland gave offence and was meant to give offence.

He is also a clubland *boulevardier* (in intervals of working hard) with a taste for unThatcherian activities like backgammon and keeping an eye open for something on the side, or so he likes to give out. There is an upper-class underworld of chance adultery and reckless iniquity which is a simple, unbroken continuation of Regency mores. Clark has some affinity with it and one can't read about the Baccarat Scandal without expecting him to be a player for modest stakes at a baize table somewhere in its midst.

Indeed it seems a pity that his distinguished father, Kenneth, cultural oracle to a generation, did not receive an *hereditary* minor honour. Alan Clark has all the necessary qualities for the more irresistible sort of bad baronet.

Oddly, he has been a conscientious Minister under Mrs Thatcher, steadily doing his duty at Lord Young's sleek, resprayed Department of Trade which that Minister, one of Mrs Thatcher's recurring lapses of taste, has issued with fraudulent convertor's note-paper with a wavy, not to say marcelled, watermark and the subtitle 'Department of Enterprise'. Young, a man without shame or ear, would like to make that into the actual departmental name, the sort of adman's self-serenading which should make Gladstone haunt him.

However it is not with Young that Clark chiefly feuded. He enjoyed for a while the most elegant two-way hatred with Michael Heseltine which the rest of us could have asked for by way of entertainment. Clark, as a serious (and acutely readable) military historian, took against the Sir James Porter *HMS Pinafore* aspects of Heseltine: the military service-evading, swiftly rich civilian, given to wearing army sweaters and latterly camouflage jackets and making intestine-twitching patriotic speeches in the manner of Kipling's jelly-bellied flag-wagger.

That may have been a bit of it, but then Heseltine's attempt to stress his compassion and humane instincts towards the poor and the black struck a gusher of liquid derision in Clark. They regarded each other as respectively fascist and sham and, I always suspected, tended to accentuate any feature inclining to controversy for the express purpose of annoying each other. The friends of Clark are convinced that Heseltine did his best to have their boy fired. But the warm regard of Mrs Thatcher supervened; indeed he came close to entering the Cabinet at one stage at Transport, where he would have been a vast improvement – in a small war-starting, board-sacking way – on Paul Channon, tenth transmitter of a foolish face and doleful stopgap at that department.

Clark enjoys annoying people; it is a great part of his charm. 'That man is drunk,' screamed the fatuous Clare Short when Clark, undertaking a late-night piece of Euro-liturgy, read the documents at a deliberately slow tempo. She could have accused him of anything else with a good chance of being right. But despite derisively running the Euro-creep's jargon around his mouth like a marginal vintage, Clark despises drink and it is hard to see him past a single glass if so far. In this he follows Lloyd George, a Methodist in drink as he was a freethinker in women.

But, more pertinently, Short, with her chattering jactatory indignation, is just the sort of predictable Commons clone he would delight in displeasing. The taste for combat is not a matter only of right and left. Only a fool would try to fit him into a narrow slot however much he encouraged them. Clark has called himself a fascist with as much meaning as when the lamented David Penhaligon, a most sophisticated politician, called himself a peasant. He is a sensibility with a gloss of cad and not, as he would like us to think, the other way about.

His account of the neglect of front-line soldiers in the First War, *The Donkeys* (a reference to Ludendorff's alleged remark about the magnificence of English private soldiers: 'Lions, but lions led by donkeys'), has sent into a little pink rage the unspeakable Major Terraine, a military historian of the authoritarian type for whom the British are contemptible in their self-pity while under-fulfilling their quota of dead in the First World War.

No one who has read Clark on war – his hatred for stupid generals and his anger at the image of soldiers stumbling into battle – will ever take his rightwing affectations very seriously. His book was a major inspiration of Joan Littlewood's *Oh What a Lovely War*, not the natural fodder of normal rightwing Tories.

Clark is a professional winder-up of pompous people who think in stereotypes – which for a politician hoping to get on in the company of minds often impressively banal is a bloody silly thing to be. But the real hatreds are for conventionally good people. He abominates Ted Heath and Shirley Williams and, a touch too obviously, affects to be fond of Dennis Skinner, a professional cur with the personality of a *chevaux de frise*. 'But I am *devoted to* Dennis', he says in the language of Tories when they mean nothing of the sort.

The official Clark rubric is that all genuine defenders of beliefs are fine by him – trade unionists, landowners, red revolutionaries and monopoly capitalists. The objects of hatred are the nice-minded diluters, Social Democrats, Tory Wets, career humanitarians, finders of the middle ground, the entire pavilion of virtue. To annoy this conspiracy of competitive innocuousness he will find opinions to shock them sideways.

There are real opinions though – loathing of the EC among them. He was one of the eight who resisted Mr Heath's Whips (quite as authoritarian in the pursuit of that solitary conviction as Mrs Thatcher has ever been on anything) to the very last and most bitter vote over the Common Market. The full reason for the antipathy is not obvious except that of course 'Yerrup', as both Mr Heath and Roy Jenkins call it, is the *beau idéal* of that broad church of nice-minded, forward-looking, thoughtful people who by written application with references and co-option constitute the wise consensus. As it happens, I have no idea what Clark's views on the European Monetary System actually are. But belief in going in is so much a social requirement with the *Independent*, the Social Liberals, the higher Civil Service, Lord Roll and the *Economist* that I will bet pence to guineas that Alan Clark will spew out its name.

That very phrase 'spewing out' belongs with him, recalling as it does the one-liner in the Book of Revelations about what is done to those who are neither hot nor cold but lukewarm.

However, Clark is an excellent test of the sophistication and good judgement of other people. I should not be able to set a high value on anyone who was shocked by him or who took his repertory of offence-giving opinions at literal face-value. It is a fair thing to be irritated by his charade-playing and ostentatious, above-morality Etonianism – a kind of conformity of its own within a specially drawn small constituency. But the value of Clark is his sharp perception of other people's humbug and his dislike of using politics as a state radio to proclaim one's goodness and right thinking. So much of politics has to do with finding out the correct things to think and then thinking them ('caring passionately' about them is the favoured cant expression), that a compulsive iconoclast comes as wonderful release. If one can persuade him in the interests of prudence not to suggest in the presence of believers that the Virgin was probably scoring with the Jerusalem milkman, which is his essential style, his lack of respect will be a source of continuous pleasure.

It is incidentally a strike in favour of Mrs Thatcher that she has taken a strong liking to him. He is so much the sort of person that downy old birds warn Prime Ministers about that he must have got through the calculations and circumspection to the stubbornly original (and reactionary) part of her personality, her non-consensual (and successful) self. She may also have been intrigued by his style of not caring a damn. Life for any Prime Minister is a choice of footmen to kick, so there must be delight in the occasional non-dependent, commonly (like Clark) a rich man, for whom it is a point of honour to avoid the self-serving computation of the correct answer. There is a refinement to this. Mrs Thatcher has had many advisers and a few colleagues who are of her free-market, Adam-Smithian persuasion. But these – John Hoskyns, the future Sir Brian Griffiths and David Willets for example – are themselves the members of a consensus. The children of the Institute for Economic Affairs are their own mafia under construction.

Clark by contrast never joined a club if he found that he agreed with its members. And anyway he doesn't. Free markets are little to him and, greatest of all heresies, he is no free trader. A mercantile regard for this country as a trader and a concurrent dislike and distrust of everything that's Japanese are among the opinions worn for more than disruptive display. The drum-rolling patriot and the classical liberal co-exist under armed truce in Mrs Thatcher's queasy psyche. Clark acknowledges for her something she cannot admit to. That is a central part of his attraction.

He is that rare thing: an uncalculating, original cavalier spirit in office. And of course if he could remove any one of those adjectives he would be in higher office. We should simply be grateful to have him. For anyone with a political ear he is a warm, humane, unconfected, free intelligence and, despite having his own tastes in art, he is without that mannered arctic illwill which commonly accompanies developed sensibilities.

The connoisseur got mixed up with the military specialist and the unobliged rich man and the fleer of received opinion to leave us somebody seriously interesting.

# CHAPTER 5

## Tony Banks

When the leftwing GLC was in its heyday, it displayed characteristics, not often seen on the grim and incantatory left, of simple theatricality: Mr Livingstone doing that Walter Raleigh bit to a far from unwilling Queen Elizabeth II at the opening of the Thames Barrage, and cheeky messages about *GLC Working For You* on the sides of buses.

The GLC may have been involved with every sort of nonsense about sexual minorities, may have been a nagging pain on race; more gravely it paddled fingers with Sinn Fein which kills people, and its worst fringe – Brent Education Committee under the ethical police inspectorate of Mrs Sunil Engineer – went 'Sniff, sniff are you a racist?' something which turned off working-class voters from the Labour party the way reports of cyanide in tins of baked beans have been known to cut sales in a supermarket. But the old, late GLC and its borough cousins were a mixture of infantile bigotry and green-room fun. When it stopped being Gay and Lesbian it was often gay and thespian.

Mr Ken Livingstone, from whom much was hoped, has come, as a Member of Parliament, to something less than nothing. The more cynical and hysterical Tories liked to talk in the Commons about 'the coming Livingstone putsch' as an event to equal his Radio La Paz seizure of power in County Hall. In fact a foot not unconnected with the ankle of Neil Kinnock descended on the dapper municipal profile in the manner of the opening credits of *Monty Python* as soon as he scrambled into the Commons. Something he did, with an exiguous majority for Brent which (poor Brent) he shares with Sir Rhodes Boyson who gives 'morality' as one of his interests and is Central Casting's notion of a reactionary Bolton alderman.

The one recent triumph from the ranks of the left has been that of Anthony Louis Banks, formerly a Livingstone lieutenant, who has managed, far better than his boss, to maintain a free-range personality under battery conditions. Mr Livingstone wilts, mutters and periodically stages the sort of denunciation-cum-revelation about our crimes against the innocent IRA. True or false, they fall like plumblines on to a foam mattress and demonstrate a collapse of Mr Livingstone's populist instincts and a humourlessness worthy of the thin-faced Irish eliminators themselves.

By contrast, Banks has become, perhaps to his horror, a House of Commons notable. His jokes and improprieties are delighted in and repeated in the smoking room, and he is a little bit marvelled at. The remorseless journey from 'That man Banks' to 'Dear old Tony' has reached the stage of 'Have you heard Tony's latest?'

His status is guaranteed by the effective supersession of the far left as a credible force. Perhaps we should have known all along that its apparent eminence was something of a mirage. Even within the Labour party, it took an assertion of courage by Mr Kinnock and evidence of general Labour decline to blow away the 1981 impression of a sub-Carpathian republic about to be taken over by women in romper suits. The idea of life as a *Tribune* meeting addressed in perpetuity by Mrs Margaret Beckett, with pictures of Wedgie smoking his pipe in every public office in the republic, turned out to be overstated. The left has shrunk to a little frazzled, wrong-end-of-the-telescope image of itself. Benn, Livingstone and Scargill, yesterday's bone-grinding monsters, have become homunculi calling from the depths of a bottomless well. We have normality back in the Labour party as though we had never lost it. What remains of the old new-left must either, like Chris Smith of Islington, adjust itself to constructive mainstream politics or, like the unreconstructible Bob Clay and Jeremy Corbyn, wander the corridors and Chamber, like ghosts looking for a bus not so much missed as de-scheduled.

Accordingly, Tony Banks is a cherished member of the Commons circle of leading personalities. His odd combination of St Just and Max Miller frightens nobody. His contempt for the pompous, authoritarian, lackeyish side of Commons life pleases all sorts of people, including the less official Conservatives. Banks is the defiant, democratic, levelling free spirit showing most attractively now that he is a man on his own. The act and its props are much retailed: Banks denouncing the pollution caused by lead piping and speaking with melancholy of his African grey parrot Chunky. 'I regret to say, Mr Speaker, that he's been quite poorly recently. The doctor thought it might be the effect of the lead in the water so we've been nursing him on bottled mineral water.' Not even the subsequent death of Chunky, a pathetic anticlimax, altogether spoiled a good story. In the same way, his shrewd last-minute return of the silver, kept in safe keeping for the estate or soul of the GLC, did not occur until just this side of a potentially interesting action for detinue (the sort of original tort Banks *would* commit), and Banks is remembered as the man who collared the silver and cheeked the authorities by not letting it go.

The day he decides to become a serious politician will be as auspicious as it will be lamentable. Banks as Minister of State at the Home Office in some future Labour government sounds anticlimactic, despite his talent to play even Ministries of State for fun. His one formal position within Parliament was to be a Whip and he resigned for an absurd reason: compassion for Ron Brown, the erratic Edinburgh MP who took to throwing the mace on to the floor.

Now Brown is a slightly crazed person of no personality or intelligence before one gets to the crazy bit. The instinct of Neil Kinnock and the conventional safety-first politicians – march him to the parade ground and tear off his stripes – could have been bettered only by a decision in favour of humane euthanasia. In resigning as a protest, Banks obeyed the reflexive call of drum to rebel: 'Here is an injustice. I must protest against it.' But really there is no injustice which doesn't give the scrambled-brained, piping Great Twit of Leith too much of an even break.

And Banks was too intelligent for the Labour Whips office

to spare him. Under Derek Foster, the dumb buddy from Bishop Auckland, it has – give or take a couple of exceptions – the reputation of a charabanc outing, a mystery tour run by one of the less clear-minded Labour clubs. Although, by all accounts, Banks does a certain amount of unpaid moonlight whipping for his chiefs when they are short, his compassion for poor Ron may have played a smaller part than the desire to get away from over-exposure to such Kantian intellects as Ray Powell, Allen Adams and Don Dixon.

His brief excursion into the municipal equivalent of power in the GLC had much to do with 'the Arts', where he gloriously stopped the grant to Covent Garden in favour of what was unhappily called 'community-based ethnic art'. He also closed the Festival Hall champagne bar on the grounds of its being élitist, renamed Jubilee Gardens 'Peace Gardens', and generally devoted himself to cheering us all up. That of course is the phrase which Bennett uses to describe Denry Machin in *The Card* and Banks, a card if ever there was one, has powerful affinities with the fictional organiser of trips to see the wreck off Llandudno and the proto-inventor of, ironically, the credit card.

In his seat at Newham North West (or West Ham as we used to call it) they are accustomed to cards. His predecessor was Arthur Lewis, a mountainous, money-minded stage proletarian in braces who would occupy a couple of seats below the gangway. Lewis was one of those sour, complaining men to whom privilege was a freebie he hadn't been booked on to. He railed against the evils of the Privy Councillors because they were called before other MPs and anyway *he* was not a Privy Councillor. Lewis hung out just enough of his inadvertence as deliberate humour to have the name of a humorist, but he was essentially mean, and unengaging, very much in the school of that other ungenial fat man, Cyril Smith.

Banks is not only a five hundred per cent improvement, given his diligent and unselfish approach to the Commons, but despite perfectly serious leftwing convictions he is good-natured and rather soothing. The abrasive manner is as much an unsustainable affectation as the Smith and Lewis claim to be lovable old cusses. Part of the Banks act takes place as dialogue for which a portable heavy is engaged as stooge, a strange man called Andrew Faulds, once an actor and always – by his own shouted account to the Commons – a lover and a man given to bursts of solemn pompous rage which are devoutly hoped to be part of an act. Faulds has been known to hit Banks in the Commons with a rolled-up newspaper and to refer to him as 'this whippersnapper' and accuse him of 'diarrhoeic loquaciousness'. It is very odd and unlegislative and Banks sometimes gives the impression of unease as though riding if not a tiger then a scratchy, self-alleged tom.

Two things distinguish Tony Banks from the dismal ruck of leftishness. The humour speaks for itself; most leftists respond to humour the way oarsmen lean to Proust. The other talent of this sceptical, engaging personality is an exuberant gift for words. His dismissal of the Tory tabloids as 'these fascist comics', the description of the abolition of the GLC as 'a sort of South Bank *Belgrano*, done to gratify the Prime Minister's power lust', and his proposal for selective vindictiveness against London Tory MPs who voted for that abolition, all have that little kick of unpredictability which marks the original user of words. Even when he embraces the awful jargon of his feminist convictions and addresses one colleague as 'Comrade Sister Chair' there is something different and comic. The solemnity of the practising left cannot be kept up. The words are sharp, the clichés either avoided or have variations played upon them.

Not that Banks's style, nor the comparative mellowness of recent contributions, has diminished his talent for the ferocious. During the Peter Wright affair, with the government inspired by a Prime Minister beside herself in the search for vengeance, a group of dachshund-level backbenchers, led by the grievous Harry Greenway, were making sycophantic competition with one another as to revenge by royalty snatching and denial of pension. The voice from the backbenches wanted to know why they 'couldn't rip his balls off'. More amiably he responded to the Karl Madden character sitting for Northampton by saying that Mr Marlow had indeed called him a worm. 'But that's all right Mr Speaker, I don't complain. I called *him* "a witless moron".'

In a sense the mellowing, if only from GBH to simple bodily harm, is part of a historical process. The far left had a purpose and, as *A Very British Coup* (the bad fantasy novel of Chris Mullins MP) demonstrated, really did believe in an elected destiny for themselves. Even without hindsight that was nonsense; such a majority never existed and never looked like existing. An intentionally elected, truly leftwing government in Britain is a case of the adjectives annihilating the noun.

But the GLC majority, achieved by a con but rendered palatable by style and persecution, turned into a fairy story and fulfilled every leftwing daydream. They had their 'government' even if it was only a municipality in charge of concerts, buses and canals. Mrs Thatcher, most satisfying of legendary dragons (a monster without being a myth and very fair casting for Grendel's mother), proposed its annihilation. The battle was fought hard and long with a mighty glitch in the House of Lords serving as a battle victory before – equally satisfactorily – ending in martyrdom.

The GLC lacks the coherence or competence or sharp definition of its purpose to stay long in power doing things. Its programmes were like the fireworks for which it had a collective weakness. Apart from the one excellent notion of subsidising London Transport back into popularity and tolerability, the GLC was mostly an existential exercise. It was more important to be, better to be *seen* to be, than painfully to construct the deep-founded architecture of government, which involves more than daring innovation and catching the press deadlines. It requires patience, compromises and the psychology of long duration.

Extinction at the hands of a vengeful right, though it far outruns the emotional capacity of most Conservatives (the once-and-future Tory party), is as acceptable to this Prime Minister as it is psychologically necessary to the far left. Mrs Thatcher on one hand and the Ken Livingstone Brigade on the other maintained a Gog and Magog relationship: they needed each other, they expected each other, they fulfilled one another's happiest and most paranoid dreams. As therapy all that was very well, but for the Labour party, which exists to do things, to hold jobs and maintain the hope of holding them, it was simple, broken-roofed calamity.

Labour under Mr Kinnock has spent four years mending, slowly putting together the pieces smashed in the great leftwing carnival of 1979–83. But as long as the parallel play government of the GLC co-existed across the river, as a sort of Punch and Judy satire on any left in power, Neil Kinnock could not seriously begin his task. Arguably, for all the quick-profit credit she took from the suppression, Mrs Thatcher wasted a priceless asset in not establishing a GLC preservation order so that a running show of ever more publicity-obsessed nonsense could occupy prime time to the grief of the working Labour party.

What distinguishes Tony Banks is that once the play within a play ended and the Player King had been reduced to his walking-on part, he – the Player King's best friend – has blossomed as the man best able to survive in the almost real world of Westminster. Quite why this should be so isn't entirely clear. The sense of humour has helped of course. Ken Livingstone used to be a formidably sardonic man, but the god who loved him is taking prolonged industrial action. Possibly there were always fewer delusions on Banks's part. Certainly he was never a close follower of the Irish obsession which betrayed Livingstone into earnest, serious purpose. Given the relaxed mixture of contempt and derision of the English for all Irish causes, including the bloody ones, that preoccupation disqualified Livingstone as much as it commanded him.

Again, Banks can and Livingstone cannot become part of the orthodox leftwing strand of mainstream Labour politics. No one fears a Banks *putsch*, no one feels the acute dislike aroused by Livingstone's jaunty near accomplishment of Leninism by the means of Dick Turpin: socialism in one nursery. So Tony Banks sits on the furthest backbenches, his elfin features grinning like a politically motivated Bilbo Baggins. He slaps his knees, mocks the Banquo dynasty of heavy ceremonial, toadyish or merely barbarous Tories. He has become an extension of the press since the best of Banks is irresistibly quotable even by journalists of a Conservative nature. He has stature, he is listened out for, his nagging written questions have become a fund of embarrassment about office creation and self-expenditure to a hubristic and often venal government. Despite the rough words and the taste for a fight, he has kept the essential good humour. Perhaps most of all he has found out what he is good at and is doing it.

He has carried the satirical impulse into the Chamber. Forswearing high seriousness, he has done the general left more good as light guerrilla cavalry, harrying and raiding, than the Deputy Chairman of the GLC and 'snarling Czar of the arts' ever could. He must know this because he gives an impression of cheerfully employed contentment which most of his party has, until very late, been without. He has lost his part of an empire and most emphatically found a role.

# CHAPTER 6

## *Kenneth Clarke*

I first watched Kenneth Harry Clarke speaking as an Opposition spokesman in 1978. He differed from what was then the norm of Tory diffidence by his knock-you-down, 'Oh yes you did, oh no I didn't' brand of truculence.

After the velleity and limpness of so many Heath appointments it was refreshing. Today, when the Scuola di Tebbit is beating up old ladies with bicycle chains to prove its strength of character, it is less so. But I asked an elder and experienced colleague who that fellow was. 'Ah yes,' he said in the way of Mr Jingle, 'Kenneth Clarke, brilliant debater, very good, can't trust him though, Heathite.'

He was rather more than a Heathite. At some time in his youth he must have given careful consideration to crossing the floor. At Cambridge he was a member not only of the Conservative Association and the Bow Group but also of the Campaign for Social Democracy, the Bill Rodgers-run Gaitskellite connection. The possibility that he might have followed the example of Phillip Whitehead, President of the Blue Ribbon Club and OUCA, later a Labour MP and Chairman of the Board of the *New Statesman*, must have been a flower he thought of picking.

Not surprisingly, he made no secret of his annoyance when the lady in the hat replaced Ted Heath in 1975, but he is not to be blamed for making terms and biting on the Thatcher shilling. The lady is not generous towards opponents, and even with submission Clarke made painfully slow progress. He had to wait six and a half years before making the Cabinet. And even then he was shoehorned into the half-job of being Lord Young's vicar on earth, representing Trade and Industry in the House of Commons. He had by then been in Parliament for fifteen years.

It is an irony – and an interesting one – that the Tory party is rich in liberal talent at Minister of State level and in dries or nasties (heavily distinguished groups) at the level of Parliamentary Under Secretary or PPS. This is so simply because those who made their entry in an atmosphere created not just by Heath but by twenty years of Bow Group liberalism are working their way through. The right, virtuous like Peter Lilley or atrocious like Eric Forth, are broadly the children of 1983 and after.

Clarke is ahead of but not greatly distinguishable from the two Pattens, Waldegrave and Mellor (though of all aspirants Waldegrave is the most ruthlessly adaptive), in not quite being one of hers and having to make the best of it. Socially he is every bit as upwardly mobile as Norman Tebbit. The son of a colliery electrician turned jewellery shopkeeper, he passed examinations through Nottingham High School to Cambridge and the Bar. But unlike many risers he retains rough edges and working-class habits. His diet is outrageous: he is a beer, cigarettes and fried-bread man and to hell with the consequences. He is suffused with an unhealthy roseate colour and badly overweight; indeed our Health Secretary is a quivering bodymass of pericardial hazard whose slim-gilt soul wheezes between passion and poetry. Considerations of whether he will one day be Prime Minister must be tempered by interest in whether at the likely hour he will still be alive.

For a man who through no choice of his own had to live in proximity to the publicity-crazed, celery and Ryvita fanatic, Edwina Currie, at a time when the Conservatives have been quite sensibly concerned to contain National Health Service costs by promoting preventive medicine, the Minister who at all times looks ready for slaughter must have felt slightly hunted. Having Ken Clarke for Health Secretary is like having a Grade Six illiterate in charge of the Department of Education or Oblomov as Secretary for Energy. While Currie lasted, a régime of crispbreads and *acqua minerale* with the occasional green salad – all of it on camera and perhaps accompanied by one of Lord Young's advertising campaigns – was always likely to be prepared for him by one or both of two bossy women.

As the *Sun* cruelly pointed out, he is fifteen stone and five foot nine, his hobbies of modern jazz, birdwatching and Nottingham Forest, though commendable, do nothing for his condition. Realistically, Clarke must yearn for the advancement to the supreme place of Sir Geoffrey Howe, not merely because Sir Geoffrey, who has accommodated to Thatcher over the years without losing sight of civilisation, must be a sympathetic role model. He was also Clarke's first boss (PPS when Howe was drafting the Industry Act in 1970–1), and in a modified way – with his comfortable shoes, gins-and-tonics and mild inclination to the Spherical Tendency – Sir Geoffrey is a comparable pudgy fist shaken at the joggers and abstainers and one who seems no worse for modest quantities of alcohol and decent nutrition.

Clarke is indeed spoken of as future Prime Ministerial material. His reputation rests upon a good lawyer's grasp of detail without fuss, a general good humour which makes few enemies, and an understanding that he is very ambitious indeed. He is also, untypically for the Tories, a dominant figure in the Commons. He can dispense with notes, not in the word-perfect nightmare way of Malcolm Rifkind day-tripping from Alpha Centauri, but with a good rough bantering authority which does what his side wants without really offending Labour.

It is instructive to compare him with Nicholas Ridley, whose Environment brief probably contained fewer natural trans-party hazards and who was the object of sincere hatred. Clarke can machine-gun COHSE, starve the nurses and spurn NUPE with the side of his foot and it is still only old Ken going on a bit. If the Tories ever resolve to do something quite outstandingly barbarous, he is the man to entrust with it. His style is one of deliberate, cultivated pomposity and self-celebration of a kind intended not to be taken seriously. The achievements of the Conservative government are uniformly quite splendid. He and his colleagues are magnificent; he doesn't know what the other lot are bothering to bang on about. The effect when he was partnered by Michael Meacher, a deadly pedant with an index finger on red alert, was gratifying. He would wind his opponent up and fly him.

He is also the master of quite breathtaking *chutzpah*. Take his assertion to Conservative conference in 1988 that 'the National Health Service happened to be set up at a time when Labour occupied office'. On that reckoning the recent tax cuts for the well-to-do are the products of an indifferent providence and Mr Nigel Lawson is best seen as a random circumstance.

Clarke is the occupant of a politically sensitive department – Health – where, on and off, and at different levels he has spent much of his time. The combined DHSS was taken apart after John Moore had crashed the car. That was in respect of the other flap of the diptych, Social Security, where he managed with nice scruple to do down the not-well-off and the middle classes in one calamitous afternoon. But Health is quite explosive enough. The balance between money spent and services received makes no kind of sense: bang for buck the NHS, though an indispensable support to us all, is like one of those petrol-hungry cars in which the Americans used to delight.

Nobody denies what the government asserts (Clarke in the bellicose way of a man starting a civil war in a bar parlour): that the Tories have indeed heavily upped expenditure. But then neither does anyone seriously deny that nurses are poorly paid (and have to shout even to obtain what they do), that waiting lists are very long and that fully equipped wards are standing empty. It is very difficult to see the new Department of Health avoiding substantial additional spending. Indeed, after a great carry-on, he has already made substantial concessions to the nurses as he will later do to the doctors. Yet we face huge deficit problems – too much consumer credit and towering interest rates. All thinking at the Treasury for at least two years will be bent towards spending money by aspersion as if it were holy water. Ken Clarke will be faced with a circle requiring to be squared. On past form he will kick it, shout at it loudly, proclaim the matchless wisdom of what he is doing and, confronted by a subverted oblong, declare it to be the very square he wanted.

This job is make or break for him. He has been kept waiting for a department of his own for nine years of wonderful Conservative government. Long years toiling as a PPS, as a junior and full Whip then as a deputy to his old Cambridge friend Norman Fowler, combined with general agreement that he was superior material, have finally given him control of half a giant Ministry but one perfectly capable of damning him for improvidence or running into the sort of street-based unpleasantness which can occupy the late news on television.

He has been mobbed by hospital workers once before. In COHSE he has some unsubtle but publicity-conscious opponents. NUPE, despite the departure of the gruesome Bernard Dix and the overwrought Alan Fisher (now dead), is inherently as stable as nitro-glycerin and entirely capable of excess on the streets. NUPE is the nearest thing there is to a union of the disinherited: it represents kitchen porters, mortuary workers and gravediggers, pushers, shovers, carriers and heavers. If a Union of Hewers of Wood and Drawers of Water stops, it stops lots of other things, like the last Labour government.

Clarke in the appallingly named office of 'inner city supremo' – a piece of sub-editors' anti-prose better disregarded – symbolically arranged, to much derision, a series of working breakfasts up and down the country with all concerned. Both the fleeting visit and the consumption of food put a patina of absurdity on the project. Indeed, like any number of politicians, he has a weakness for running about to create an impression of useful activity. There was a fact-finding mission to the United States in the same connection. How far contact with Lord Young, a silky-mannered confectioner of stopgaps and good images, has coarsened the boy idealist who shall say?

Much of his tough side is bluster, actually much of *Clarke* is bluster. But he can make the Thatcher noises denouncing scroungers, and he worked out a plan to outlaw the closed shop and permit union members the right to break strikes even where the union had voted for them. That last may be opportunist tagging behind Thatcher and Young, but it might just as well be the reaction of a son of the Nottinghamshire coalfield which being historically economic has its own strike-avoiding traditions. There is no vast social gulf between Clarke and Arthur Scargill, only the thirty or so miles which constitute an alpine barrier between the adaptability and solid expectations of one county and the curled-up condition of soured siege which leave even visiting Fife communists gasping for air.

In a happier way than Norman Tebbit and without his hang-ups, our boy – who shares the master's talent for debate if not his elegant three inches of epigram – is modern Conservative man. He is someone without connections but with exam-passing facilities who kept humane company at first and is now, just below the summit, mingling on affable terms with the very rough trade of Mrs Thatcher's inner circle. It is doubtful if she trusts him. One hopes for his sake that she is right not to do so. But, though he has not precisely discarded the liberal conscience of his early days, he is highly adaptive, an ambitious boy from the North Midlands who wants to be Prime Minister.

By the standards of other hopeful men – Moore, Fowler and the nameless vanilla-flavoured pixies of recent intakes – he has not lost his savour. There is an individuality there, the burps, grunts, and occasional bawlings of an identifiable human being. This is a drawback in modern Conservative politics, but by no means an absolute bar. To adapt the words of Richard Nixon in another context, we shall have him to knock us about for a long while yet.

# CHAPTER 7

# Tony Benn

All political careers of any moment have some sort of shape. There is usually a prelude, a swelling theme, a climax and some sort of diminuendo. Because the company of politics is unmaliciously realistic, it is not hard to distinguish those, however languishing, who have something to play for from those whose game is run.

But there are all sorts of comfort for the old age of one's aspirations, and some politicians fit into elder statesmanship and enjoy it better than the real thing. They enjoy giving advice in a good humour without having to live edgily with decisions and the prospects of getting them wrong. Others – like poor Mr Heath – are so oppressed by failure that they deny it diplomatic recognition and continue upbraiding those in power like long declined, not very competent occupants of sheltered housing talking to their grown-up grandchildren like aberrant tots.

Mr Heath reminiscing about the great days of heavy-duty administration, when there were minds big enough and visions equipped to cope with the DHSS, his own lumpen Brobdingnag of a DHSS, is pitiful. He recalls his own most absurd hopes in office, that passion to be massive, to build big whatever you built – never mind the cracks in the ceiling, feel the size. So unadjusted is he to that world over which he has not ruled for fifteen years, that long overdue correction of a notion of his is taken as a monstrous affront, an amendment by minnows to the decrees of a Triton. In becoming a pathetic echo, uninstructed in the fact of his own fall, failing first to practise damage limitation as he could have done after 1975 and then failing again to be an intelligent, dignified and thus injurious presence in Opposition, Mr Heath has demonstrated that he was never fit for the office he held. Tony Benn, whose latter days have been not much happier, confirms a general public relief that such greatness evaded him.

But Mr Benn's fall was quite different from Ted Heath's. As recently as 1981 he was candidate, nominally, for the deputy leadership but actually expressing his plans for the senior post; and if he fell short it was by two-thirds of a single percentage point! Yet for several years now Mr Benn has not contested the Shadow Cabinet in the perfect certainty that his vote would be insultingly small. The words of Brian Wilson, an extremely gifted new Scottish Member, are instructive. 'Benn,' he said, *à propos* of some pitch the old hero had made, 'is an odious hypocrite.' Yet Brian Wilson of the West Highland Free Press has excellent leftwing credentials himself. But the contempt for Benn there is bottomless.

When every allowance has been made for physical illness and his (short) absence from the Commons betwixt losing Bristol and gaining Chesterfield, the drop in his standing is of the magnitude of the worst found-out dud share falling gracefully down the cliff face of the Stock Exchange. Benn may not care for the image, but he is very much the Rolls Razor of Parliament. He has gone to nothing without a coup. There was no Milk Street conspiracy to remove the levers from his hands. Logically, Benn, though short of the artillery to attain the defended mountain, should be in there in good standing, the leader of the left, a serious bogey engaging the witch-finding talents of the *Daily Mail*. He should, at the very least, be a major obstacle to the Labour party behaving sensibly.

Instead he is nothing. The recent candidacy was merely a forlorn advertisement for that condition of nullity. Benn today is a man not feared, not admired and (if at all possible) not listened to. Yet his gifts have not deserted him. On his day he can make an impressive speech; he made one during the debate on Richard Shepherd's bill to end the Official Secrets Act. Ironically, so did Ted Heath. It is depressing that men so totally marginalised can speak with such authority in the sinister territory of secrecy and security, as if the conspiratorial and paranoid caste of mind acquired validity on certain issues.

But Benn's verbal felicity – mostly a matter of going on – which was once admired even by those who detested him, has slipped into self-parody. The little tricks of speech which were supposed to make him less upper-middle class, like the habit of saying 'ye' for 'you', are hilariously acclaimed; the instant E. P. Thomsonry of his compulsive historicising has become a crutch rather than a tool. He remains as preppie as he always was. We know what we are going to hear, we are not surprised, still less shocked and – most deadly of all – an element of condescending affection creeps into the observations of Tories and orthodox Labour colleagues. He is not quite 'Dear old Wedgie' but the epithet can't be far away.

Algernon Moncrieff, pursued about the whereabouts of Mr Bunbury, observed: 'Bunbury was exploded, Bunbury was found out. That is, the doctors said Bunbury couldn't live, so Bunbury died.' With hindsight it is evident that Tony Benn, otherwise the Right Honourable Anthony Wedgwood Benn, has never had much more substance than the creation of Wilde's genius and the necessity for Algy's out-of-town excursions. The great crisis which split the Labour party, brought the SDP into existence and gives the appearance of having conferred political immortality upon the Conservatives, is best seen as a great and glorious Bunbury, a Bunbury to end all Bunburies.

Benn is a product of family connection. His father, an affable Liberal who joined Labour to win the kindly condescension of Mrs Webb, occupied office for a while without upsetting anything very much and was duly rewarded with an hereditary peerage, the Old Haileyburian being rather keen on that sort of thing. His second son Anthony had one of those pleasant university and service careers after leaving his public school: commissioned in the RAF, a respectable Second at Oxford, and the friendship of Anthony Crosland, who insisted on calling him 'Jimmy' and observed, 'Nothing wrong with Jimmy apart from the fact that he's a bit cracked.' He entered Parliament in his late twenties, something less remarkable now but quite Pittian in the Attlee era.

During the last big Labour party spasm before his own, the

one involving Hugh Gaitskell and the unilateralists, he at no time took the side of the rebels. He was seen at that time (and for a while after) as a brightish, fresh-faced, inoffensive younger utility politician, a touch anaemic if anything, but your standard-issue, gleaming white, caring passionately about something or other, wanting-to-get-on serviceable MP, the sort you give a job to because he wants it so much. There was a thesis which is unfair: that Benn's ambition was the father of his radicalism, that in the words of a Portuguese general who actually declined to lead a coup in his country, Jaime Neves, 'I kept seeing this horse crossing and recrossing before my front door', but that in Benn's case he jumped on.

Usually, when politicians tell you that they care passionately about something, you know you are perfectly safe, that this is banal careerism looking for a knightly helmet and coming up with a passable plastic article. Benn, alas, landed himself with the Tarnhelm! Something very funny happened to us all on our way to Mrs Thatcher.

There was a period, roughly between 1968 and 1981 and lingering in the mind a little longer, when all destiny seemed bound up with a conquering and triumphalist left. Chris Mullin's perfectly unreadable novel, *A Very British Coup*, a trudge through a six-inch bog of untalent and prejudice, but made to shine bright on television, perfectly expresses the delusion of the era. An unapologetic Labour government of the sort which expels US bases and sets about distributing the means of production, distribution and exchange to workers by hand and brain, is freely elected by a landslide. That is not the expectation of anyone intelligently interested in British politics this side of the next ice age.

But Benn lived his key years through a time when it was, sometimes tenuously, sometimes vividly, very thinkable. The era began with the public nonsenses of student indignation in 1968. That was fuelled by Vietnam and found expression in the Grosvenor Square demonstrations. It was accompanied by – but wholly unconnected with – a shift reflecting tiny movements within a Lilliputian electorate in the trade union leadership. The emergence a little earlier of Hugh Scanlon and Jack Jones, men of a certain decent rectitude but with a narrow, single-purposed, 1930s *Pravda* editorial subtlety of mind, created a thumping power block. And, as George Orwell observed, power worship, reverence for other men's muscle and brutality are formidable factors. As he also remarked, 'There is a tendency to play with fire by those who don't even know that fire is hot.'

By the early seventies the European and American components of this parakeet echo of 1848 had run themselves very thin. The candidacy and humiliation of George McGovern – a sort of calmer, less obsessive version of Benn – had seen the fashion put by American politics to the only test that matters. Kevin Phillips was already publishing in that year (1972) his thesis of long-term Conservative domination.

In Britain things were less clear-cut. The Conservative government which came to power in 1970 was a fortuitous thing, trembling with the sort of imperious self-doubt which was Mr Heath's speciality. It retreated from early dabblings in freer markets and less statism but, although gently mocked by a tired and ageing Harold Wilson, it was troubled less by orthodox Labour already enfiladed to its left than by the unions. At about this time the journalist, Paul Ferris, published a trumpery book for Penguin on the new unions. It expressed, in the language of a groupie at a rock concert, the wonderfulness of the splendid, abrasive new tank-drivers of the union revolution. It even managed to see Clive Jenkins, that buffoon's understudy, in a heroic light. Union leaders – sclerotic, cantankerous, old mediocrities of slender talents – were the chic of the decade. And Mr Heath in his dealings with the unions conceded as much.

Just as the feebleness of Mr Heath ultimately created Mrs Thatcher, so it temporarily set Benn on fire. The leftism into which he had already been drawn as the coming truth for mankind seemed to be moving towards apotheosis (nothing in this life ever does, but no matter). Not only was it inevitable, but the unions would make it happen. When the first fissure appeared in the Labour party with the appeal by the de-selected MP, Dick Taverne, to his constituents of Lincoln (which the Conservative press, being human, delighted in), Benn made his notorious speech as Chairman of the year to Labour conference. He indicated that if any workers in a newspaper (liftmen was his suggestion) wanted to stop publication of articles hostile to the Labour movement he was not saying that they shouldn't.

This was a straightforward appeal to the trade unions to institute political censorship which sits with bitter hilarity beside his recent defences of freedom against Mrs Thatcher's clucking intrusiveness. The Lincoln candidacy was a trial run for the SDP and Benn's response was an earnest of his potential for saying frightening things and talking perfect nonsense at the same time. There was never, in fact, a sympathetic public response to Benn. The rise of the left was largely a matter of filling a vacuum in semi-derelict constituency parties.

It was also a factor of the paralysis and inadequacy of almost everyone at the top of Labour politics – Harold Wilson, Jim Callaghan and trade union place-holders like David Basnett. A modest amount of courage would have sufficed: left strength in the unions was mostly bluff and, even without Mrs Thatcher's slump, could and should have been seen off by articulating the opinions of the members. But the crushing of Harold Wilson's spirit over *In Place of Strife*, a sensible piece of reform, was a perfect illustration of the over-rated reverence and fear which the unions inspired. It was cut from the same cloth as Benn's exaltation in the power of the workers, a harvest of 'orient and immortal wheat which never should be reaped nor was ever sown'.

All political judgement for the best part of a decade, with Tories like Jim Prior very much included, was hooked on mysticism about the unions. Atahualpa confronted with magic pistols by Pisarro's thieving Spaniards was not more impressionable than the two halves of the British political establishment. The young Ken Clarke calling for us to come to terms with the closed shop was only speaking the reverent language of his day.

In this atmosphere – unions riding like Tamburlaine through Persepolis, Heath begging the miners to accept 16.5 per cent,

Arthur Scargill (another hairy muscular wonderful proletarian) calling that offer 'a bag of crisps' – Benn shared the
perceptions of the *Daily Mail*, his spiritual pair. But, where
the *Mail* perceived dangerous reds who must be resisted from
the hills if necessary, Benn saw in his own words 'the
irreversible transfer of power to the working people'. Well,
he was wrong wasn't he? Benn is the man who went nap on a
future that didn't happen.

Ironically, if he had followed a different game plan for his
ambitions, which meant assuming that Labour remained both
gradualist *and* influential, it is hard to see his being stopped.
For Benn was once politically golden: he had started early
and retained the looks of youth late; he had an honourable
family connection which accelerated his early career as it did
those of John Silkin, Tony Greenwood and Roy Jenkins; he
was a gifted talker, genuinely fluent, facile and charming.
And his original political stance was almost perfect: middle of
the road with a little dab of radical gesture behind the ears.

He even brought off an early draft of Baker's Indian
Defence, safe immurement behind a couple of high-technol-
ogy pawns which caused him to be designated a science and
gadgets wizard. This device – elegantly perfected by the far
cleverer Kenneth Baker to get him out of the hole of being a
literary liberal in a government dominated by a philistine
reactionary – has the singular beauty that it leaves a politician
looking apolitical: 'I'm afraid Ken doesn't have any views on
the money supply or public spending. He's too busy worrying
about fibre optics.' And who in a Christian country could be
*against* fibre optics?

This was Benn's glorious position in the late seventies: not
unpopular, a debonair good-looking politician (not at all like
Baker), wrapped up in a neutral topic which was acclaimed,
without any very serious interest, to be a good thing. All he
had to do to take intelligent advantage of the radical mood
of the seventies was to shift a few conciliating steps to the
left while keeping his base firmly in the world of bankable
politics. If the left had been the future, he would have had a
useful investment; if it had blown out as it now has, he would

have been cheerfully excused a spot of opportunistic rhetoric and would have been sought out as a conciliatory figure with all the unity guff at his finger ends.

This is the low politics which Benn affects to despise, but without it there is no high politics. Low politics involves hedging against a changing market, it requires never being hopelessly exposed. To pursue the hateful capitalist metaphor a little further, Benn's reaction to the frothed-up but ultimately insubstantial leftism of the seventies was that of the glinting-eyed, overwrought million-maker who in a bull market believes only in bulls and goes a bundle – second mortgage and all – on margin, just where one of those monochrome Tuesdays can hit him for his last half-farthing. If you believe that every streak in the sky is the dawn or at least the first fired hayrick of the revolution, don't be surprised if night lasts a lot longer and the county militia come along to hang or, as it were, surcharge the rickfirers.

Benn stuffed everything he had – prestige, irreversible commitment but also friendship – into an increasingly hysterical and bitter dedication to a hard left whose beauty, obscure to most people, left him dazzled and half blind. He also, quite ruinously, found an outlet for his vanity. All politicians like being applauded but they mostly have the sense to treat the stuff like alcohol, agreeable but not good for you in quantity.

Enoch Powell's departure from the mainstream may have had some parallels with Benn's, but it owed little to a desire to be cheered to the ceiling by the rather unpleasant people on the far right (witness Powell's resolute dislike of capital punishment and his dedicated ice-coolness towards the United States). But one should not be comparing the two men; they are not in the same league. What became apparent, perhaps fastest of all to a key part of the left, was that Benn is a fool. No sensible man throws away so much so lightly. No one possessed of wisdom pursues vendettas as Benn did when he was up. No one playing the market wisely puts a second mortgage into equities.

The Benn venture did not last but it was for a term both believed in and exploited by the right and instrumental in paralysing the old established Labour party. The constitution of 1980–1, the exodus of the group who formed the SDP and the institutionalisation of Conservative government under the most consistently rightwing leader that party has had since the end of the First World War, would none of them have happened without Benn's personal adventure. The irreversible transfer of power to which he had gloatingly alluded took place indeed, but it transferred power away from unions, away from the Labour party, away from the poor and their friends. If a world has been created in which Sir Jeffrey Stirling is comfortably at ease, Tony Benn helped to build it.

Benn is owed no tenderness by any commentator. His main trouble is that he is stupid and greedy, greedy at least for power. In all his years of finding Labour morally deficient and weakly submissive to the capitalists, he did not surrender a single day of executive chauffeur-drawn, Right-Honourable eminence. He was a Cabinet Minister from first day to last, from the start of Wilson to the end of Callaghan. Eric Heffer resigned from government, the SDP people resigned from the Labour party. Benn remained and held office. He is/was always a rich man and became richer still on marriage ; he has given nothing up. He condemns the upper classes but does not leave them. A change of name is less impressive when accompanied by a resolute retention of address. The Essex mansion, unlike the double-barrelled name, has been retained.

Benn's place in history is that of the man who showed up the Labour party, showed it up as too weak to deal with him. He was a test which Labour failed. But in himself he is a vain, foolish, lightweight, self-deluded minor humbug who nearly smashed the Labour party as a force for good or indeed for anything. The only people who could have turned him to useful account were those nineteenth-century Russians like Gogol and Ostrovsky who portrayed shams, and confidence tricksters. It would be a challenge, but perhaps one not beyond the dreams of Gogol, to depict someone who so comprehensively duped himself. In American terms, he sold shares in Brooklyn Bridge but took care to retain majority control for himself.

# CHAPTER 8

## *Roy Jenkins*

There are moments when Roy Jenkins, as evidently contented a man as one hopes to see in politics, seems to have spent a lifetime working towards a slow motion, honour-lapped and wiser-after-other-people's events, old age.

There can at times be a maddening lassitude about Jenkins going clean against the way of politics, which, far above professional gymnastics, is an energetic trade. But some things are immutable – the smile for example is the smile of a salamander who has done well in life. The same expression of rational self-content looks out of the blurb fold of a book published when Jenkins was thirty-nine and a coming man: 'A Younger Turk the very cream/And essence of the new regime'.

He was a child of the Labour party's own aristocracy, son of Arthur Jenkins, Welsh miners' leader and notable trade union moderate, and of his ambitious wife Hattie, who hid from her son what might anywhere else have been a source of pride – Arthur's short but criminally stupid imprisonment for his honourable but constitutional and reluctant part in the General Strike.

Roy Jenkins's political stance seems to have been compounded from both elements. By every account his father seems to have been an intelligent man of notable good sense and restraint, too wise to bear a grievance. The best of Roy Jenkins – well-intended social reform at the Home Office, a cautious budget-balancing term at the Treasury – seems to be everything that Arthur, equipped with an advanced formal education, would have wanted to achieve.

The side of Jenkins which likes duchesses and other titled folk, which hugely enjoyed the pantomime grandeur of a Brussels Boyar, which developed the lisp, the taste for claret and sent him via Lady Violet Bonham-Carter on the worrying historical trail of the futile Asquith, sounds like pure Hattie, according to her most unsympathetic observers. Asquith should have been a warning to Jenkins's friends. Nothing like as nice a man as his biographer, he was also the arch apostle of listless and gentlemanly negligence.

It is good to be without resentment and Jenkins, like many hedonists, is an easy, comfortable, good-humoured man. It is good not to be the politician governed by a committee of ulcers. And yet how much the socially rising Jenkins has diluted Jenkins the intelligent Minister . . . and how grievously obstructed him! Jenkins rose by his merits, accentuated by his connections, actually starting his career after the long hiatus of Tory government as a full Minister (Aviation) outside the Cabinet.

Like Nigel Lawson, he was far better known, at least to an insider audience, than most new Ministers. He had written his *Mr Balfour's Poodle* and his *Asquith*. He had made a reputation in the Commons in that uncommon stretch of thirteen years as both wit and liberal reformer. The Jenkins Home Office had a kind of inevitability about it, but he was also known as a senior member of one of those fighting factions in which Labour delights. Along with Patrick Gordon Walker, Douglas Jay and Anthony Crosland, he was a Gaitskellite. Thus he was part heir to a quarrel thirteen years old, going back to charges on teeth and spectacles and barnacled with Schleswig-Holstein type atrocities like the Stalybridge Speech which only Alan Watkins can be expected to remember. The hatred between old left and old right was something else. It was very roughly a war between two coalitions: gentlemen socialists, trade union steadies, careerists and ordinary sensible people against sentimental rhetoricians, trade unionists with clenched minds, and individuals grateful for the warm benevolent intentions of J. V. Stalin.

By joining the first gathering Roy was doing what Arthur would have done. But by making it on his talents, he was also into an inner group, fulfilling Hattie's aspirations and becoming an honorary Wykehamist. Public-school socialists are usually defensive about their advantages in life. And Gait-skell, who came from a civil service family and embodied the cool, conscienced qualities of a high functionary with a serrated edge, could never have prized the little joys of social one-upness the way they have always mattered to one so dangerously proximate to the coal face. Crosland was much more of a leveller though alas it was us, the class two groups below him, the grammar-school entrants, who received the full force of his Robespierrian imperatives.

There was asperity between Crosland and Jenkins at all times. Not only the increments of radicalism but an ambiguity between two clever men as to which was actually the cleverer spoiled a perfect mutual appreciation. Jenkins, the product of Abersychan Grammar School, might not have felt ties to his upper-working-class roots, but he would have been less likely to bust a system which roughly worked than a minor public schoolboy trying to kick rungs out of the middle part of the ladder.

If one thinks about it, Jenkins had a blessedly sweet run, mostly at the hands of Harold Wilson, who despite a mild and wholly justified paranoia always played safe (and gently) with cheeky talents and tried to make troublesome people happy. Jenkins was a reforming Home Secretary, at least first time round, if an unduly optimistic one, full of rather windy talk about 'a more civilised society'. But he helped see off hanging and the remnants of corporal punishment and he reorganised the criminal law. The beauty of all this was not its success but its perfect uncontentiousness with any halfway serious member of the political class. The public is another matter. The public is broadly in favour of an uncivilised society, walloping offenders for lesser offences, stringing them up for greater. But the public has never played a very significant part in the calculations of any politician making his way in Britain. To his entire party, including the likes of Sydney Silverman (that devoted apologist for Stalin, and a great capital punishment man) through to Willie Whitelaw and the nice Tories, the stance taken at the Home Office from 1965 on was better than unexceptionable, it was the glittering embodiment of all right and proper thought. In terms of the career beautiful, it was excellent politics.

That was of course simple good fortune. The bitterest critic of Jenkins has never charged him with trimming. He stuck to Europe, to the exasperation of Hugh Gaitskell who came to detest the notion. As Chancellor, he was as tough with the citizenry as only a Labour Chancellor can be, and though he won credit again with the political class over all, he upset parts of his party. The significance of his good luck was that Jenkins was temperamentally ill-equipped to exploit it.

The seventy-four votes he received in the leadership election of 1976 were a fascinating commentary on an enlightened Home Secretary, a successful Chancellor and the Labour Minister with the best press this century. The Parliamentary party was not very leftwing at that date (it isn't now), and yet they clubbed him down. Jealousy and malice have always had good soubrette roles inside the Parliamentary Labour party (witness Robin Cook's diagnosis of Dagenhamitis – talent, charm and style in Bryan Gould beyond what is acceptable), but they really are not enough to stop rising gifts. You can make it to the top even with ability.

Jenkins, however, is one of those people who notoriously hover between the shy and the aloof. He had never mixed convincingly. He disliked the smoking-room aspect of politics, and, while not unkind, he was inadvertently patronising. Something is quite seriously amiss in a Labour politician who acquires the distinguishing characteristics of one of the more distant members of the Royal Family. There was a good deal in Neil Kinnock's crack about Jenkins canvassing in an election and being told 'Oh no, sorry love, we're Labour here.' Grandeur had got at him, so had pleasure at himself, and there have been times since then when Jenkins sounded like a parody of himself, kneading his fingers, observing 'I feel bound to say' and generally putting on the Jenkins. The flaws come out sometimes in his writing; he writes very well indeed, but there is a too amused elaboration of style which suggests a pleasure in wit anticipated at source. He has also suffered from his admirers, the Friends of Roy Jenkins as they were called. A small cult of Roy the Good and Beautiful among fellow European enthusiasts and natural emulators, some of whom – like John Harris – actually adapted their speech and mannerisms to sound like rough drafts of the master. As Beethoven said of Ferdinand Ries, 'He tries too hard to be like me.'

The decision to go to Europe as Commissioner was a logical follow-up to conclusive rejection by the Labour party. It was also, despite the spoils, an extremely bad move. Jenkins was already quite sufficiently remote from commonsense, wet-finger politics. A worse atmosphere than that prevalent in the Pagoda of the Elect among the scurrying footmen of the Belgian capital cannot be contemplated. Jenkins was fed like Tantalus upon unfulfilled expectations of power, given all its ceremonial, first as a Commissioner, then as President and generally made to feel, truthfully, that his real friends – the enlightened ones, nothing to do with the brute public or the Labour party – were making it up to him for not having been Prime Minister. Though it is no contemptible thing to have the admiration and affection of so many capable people and, as the *Diaries* show, serious business over an EMS was in hand. Even so, that was no fit mood for coming home at the end of his term to form a new party, fight elections and win over the mere public.

We will never know whether the Conservatives, without the intervention of that ludicrous but advantageous war in the South Atlantic, would have survived the onslaught of serious social democracy. But everyone forgets, as once nobody would ever forget, that the SDP at one stage had gathered in more than fifty per cent in a serious, properly conducted poll. Jenkins demonstrated rather splendid conduct at Warrington, one of those few defeats which really *are* victories, something measured by where you have got to against where you started from, also in the faces of the other side. The excellence of Jenkins here was in his good humour, his sophistication and in a burst of energy which we were almost never to see again.

The long-term failure of the SDP (and they got their failure into six years which is a pretty short kind of long term) is not attributable directly to Jenkins. The foolish talent of many people for petty quarrelling, the mixture of defeatism, sloppiness and ill-targeted opportunism which was David Steel, and the Donald Wolfit-like personality of David Owen – an Othello hiring his own Iago and requiring the spotlight for his exclusive use – combined to do the harm. The leader simply looked on and was appalled.

But to Jenkins falls the doom of the non-playing captain. If his colleagues, unled, rapidly demonstrated the qualities of a bunch of professional misfits capable of quarrelling only on camera or the record, the leader who doesn't stop them but instead murmurs something about 'having a bit more love in our relations' is very much to blame. Jenkins was indeed far from well. Hashimoto's Thyroiditis is a complaint which decelerates the performer. Jenkins has in the past been a notable Parliamentary debater, witty, expert and authoritative. From the moment he returned to the Commons after his Hillhead victory, all energy seemed to leave him. At that time he had, remember, thirty plus ex-Labour MPs and a dozen or so Liberals, including some notable talents like George Cunningham and John Horam. If that party had played Parliament hard, if it had attended in full numbers, used question time intelligently, organised its set-piece speeches and generally gone for impact, the outcome would have been very different.

Alas, a central flaw in the original SDP, and what must be called the clique at its centre, was a certain fastidiousness about such a ragged-trousered institution as Parliament. It isn't an accident that with a couple of exceptions – Cunningham and Douglas-Mann – the SDP were all sacramental Europeans of the most open-eyed, Edward Heathian, awful sort. That sort of opinion goes with a degree of disdain for native assemblies, a love of the civil service mentality and a sense that the good and wise, over coffee and cognac, will better order the universe. They were not fitted for rough domestic politics and Roy Jenkins, thin-skinned, hurt by rough play in the Labour party, snobbish, aloof, shy and playing aristocrats, was especially not fitted. Considered as a leader, he was a perfect calamity, a constitutional monarch all prestige and no function.

To him applies the old Roman maxim: *Capax imperare nisi imperassat* – Fit to govern if only he hadn't. As leader of a small Opposition party with the potential for becoming the Opposition if not indeed the government, Jenkins, like Steel after him, let himself be bullied by Dennis Skinner, a noisy oaf equipped with a minimalist repertoire of derisive slogans, of which 'Yer what?' was probably the most subtle. Three minutes' harsh irony should have carved up Skinner so that he never walked again. But the entire spirit of Jenkins's leadership brought together in the worst English way (James Prior does the exact same thing) otherwise irreconcilable faults of complacency and despair.

Jenkins never summoned the energy to lead. He was not by temperament a fighter. Illness and office had done their share in debilitating him. A want of impact, apparent almost from his return to Parliament, indeed from his second successful but limply fought by-election contest at Hillhead, became public property during the 1983 election. David Steel who had admired and looked up to him, who indeed had helped persuade him to return and join the new enterprise, had reluctantly to wrest executive control out of his hands to conduct the election himself.

As fighters' comebacks go, it had not lasted very long: a little blaze of choreographed advertisers' publicity in the Connaught Rooms with the four great ones sitting on a raised dais to address the press at breakfast; a link made with the Liberals at their Llandudno conference; the Warrington, Crosby and Hillhead by-elections, and that brief moment when the SDP (the SDP!) in a fully accredited poll had held fifty-one per cent of the hypothecated vote.

Jenkins was not answerable for the Falklands campaign, the heroic irrelevance of which burnished the reputation of an unesteemed government, and he showed throughout that melancholy episode a degree of fastidious distance which did him more credit than good. But even allowing a government recovery and the tricks and rigs built into the electoral system against third parties, Labour was still nowhere, still led by Michael Foot, a good man out of his time. Jenkins was the man with an opportunity who seemed content to gaze at it admiringly. With a team forty strong and not short of talent, he could and should have made the Alliance a Parliamentary force and a national one. To the limpness was added that imperfect enthusiasm for Parliament. He had the tools and he did nothing about the war. The initiative was lost, the target drifted out of sight. The inadequacies of the '83 election only pointed up a wider inertia. When his removal came at the hands of David Owen, it was unresisted and unregretted. The fact of Owen's being the pathological opposite of Jenkins – hyperactive, intolerant of great tracts of the human race and incapable of common-sense cosiness with allies – was suspected and of course fulfilled in a finale reminiscent of Jan Pallach. But at the time he was seen as electric current replacing a flock mattress. The full vitality of sudden death was not altogether perceived.

Yet Jenkins lives on in a happiness which Owen will never share. He is a natural member of the Upper House. He is still clever, still sensible, still a pleasure to listen to as a cool interpreter of events. And his judgement of the political stance of a centre grouping – much more critical of the Tory government, very cool indeed about Mrs Thatcher's wonderfulness – was almost certainly right. He survived to enjoy a happy retirement, hung around with pleasant little garlands like the Oxford Chancellorship. He had had some affinities with Asquith: the culture, the bland, natural, unasserted authority, as well as the lethargy, but he was never touched by Asquith's sour, destructive enmity of those who removed him. Asquith worried about his revenge and the historical record and began the great tradition of Liberal self-evisceration which took that party out of the frame of active politics.

Jenkins lacks such dogged malice and anyway it would be supererogatory. His opponents extinguished themselves, leaving Jenkins as a solitary witness of an accelerated political ice age, a green but thin-soiled paradise converted to a wilderness in seven years. It was Roy Jenkins's fate to re-live his political life at speed through the medium of a dream. Yet considered over his whole career, despite the vanities and the cliquishness and the lack of political as against governmental skills, he leaves a pleasant taste behind him, one of pre-Thatcherian enlightenment, good temper and the absence of hysterical compulsions. It is not a bad thing to lack the defects of character necessary to lead a nation.

# CHAPTER 9

# Terry Dicks

Norman Tebbit is fond of the theory that the Conservative party draws its strength from the adhesion of C1 and C2 voters from the working class who hold opinions radically at odds with most humane, moderate and socially conscious Conservatives, never mind the reds and perverts in Walworth Road.

There is a lot in this though many Conservatives try not to let logical conclusions be drawn from it. If they did, we should probably get back the public hangings yearned for by Mr Harry Phibbs. The point about Terry Dicks, though it is hardly his justification, is that he is the vivid public projection of this bundle of views and attitudes, even though his own social position is rather different. There are nice people who periodically try their hand at 'Terry isn't so bad really. He speaks his mind but he isn't altogether the monster he is taken for.' As an argument it is on a rough par with 'the surprising intelligence and application of Vice-President Quayle' school of conversation-provokers.

Anthony Marlow put it better. 'Nice having Terry about,' he remarked, 'makes me look like a pinko.' Given that Mr Marlow can see the therapeutic value of the Hitler Youth, that puts things succinctly. It is, we must suppose, desirable that MPs should not all conform nor all defer to the same prejudices or drop incense on the same highly regarded altars. In other words, when a man talks about all West Indians being 'bone idle and needing a kick up the backside' he may be many things but not mealy-mouthed.

There is a gap of sorts between Dicks's personal style – which is unmalicious and decently affable – and, well, most of his public utterances. This is all the more surprising as he speaks spontaneously and from conviction; hardly at all does he belong to the Friday Club of people trying to make it into the weekend papers by accommodating Mr Christopher Moncrief. One Bruinvels, a once and I fear future MP, is said to have informed Moncrief that he would put his name to any confection he liked to print. The object was publicity, the intent behind it superfluous. Some statements are then like absolute offences in law. They need no *mens rea*.

Dicks, by contrast, says only what he wants to say. And he has a heroic contempt for right-thinking opinion. His Queen Victoria-like unmoved indifference to the sentiment of others makes him genuinely different from those only *seeking* to shock. Dicks simply *is* shocking. He roams Westminster like a freelance *id*, saying what remain for other people unvoiceable notions not fully admitted to themselves, never mind something for the public domain.

In how many souls was there a corresponding tinkle of recognition when Dicks dismissed the opera as 'an overweight Italian singing in his own language' and ballet as 'men prancing about in a pair of ladies' tights'. Signor Pavarotti, definitely an overweight Italian but a little else as well, hates and loathes the British (not a general Italian view) because he feels that we do not respect him. It would be interesting to engineer a meeting between the two, a case perhaps of Nemorino meets Godzilla.

But you can damn the ballet (Russian) and the opera (Italian) and really suffer social death only in the first division of the civil service where candles burn quietly in niches for Mozart, Verdi, Wagner and other layabouts.

Talking about black people in terms of undisguised contempt, with the word 'tribal' coming readily on to the tongue, is another matter. It is wrong, very seriously wrong, to underestimate the earnest dedication to racial goodwill among the bulk of the Parliamentary Tory party. There are people notably stroppy on the need to cosh the monetary aggregates, for unit labour costs to be the pole star of economic navigation and for general dehydration, who will, without affectation, make a mighty stand on racial justice. Dicks speaks by contrast a brisk street language about people who come over here or asserts that certain Indians seeking entry are liars and cheats.

He is not a systematic theorist of race or a systematic theorist of anything. He is most unlikely to be a friend to organisations actively promoting racial hatred. He is an unconscious speaker of his mind. He could construct a case which argued that he made charges which were broadly true. Deceit by aspirant migrants is not unknown. There are West Indians uncorrupted by the Calvinist urge to endeavour (along with great numbers working – as Mr Dicks might say – like blacks!). Also Dicks would be a sincere enemy of any racial persecution and he would claim that speaking plain never did any great hurt. It is open to him as well to claim, though he never has yet, that his virulence reaches out and strikes cheerfully against his own tribe. He has denounced the inflow of young Irishmen to this country as a 'crippling burden' which, coming from a Roman Catholic with the given names Terence Patrick, may be many things but which as sure as hell is not racist. Yet, despite his forthrightness and distance from the weekend publication school, Dicks is something of an act. He is, for example, to be violently distinguished from Geoffrey Dickens, the fat and eye-rolling MP from Saddleworth, as a cool-eyed buffoon is to be contrasted with a natural fool. Dickens, obsessed by sex crime, desperate for publicity, oblivious of the tolerant contempt of his colleagues, is a blob of soft flesh prattling away like a prurient simpleton. Dicks is rough, hard and listened to with a mixture of disbelief and near respect.

For the moment we are going through quiet times, at least on the surface, but if the race thing (as George Bush would call it) were to come back hot and strong, Dicks is better placed to exploit it than anyone. Precisely because he has kept many arms' lengths away from official race theory or street fascism while being a very apt and on-target populist, he will, in any conflict, use words which chime in with the anxious native British population.

The actual faults of migrants go unvoiced by official Britain for all sorts of creditable reasons – Willie Whitelaw reasons, ones concerned with not torching petrol or hurting people's feelings. But there is a case for saying that a measure of direct speaking, which comes to the point about West Indian crime and the elements of exploitation (and self-exploitation) among people from the sub-continent, would be healthy. 'Better,' one might say, 'that Dicks should talk the way he does than that such points be made by hatemongers, but better still that somebody less candidly brutal should find plain but better words.'

In New York official multiracialism has existed side by side with a terrible state of affairs, incapable of good resolution. The South Bronx is a moonscape inhabited by people, the people who burnt it down. Piety about blacks co-exists with an unspoken dismissal of the great mass of them. A religion of right-speaking has stifled argument and recognition of problems and has become anyway one of those religions which involve going to church rather than believing. Dicks at least acknowledges gaps we don't like to talk about. And if some Indians do cheat, it isn't actually wrong to say so. The difficulty is that we are in the early days of a new set of problems. The old, properly dismissed racism, mostly directed against Jews, was the idle venom of an instinct only shallowly entertained. With new, poorer, but often competing minorities, set down among unprivileged British people, more may be imagined occurring than has happened so far. The worst racialist remarks have sadly come from black sources.

The British may not feel sweet but we are a people with a flair for turning hypocrisy to enlightened account. The stiff upper lip of the upper class and the 'better not make trouble' instinct of working people are both very wise. Terry Dicks rows against them. He does so for satisfaction of his feelings, for short-term advantage and popularity. He feels better for it, but nothing he says will not have been taken on board by the minorities and cherished like a dead baby. One stereotyping generalisation about immigrants which he hasn't made to my knowledge, but which happens to be true, is that they are touchy!

The gratuitous giving of offence is the single least constructive thing an MP can do and Dicks does it all the time. The pity is that he is an intelligent, quick-minded man. He has been brave about dishonest builders and contractors ; in many ways he is a good, conscientious MP. But he has chosen a soft and destructive option.

At a less earnest level he risks becoming a bore. Like all decisive men holding strong opinions, he does not care to leave them unaired. There is also a sort of suppressed violence in his nature, not just the endless tedious calls for flogging and what he calls 'swinging' but a desire that football hooligans should be dyed so they can be identified. Football hooligans are a very great plague, but this is four-ale-bar fascism of a wearying type, a condition above which Terry Dicks normally remains deftly but perilously perched.

# CHAPTER 10

## *Gordon Brown*

It sometimes happens that a public figure becomes too quickly famous, too soon proclaimed the best thing since single malt, and before you know it the poor chap is standing on a hilltop waiting to roll down again as his inability to meet the expectations of perfection and the loving, downward-pushing hands of colleagues sweetly combine.

Gordon Brown, so suddenly a public stock and riding a bull market, *could* be like that. He is, as the Australians put it, 'a tall poppy' and there will be plenty wanting to scythe him down.

It will also be argued that Brown, like the Victorian suitor, is 'so sudden'. Hardly anyone outside the ranks of us political obsessives had heard of him before John Smith's heart attack grimly created a long convalescent gap for Brown which he strove to fill with an eloquent, fact-bejewelled, gracefully scornful speech which made Nigel Lawson sweat. 'One speech,' they say (one and half if you count his crisp comeback to the autumn statement) 'and we get ourselves a new messiah. Garn.' Before that his public fame had been limited to a short resonance in the hollow and echoing skulls of gossip columnists by reason of a forlorn love-affair with one Maggsie, otherwise Princess Marguerite, the daughter of the former Prince Michael of Romania.

Scepticism is very useful in its way, but the private reputation of Gordon Brown has been high for almost as long as he has been in the House. You do not get yourself elected to the Shadow Cabinet after less than four years as an MP without having impressed cynical colleagues that there is some exceptional merit there. Together with the mild but annihilatory Tony Blair, he is coupled as the new-style meritocrat, representative of Labour's improved public face, trying to win back authority by rational argument. I have a recollection of hearing Brown preferred to John Smith as a replacement for Neil Kinnock, at that time stumbling badly, *before* Smith's illness, by one of the most intelligent and independent minds in his party. To the Scots who knew about him before that – on Scottish Television and at Edinburgh where he was student rector in a bitter battle with the university establishment – the reputation goes back further.

Brown is close to prodigy status. Because of an educational experiment, he was one of a group of gifted pupils permitted to take 'A' levels at fifteen and go to university at sixteen. He emerged with the best degree in history Edinburgh has awarded since the war, an echo incidentally of Franz Josef Strauss, Munich's finest graduate in his subject. A doctorate, the foundation for his book on Jimmy Maxton, followed, as did a job on TV, but a seat in Parliament was hard going. They were scything at distinction then, in a way which, gratifyingly, the Scots appear to have given up recently. Also, at that stage, they were resisting a distinct leftwinger who had also dabbled in nationalism, fashionable in the mid-seventies as it seems likely, in a sour, abrasive way, to become again.

Two things are certain about Brown now: that he will function neither as leftist nor nationalist. The election of 1983 put an end to any dabbling with a far-left stance. 'A flash of lightning which brought us to our senses', was how one colleague put it. Brown himself spoke coolly of the Livingstonian Rainbow Left as a policy of 'sending out search parties in search of ever more discontented minorities'. You will not be hearing about lesbian day centres from Mr Brown.

As for nationalism, Scotland at present is enjoying a curdled moment of hysterical self-pity, cheered on by the charming but autocratic personality of James Sillars and drifting at times into a near racist hatred of the English. It could all get much nastier before it stops. Sense, civilisation and the interests of the Labour party, all of which concern Brown, require a fight with the Nats. There are interesting and nasty moments ahead in Scotland.

It is part of the irony of things that Brown should be

emerging as the rational voice of the sort of humane, appealing Labour party which could win back support throughout Britain at the very moment when Scotland, in a tantrum of particularism, threatens to take away the northern base without which Labour doesn't get to play. Yet, despite the blight of Govan where a safe seat slipped through the tattooed fingers of two-syllable Bob Gillespie (a better candidate for retarded Liverpool), Labour has to soldier on and Gordon Brown is part of its consolation.

He demonstrated in an afternoon that the talk about him had not been vapidly hopeful. You do not fillet and bone this Chancellor by way of a fluke. What made the speech so effective was that it took in the entire record of the government – its taxing policies, its stand on benefits and expenditure – but did so without the usual mix of moan and outrage. It argued both that tax policy was tilted absurdly to the country-club element: 'The two thousand wealthiest citizens would gain as much from cuts in inheritance tax alone as it would cost to uprate child benefit in line with inflation for twelve million children.' Also, in the serious long perspective, Mr Lawson had failed to generate investment despite the fillip of selling oil instead of buying it. As for Lawson's forecasts, they had been conclusively wrong – on imports, on the deficit, and on inflation. Now that his forecasts had failed, the Chancellor's response was to do away with forecasting. 'Most of us,' said Brown drily, 'would say that the proper answer is to keep the forecasts and discard the Chancellor.'

Almost never do Labour MPs, even when pleased with a speech, wave their order papers. It is not the tribal way. This practice is, for some reason of political anthropology, a Tory habit, but when Gordon Brown sat down they waved their order papers! It was that good.

One might not go quite all the way with Trevor Kavanagh, the *Sun*'s excellent and experienced political correspondent, who reckoned that Brown's critique of the Chancellor had had more effect in half an hour than five years of *kamikaze* attacks by Labour. It would be a pity if in instant admiration for Brown we had lost sight of John Smith in his sickness. For

Smith has seemed at times to hold Labour together through a long dark hour. And Smith – slimmer, fitter and no more forgiving of the government now he is back – still strikes me, if his health would permit it, as the person capable of communicating enough warmth and sense to the voters to roll Labour substantially forward.

But it is the irony of things that Scotland, at the same time that it is playing ineffably silly games with nationalism, has contributed to Parliament, not the 'feeble fifty' as Jim Sillars in his cheapo sloganising way calls them, but people as gifted as Smith, Brown, Donald Dewar, Robin Cook and perhaps a dozen of the brilliant '87 intake.

Personally, Brown is a quiet unassertive man, good-looking in a vulnerable, wounded way. As indeed he is. A head injury when playing rugby has left him blind in one eye and partially sighted in the other. He is unlike any other prodigy I have encountered in being notably shy and modest. The arrogance and insufferableness of many of the clever and successful, or even the sort of jolly unself-doubting optimism of Michael Howard (working long for Captain Hook at the Environment) who may be the Tories' best find for high-stacked IQ, simply isn't there. Perhaps his being the son of a Church of Scotland minister in a poor parish, with first-hand knowledge of other people's wants, has played a part.

Brown is mild, self-deprecating, civil and understated. The respect which the Conservatives have for him is enhanced by this delicacy of manner (they also rather enjoyed watching Nigel Lawson being boiled alive). His nickname among Scottish friends is 'Broon' after a strip cartoon family of loud, assertive, prolish fitba-watching, many-prejudiced *ney kulturni* Scottish neanderthals. Subtle, elegant-minded, puritanical, rational, Dr Brown is so far from the Broons that the name fits nicely as an irony. He is everywhere described as very ambitious (and why not?), but the consensus seems to be that the shyness is as genuine as the ambition.

Yet he did not have doubt about his ability to walk unaided. Having made a name before he entered Parliament, he was wanted on election for immediate recruitment to the frontbench to share what are now the tribulations of Donald Dewar, as a junior spokesman on Scotland. Interestingly, he shied away from the annals of the parish and opted for a brief period on the backbenches and the Select Committee on Employment. He made a formidable reputation, notably as a someone lucid on finance, and in 1985 was given regional policy and shipping, interests impinging upon Scotland but blessedly remote from the vortex of pettifoggery of that narrow defile.

He was aided in his performance by the fact that he has cultivated excellent sources for the transmission of involuntary leaks, on plans to abolish wages councils, mortgage tax relief and, fascinatingly, the present system of child benefits. Together with Robin Cook, he has been able regularly to pre-empt the government's own taste for trailing the news. This is of course a species of treason and sends Mrs Thatcher into pink little rages about 'stolen' information. In other words, it works.

Brown had his leftwing phase and his dab at nationalism. He had been seen by the scary and resentful academic establishment in Edinburgh as a dangerous conniving red (he and others had discovered that a student could become rector and that he had a right to chair the court of the university). Sir Michael Swann, Mr Heath's favourite strong Chancellor amid all the student troubles, took a particularly bleak view of the boy. The Brown student career was representative of its times – aggressive, learning to throw the rule book at the establishment, able to play a crowd, display an intelligence which could be seen as cunning and possessed of a fervour representable as demagoguery. There is a parallel with Jack Straw, the boy Kossuth of LSE, who has developed a wisdom sometimes braked by circumspection. The period was one of extreme dislocation inside the Labour party. But for the savagery of 1979–82, when the Benn drive for the leadership and the presence on full voice of Scargill, Livingstone and the Militant Tendency produced fever and crisis, perhaps Brown might have remained for rather longer a conventional left-winger and rebel.

But those years of the early eighties were a telescoped and accelerated education, not just for Brown and his fellow student generation but for Labour as a party, perhaps especially in Scotland. In that country Labour was emerging as absolutely dominant at the very time it was slipping to the margin in Britain as a whole. The improvement in quality in Labour candidates was a reflection of the combined ambition and seriousness of Scottish Labour's response to its opportunity and the party's national calamity. Just as Scottish Labour could not afford more duffs, deadweights, city councillors or histrionic exhibitionists, so likely talents suddenly had no time for the self-indulgent pursuit of true socialist perfection. Brown matured, grew more reformist, was perhaps struck by lightning by that '83 election. Also arguably, he learned from his doctoral study of James Maxton that it is possible to be a much-loved romantic socialist impossibilist and accomplish nothing. His move to the centre, masked to the unobservant by his membership of the hollowly and rhetorically leftwing Tribune group (all sentimentality and bet-hedging), is not more opportunist than that of the hundreds who have trodden the same path.

He has become no routine careerist. Nobody listening to the banked-down fervour of his speeches will mistake the old Scottish puritanical scorn for the cheaply rich, the detailed grasp of where the poor have been the losers, or the ability to turn measured anger on to the government. The contrast with Neil Kinnock *has* been noticed. Where the leader at his worst tosses his head like an inside forward looking for a cross, uses all the clumsy tropes of rhetoric and always seems happiest shouting, Brown is almost immobile, uses apt little ironies and talks in a deadly conversational voice into which scorn enters like an assassin.

To anyone who watches politics it has become apparent that Kinnock – despite his courage, despite a wise return to fun and wit starting with the eggs-and-cheese speech – still has problems in the Parliamentary half of his job. The Prime Minister has treated him as an irrelevance; poll after poll until July 1989 ranked him behind every other Labour leader ever with the exception of Michael Foot. And the man who was best equipped to replace him has spent more than a month in Edinburgh Royal Infirmary!

It will do Brown no good after half a dozen excellent speeches to have been talked about so young as a quick successor. He is thirty-eight years old, and has been six years in the Commons. But he has managed to wound and injure the strongest Chancellor of modern times, helping lift Labour morale off the bottom of the sea in the process; he has struck the precise note of combined reason and intelligent compassion which is right for a reformist party trying to re-establish itself with the electorate. The longer-term witnesses to his career reckon that he is as good as he looks.

As to the alternatives, if John Smith really is out of the running, Robin Cook – despite brilliant performances like that machine-gunning of John Moore – has too many enemies and is seen as a master manipulator. Bryan Gould is liked and admired, but his status is that of the consultant. He looks too much like the first-rate man sent along to reorganise the management structure.

Along with his other virtues, Brown has deep roots. Despite that fine degree, he seems able to talk to working people and find the words. We should not look to see Gordon Brown being chosen to lead Labour before a further large Tory election victory. But if Labour's renewed hopes are balked by a substantial margin, it is very hard to see what will stop Gordon Brown from taking the uncomfortable coronet of Opposition leadership . . . and if his present performance holds up, filling it.

# CHAPTER 11

## *Ian Gow*

Some men are eminently mockable and yet not to be mocked. When Ian Gow was Mrs Thatcher's PPS he struck me as being like a Muslim wife, waddling four paces behind her lord. And since Mrs Thatcher makes a pretty fair Muslim husband that passed fairly enough at the snap epigram level.

However Gow deserves something better than snap epigrams. The manner may have been extraordinary: the abrupt speech, managing in a sublime way to be staccato and orotund at once, the heavy florid irony which usually finished up with a goodish to good joke. Then there was the man himself: plump, balding, and given to inquisitors' spectacles and hand gestures somewhere between Heep and Pilate. But he was, for a start, good at his job, if in a slightly awful way. The notebook went with him everywhere. At meetings and immediately after conversations, he scribbled earnestly away. As a result, Mrs Thatcher was exceptionally well served with a flow of intelligence about how the troops felt. She was the better able to play the populist with her troops for knowing what they wanted.

Despite best efforts she has never been kept quite so well in touch since. Gow's predecessor, Fergus Montgomery, was a thickheaded loyalist; of his successors, Michael Alison, an unfulfilled archdeacon, was far too shy to do the search-and-find operation with conviction, and Archie Hamilton, though shrewd, would never rush around in Gow's mad but very useful way.

Gow might be seen, oddly enough, as the other wheel, with William Whitelaw, in the stabilising of a dodgy tricycle. Thatcher was restrained by Whitelaw from, for example, rushing up to Leeds to take over the investigation of the Yorkshire Ripper case. Gow told her at all times what people thought, for and against, guiding her simply with factual reports. Now all Prime Ministers are slightly mad simply to have had such ambition so badly; but with a diet of sycophantic devotion of the 'Maggie lashes Foreign Devils' sort from our gruesome newspapers, some of which read like Habsburg gazettes without the taste, the crazy uncritical instincts become disinherited.

Although Gow was a doggedly loyal protagonist of the lady, he was also giving her objective accounts and Prime Ministers need all the objectivity they can get. And as a wise piece in the *Guardian* noted about him, he wasn't a sycophant; he was something different, an honest supporter of Mrs Thatcher and what she stood for! Never sick in love with office, he found promotion when it came – first to housing then to the Treasury – rather depressing and finally resigned of his own volition over Northern Ireland.

My impression is that although he did have strong Orange sympathies he was at least equally fed up with office itself, where he had earlier threatened resignation over cuts in housebuilding funds, not incidentally the natural act of the hard dry he had believed himself. But the Orange thing is still instructive: bad cause though it was, it put him in the opposite camp to Mrs Thatcher. And sycophants do not go into opposite camps. She was, rightly I think, in favour of the Anglo-Irish Agreement which has the virtue that it cuts Irish Catholic leaders inside the Republic modestly into Northern Irish affairs. This is the sort of irregular action which, pushed far enough, may intimate to the gnarled men of the Six Counties that they are not immortal.

The point against it is that its execution, in secrecy from Protestant leaders and wide open to the SDLP leadership, was the product of the personal spite of Robert Armstrong, who had been humiliated years before during the Ulster workers' strike. This vitiates it badly and is representative of the malice of which conceited authority is capable when cheeked.

Gow was sincerely horrified by the whole thing, including its best parts. On this he joins with a group which, though it includes the excellent Nicholas Budgen, is mostly made up of bristly absurdists, legalistic patriots with a transferred persecution mania. However it has its consistent and honest element and Gow is at home with that group. Oddly, his resignation made him a hero to the *Sun*, which for years afterwards regularly plugged him as a man for restoration to high office, especially the Northern Ireland Office.

In fact, part of his anger at the Anglo-Irish Agreement stemmed from his hopes of getting just that job. It wasn't petty ambition at all, but the one thing he dearly wanted to do and held passionate views about. Perhaps he could have gone despite his Jaffa-flavour since, contrary to what he thinks, it probably doesn't matter who is in Belfast. Life will remain a matter of holding the ring and making gestures; the debate is only about the gestures.

The other post for which the *Sun* fancied its hero was Party Chairman where they have a point of sorts. The Chairmanship was done very well by Cecil Parkinson, Gummer was his own squeaky self, Norman Tebbit was the object of great, undeserved fusillades of sniping, Peter Brooke was a Lords Long Room lovable silly ass. Gow only *looks* like a silly ass.

He is a brilliant operator. Long before the Tories came to power he used the ten-minute rule to proclaim a whole series of mock privatisations which are law today. In a creditable and decent way, he is Thatcher's man. As a debater he has a gift for what might be called 'light heaviness'. He understands the vein of pompousness to which he inclines and, instead of suppressing it, has wittily sent it up.

His obituarial speech on Stuart Holland's departure for a highly remunerated Euro-chair in Florence was a little gem, and his risqué invitation to the excellent Paul Boateng to visit him at the Gow residence near Eastbourne where he would offer him 'one, perhaps more than one, White Lady' (he is addicted to the gin and Cointreau mix), should theoretically have been offensive; but so patently is Gow *not* offensive, so shrewdly treating the adversary as a friend to be bantered with, that he probably enhanced good relations.

One could see a Gow Chairmanship, though highly improbable, being enormous fun.

He has the great qualification of selflessness and the greater one of capacity for enjoyment. He likes to knock the other side about but without rage or malice. He is nicely in the Tory mainstream – a dedicated friend of enterprise and the market, a healthy patriot without hysteria – but, terrorism apart, he is against the death penalty. We have not seen too much under Mrs Thatcher of Tory geniality, and Gow bubbles with it. He is a genuinely nice man lacking the carnivorous impulse, which oddly enough makes so many politicians downright boring.

He would actually make a rather good Chairman. He would cajole and bounce sweetly, he would bring the house down and would never, like David Young who wants it too badly for wisdom, become a focus of serious dislike. The Tory Chairman who for a few weeks becomes the party is a reflection of how people see that party. He needs, in difficult times, and these *are* difficult times, to be its friendly, sympathetic projection. For once the *Sun* may have got it right.

Gow's agreeableness is odd and very much an expression of the whole rather than the sum of the parts. He was not wildly loved when he went about with notebook and pen. His nickname in those days was 'Supergrass', though he was more like an efficient Inspector Clouseau or a blue-rubber KGB man. Politicians do not like other politicians who report on them. And Gow reported more efficiently than anyone since Fouché. But he did it all in an ingenuous and funny way, and then again he is a compulsive smiler with mouth and eyes. Time and again one wants to be hostile to Gow as a rubber-soled loyalist and is disarmed by the man himself. He is also a jolly hedonist, good at finding restaurants, devoted in an age of yoghurt and jogging to White Ladies. There is no reproach in either his manner or, better still, his conduct. This, incidentally, is very odd in a Wykehamist, another link with Whitelaw.

Winchester is an institution identified with thin lips and elevated minds, a private-sector equivalent – as sauntering Eton hardly is and louche Harrow is not – of a French Grande Lycée. Yet Whitelaw and Gow, who have Wykehamism in common, also share the distinction that they are not embarrassingly clever (Gow's academic record was anonymous). Both are shrewder in the gut than distinguished in the cerebellum and they operate on good nature. Ultimately, personal temperament is more important in an assessment of anyone than origins or ideology.

Gow is a natural dry, a market-minded *economic* rightwinger. Despite Winchester, he is no grandee but a thoroughly middle-class type (significantly a solicitor not a barrister). But he is an old-fashioned Tory in the same way as Whitelaw and at a friendly distance from the grave, intense circle of St Andrews' graduates who come to the cause like Cromwell's 'Good russet-coated captain, who knows what he fights for and loves what he knows.' For that matter, they come like Cromwell himself!

Despite having entered politics as a rightwinger, and for all his devotion to the political crown under this monarch, Ian Gow is very much normal politics with a free-market flavour, a jovial bourgeois without reserves of fanaticism. And despite his modest taste for office, he is rather too large a personality to be permanently confined to the backbenches. His limitations come into this as much as his strengths. Not being a first-class administrator or a creative legislator but a big personality with an unselfish desire to subordinate himself, and one with endless efficient energy, he could be used, trusted and not feared by any other leader than Margaret Thatcher. It is a personality which thrives on service without becoming servile. It apes the thing it might be and, untypically for a henchman, it has fun.

# CHAPTER 12

# *Robin Cook*

No party of the left, however constitutional, however meliorist, should be without its Robespierre. That role is filled very satisfactorily for Labour by Robin Cook – the slight, mephistophelian-bearded member for Livingston (formerly for Edinburgh West).

No one who saw his performance after the government announced the Fowler plan for frugality with benefits, which fell with sweet fatality upon John Moore, will quickly forget it. So many Labour spokesmen are trapped between limpness and noisy oration. One could hear Michael Meacher, his predecessor in that portfolio ('weak as hell', Neil Kinnock), clutching at outrage and setting up the sort of moan which cheers hearts in their hardness. One could imagine Neil Kinnock shouting, making phrases and adding thirty per cent to essential length.

Cook does not share a propensity for missing open goals. He had the facts indeed, and gave them out in the sort of magisterial voice that goes with a prosecutor demanding the maximum penalty. But he also has the right manner and the right words. Cook on the attack exudes a mighty scorn, a moral authority which induces unease in thoughtful opponents.

He had made a little-noticed speech a few weeks earlier on the unrewarding topic of withholding benefits over an extended period for those who leave employment voluntarily. There are not that many friends anywhere for the sort of youngster who gives up a job. He is deemed to be feckless, weak, hopelessly to blame for his own inadequacy and thoroughly deserving of a longer stretch of hard times without benefit for his folly. Cook reminded the House of the wide spectrum covered by the word 'voluntary': the bullying, the unhappiness and discouragement which could cause a departure. He asked that the government should sophisticate its thinking and not rest contented with the complacencies of employed prosperity. It was characteristically intelligent and notably warm.

Cook does not make sentimental glutinous speeches any more than he rants. It is correspondingly more difficult for Conservatives to discount what he says or brush him aside. DHSS Ministers whom he shadows know that they are being scrutinised, that they cannot lightly waltz through softly worded harsh acts. They know also that the man across the despatch box will not be strap-hanging on routine indignation or going over the top in the clownish noisemaking way of so much self-indulgent opposition. I have never yet heard Cook, even on occasions when little hung upon it, make a *pro forma* space-filling speech.

To compare him with Robespierre is to go only some of the way. Although he began on the left and in many essentials belongs there yet, he is practical and amenable to rational argment. Unlike Robespierre he is not a fanatic, but he has the essential revolutionary virtue of incorruptibility. Incorruptible, that is, in the sense of not being caressed or softened by the Parliamentary club or attracted by the eating, drinking, travelling and good times aspect of Parliament. There is a whiff of soda water and arrowroot biscuits about Cook which should trouble the Tories.

He is an odd companion for Neil Kinnock – a florid politician, a man constitutionally incapable of shutting up, a pan-oratorium of opinions who would sooner talk than think. Yet it was Cook as much as anyone who accelerated Kinnock, who acted as his campaign manager during the leadership election. If Kinnock was young at that time, Cook was absurdly young. He appreciated the Welshman's charm and facility and surely also sensed someone who could be influenced and helped to his thoughts. It was the perfect marriage of introvert and extrovert, of backroom and downstage, of epigram and *hwyl*.

However, it also tempted Cook, whose besetting sin is a measure of intellectual arrogance, to a rather over-apparent view of himself as the Dr Coppelius of this outfit. There was a fall when Cook was actually voted off the Shadow Cabinet, having been altogether too crisp and peremptory with lesser men and slower minds. Members of inner *apparats* are not loved, as the present Kinnock kitchen cabinet could heartily testify. Cook was seen at this time as a truculent, bossy, cocksure, ginger-bearded little dominie of whom it was very easy to have too much. The judgement was not unfair. He was still very young (born 1942); he had the hubris of many quick minds and no great store of tact. I have even heard him patronise Denis Healey at a fringe meeting, normally an act of terminal indiscretion.

If he had been incapable of learning, Cook could have ripened into the most thoroughgoing obnoxiousness. But he is hugely capable of learning. As it was, being thrown off the Shadow Cabinet was perhaps the best thing that could have happened to him. He went away and worked even harder. He took the knock as something very close to a just rebuke and, above all, he concentrated his talents for making himself feared and disliked entirely upon the Conservative and Unionist party. Labour in Parliament is collectively quite shrewd. They have a good notion of what works and who gets across (which makes doubly absurd the new method of choosing a leader through a majority of non-observers of the talent). They forgave Cook the memory of his strutting ways, acknowledged his gift for carbonising the other side and on pure merit reinstated him after a year, and with a high place on the tally.

He has not seriously looked back. Health and Social Security is an area where the government is being experimental without fully grasping the implications. Whoever was to oppose the reorganisation of benefits laboriously and furtively prepared by Norman Fowler and topped, tailed and brought forward by John Moore, should have enjoyed some success. There was enough Conservative unhappiness to work upon. But some success might have been expected from the Westland crisis and the leader of the Opposition spent that day of opportunity beating himself to his knees.

The Cook assault upon the new frugality was perfectly splendid. The facts and details were there but not in a boring abacus-clicking way. The words were good and elegant but without any froth of rhetoric. There was dignity but no high piety. What we had was the charge sheet, elegantly read and glossed by prosecuting counsel with just a hint of the recording angel. It was Labour's best day in this Parliament. John Moore happened to be below par in health, struggling with a feverish cold and his voice giving out. Even so, one doesn't get many Conservative crucifixions these days.

Although Cook has it in him to point an attack in a way which actually frightens the Tories, and although his colleagues are sensible and appreciative of this strength, a serious anti-Cook case has been made and made by responsible people, notably fellow Scots. It perceives him as a compulsive fixer with a talent for staying just the right distance between any two positions so as to exploit them at both ends. That Dr Coppelius image of someone coldly and manipulatively using his strong residual position with the left as a lever inside the team is sharply invoked. Specifically I have heard it argued that the alleged influence of Cook upon Neil Kinnock in the terrible few days between his multilateralist statement to Vivian White and his unilateralist interview with the *Independent* was calculated very long.

It is generally agreed that Cook argued for a return to the old line, something which is consistent with his general position. But the hostile view sees him as being far too intelligent not to foresee the tremendous damage such shuttle-thinking would do Kinnock as leader. 'I cannot believe,' said one astute observer, 'that Robin didn't know what harm he would do to Kinnock and didn't subtly mean to do it. He is altogether too much of a Cassius,' he added. That is a very black view based on a Machiavellian assumption about human nature. Indeed, there is an echo of the Scottish soubriquet of the sixteenth-century statesman William Maitland, known in the doric as 'Michael Wylie'. It may be wrong and it may be unfair but it is partly the price that Cook pays for his high and saluted intelligence. Being so quick-minded, he is, as it were, seen to perceive his own advantage.

An odd aspect is his perpetual twinning with another unreasonably clever Scot, Malcolm Rifkind. At high school and university, and later as adversaries on Edinburgh City Council, they may have been 'as twin lambs that played together' but whether 'they knew not the doctrine of illdoing nor dreamt that any did' is more doubtful. It is startling that two such exceptional talents should have started together so soon and pursued closely parallel routes. It is odd for the onlooking Englishman to watch significant pieces of his destiny (at one time our whole relationship with the EC) being debated together as an extension of their high-school exercises by a couple of clever Scottish lawyers who have taken up the government of Britain as a steady career. That neither of them wants Scotland returned to the kaleyard of petty Scotch autonomy is the least surprising thing on earth. An independent Scotland has all the charms of an independent Barataria and neither man has the least affinity with Don Quixote, made king of that wilderness. In assessing the seriousness of Scottish patriotic noises, never underestimate the opportunity which England constitutes for clever Scotsmen.

These two have in common great cerebral intelligence and great taste for rational argument. But Rifkind enjoys more content; his humour is less stinging. The cynicism, if that is what it is, is present on the surface in adjustments of policy from devolutionist to anti-devolutionist, from liberal Tory to Thatcher functionary. This is all part of the footwork necessary for advancement and is not taken altogether seriously. Cook is serious even as a manipulator. He has found an optimum position, part of realistic rather than daydreaming politics. But he has retained most of his credentials with the left. He is not seen as a betrayer of their covenant. Consequently he is listened to by them and is likely to be used as an intermediary in conflicts. At the same time the idea of Cook as conscience to the new realists only mildly irritates them. There is not too much of a world to be enjoyed in Opposition, but arguably Robin Cook has the best of it.

However the sceptical view in cool pursuit of low motives can be overdone. What should not be underestimated is how important the adherence of someone like Cook to mainstream politics and to a prominent place in it means to Labour's ability to function at all as an Opposition. Anyone making prophecies in the late seventies would have assumed Cook to have been part of the left destiny under Mr Benn which was going to dominate Labour politics after the next logical, implacable step. From within the left Cook was able to spot a fool when he saw one. Like Jack Straw, like Jeff Rooker and, following a rather different pattern, Frank Field, Cook is one of those once readily identifiable as part of the left who, for reasons of sense and maturity and because first-class talent does not pursue marsh gas into the middle of a devouring bog, have survived and now help Labour itself almost to thrive.

I wrote about these four together in 1982 when preparing *The Senate of Lilliput* and noted that all four – then perceived to be somewhere on the left – were, in contrast with a quartet of wellknown adherents of the then irresistible SDP, simply better talents, superior articles. In retrospect their adhesion (and their political refinement though that of Field was already far advanced) constitutes evidence of why Labour survived in what must have been the bleakest two-year period of that party's history.

Neil Kinnock, the ceremonial head of the soft left, has gone on to glory. Figures like Cook not directly caught in the full blast of publicity are not his successors, but if Kinnock should ever come to an exhausted end, a retro-rocket necessary for correcting direction but unequal to sustained flight, such people will sustain Labour as a serious party.

Of all the intelligent men available to that party, Cook is the most directly political, the one with the greatest aptitude for the frontbench. He genuinely scares the Tories, perhaps because a little of the old leftwing contempt for a corrupt world is still within him. John Smith, despite his stern prosecutor's manner, is a comfortable man and ultimately more effective with the country because of it. Accordingly, the Conservative response to Smith is one of friendly admiration. 'Here is a sensible fellow, on the other side of course and not at all a crypto-Tory, but talking a language we comprehend. It's very good for us to be given a dressing-down by John; he might well be right.'

The response to Cook is one of dislike, tempered by guilt and admiration. This is indeed Robespierre – calm, lucid, scornful of all well-set-up gentry with ribbons at the knee. 'He may have joined the Gironde, he may sound like a maker of rational reforms but what is that sharp harsh sound in the back of his voice? It has the ring of a stone against which is being sharpened the slicing edge of a heavy blade.'

# CHAPTER 13

# John Selwyn Gummer

It is given to some public figures to be more public than others. The arts of Mrs Edwina Currie in wearing spangled tights on the trapeze or, at her most useful, in finding a column of dull nutritionist information and ringing it around three times in day-glo pen, are familiar if ultimately injurious to the principal.

But the generality of junior Ministers, whatever the level of ability, inclines to a style which matches its clothes: dark blue or grey, striped (pin or chalk), and shod in black brogues. From this haze of concussed restraint, John Selwyn Gummer, forty-nine, author of *When the Coloured People Came* and *The Christian Calendar*, leaps clad in fluorescent purple and primrose, like a hallucinogenic frog.

Gummer has minor physical qualities: a voice like a cor-anglais and the body of a stick-insect, which makes him look like a tragic loss to cat burglary, and a name 'Selwyn', to which his personality seems reasonably attuned. Oddly, 'Selwyn Lloyd' sounded perfectly reasonable; 'Selwyn Gummer', as he was at his earlier election attempts, sounds like a character invented by a facetious novelist. Personal suffering has not made him a thoughtful parent – the Gummer children, poor things, are called Benedict, Felix and Leonora.

There is no harm in him, no wellspring of malice. He is a nice boy given to enthusiasms and enormously churchy with it, a natural Selwyn. Like Frank Field, a rather different sort of political Christian, he has been a member of the Anglican Synod and spreads a Christian manner wherever he goes. Gummer has religion in the way that someone else might have a springer spaniel. He takes it out for walks, exhibits it at the county show, walks the prize ring with it, calling 'heel' and 'sit' at appropriate moments, keeps its second and third prizes on the mantelshelf and brings the conversation insistently round to it.

He was born into a family of nice evangelicals, hence the Selwyn – a reference to the evangelical college at Cambridge. His father, who comes over as a very agreeable clergyman, wrote a biography of the Cold War and Moral Rearmament Bishop of Rochester, Christopher Chevasse. But Gummer opted for Anglo-Catholicism, now an increasingly sour and paranoid branch of the business, given to burning women *in absentia* and to worshipping at the shrine of Gareth Bennett, the Emily Davidson of ecclesiastical misogyny, whose sad suicide seems to have released deep underground springs of venom among the Anglos.

In fairness to Gummer, though a dedicated woman-stopper, he is drawn to the celebrants of the white mass more by its big-top atmosphere of props-basket theatricality and general dressing up than by that sub-sect's taste for character assassination. But that *piccolo mondo* of sub-ecclesiastical conspiracy and frenzy over antiquarian trifles quite becomes him. The religious aspect of the lad is trivial and for show. Gummer does not perceive a speaking fire in religion, he approaches its observance as thrill and happening, while looking on God as an influential person well worth cultivating. He is against the ordination of women, but only because 'it would deny validity to our orders which are recognised by Rome'. That is the authentic voice of Anglo-Catholicism which, in its readiness to fall downstairs to please His Holiness, always sounds to me faintly collaborationist, a sort of Vichy Anglicanism. Incidentally, what really upsets the sort of vicar who has high mass instead of evensong, is less a woman priest than the rise of a woman to the rank of bishop with an ordaining power which would break the apostolic succession (people actually *believe* this).

As a camp curate put it in the same context, 'Mere ordination simply wouldn't take, my dear. It would be like ordaining a pot of anchovy paste.' Women, it would seem, are barred by the Roman Catholic church, which Gummer continues to spare his membership. Accordingly, the Church of England, if it is to keep the apostolic ball in the air, must not lapse into permitting their ministry. It seems a long way to push an old Jewish prejudice, but it keeps Gummer off the streets.

Gummer is the product of active youth politics, a fairly gruesome thought which he has done his best to live up to. He was, like David Mellor, every kind of Young Conservative, and later president, for what it is worth, of the Cambridge Union. Cambridge produces most of the politicians in this generation, but it does not make the Union a competitive place for exciting, witty debate – two matters which may be connected.

He was unforgettable in the mid-seventies, at a time when the BBC was accused of 'leftwing bias' on an all rightwing redress programme, together with the fatuous Christopher Booker excitedly calling the odds for Conservative, Christian and very slightly creepish values. Everything about Gummer confirms the view that everyone ought, at least briefly, to have been somewhere on the left. Conservatism may be wisdom or it may be greed, but as sure as hell it doesn't look right at eighteen.

The impression lingers that, theology apart, Gummer can never have given his parents anything but joy. He is, to a depressing degree, a good boy – bright, cheerful, willing, and at the same time responsible. Thoughts of Charles Augustus Fortescue (and murder) occur:

> The nicest child I ever knew
> Was Charles Augustus Fortescue

The line in Belloc's cautionary tale which bears most heavily is the one about

> And as for finding mutton fat
> Unappetising, far from that,
> He often at his father's board,
> Would beg them, if they did not mind,
> The greasiest morsels they could find.

Gummer, a young fogey before the word was thought of, is essentially a confection. He has invented himself as an amphibious article, capable of functioning fulltime in politics; should that fail, as a character or original much in demand by the flashier sort of television programme. Given Mrs Thatcher's appalling judgement about people, she is quite capable of elevating Gummer to the Cabinet.* But in the event of greater wisdom being shown, he has a secure future compêring a news programme between the quizzes and the three-hundred-part American serials on any of the competing wildernesses. For that matter, he could take over *Blue Peter* or *An Act of Worship for Schools*. He is also perfect life-peerage material.

However, we must be serious about Gummer, we must. He has been a junior Whip, a junior Minister at Employment, Chairman of the Conservative Party and Minister of State at Agriculture. He is now Minister of State in charge of Housing at the Department of the Environment. He has played a very full part in governing us. The only job in which he really attracted notice was the Chairmanship of the Tories, a fortuitous greengage on the tree of knowledge as plucked by Cecil Parkinson.

For most of us, concerned only that nothing should be done which disturbs the horses, the sudden disclosure by Miss Keays (who certainly should not become an ordained minister of the Church of England) that she was pregnant after a long affair with that politician, was interesting but not in the least shocking. This, to be fair, was the view of Mrs Thatcher who would be something of a Hampstead Jacobin if she could be as liberal about everything else as she is about sex. But the Conservative party, as a hypothesis, and Mr Parkinson's enemies, for a certainty, were in a state of old womanly agitation and for the interim Cecil, who could be forgiven anything except his monograms and his accent, Had To Go.

Gummer's time as Chairman was perfectly timed. The election was already won, the next election would obviously be in the hands of someone important (Norman Tebbit

---

*She did!

actually); Gummer was given the presidency of the interim and required to function as talking Polyfilla. He denounced Dave Nellist as a 'red fascist' (he is actually rather a sweet kid given his daft views), denounced the BBC for its 'McCarthyism' and, more satisfying, preached a sermon at the 'purblind' Monsignor Bruce Kent, annoyingly a real Catholic but another class act in Gummer's sanctimonious egotism division of the tedium circuit. Having made only modest impact, he was, Soviet style, put in charge of a mangold-wurzel plant – that is made Number Two at Agriculture. His role as *klutz* of Smith Square was taken (as deputy) by Jeffrey Archer.

If Archer preaches the gospel of success – sex, business, power, fame, intimidation – a half-literate gospel to be read by a penthouse-dwelling, logophobic developer, Gummer is all moral intrusion, worship-in-drag, moral affront, righteousness and sentences beginning, 'As a Christian I . . .' They are parts of the same party: not quite Dr Jekyll and Mr Hyde more Dr Hyde and Mr Hyde, no-talent prose spiv and self-assembled conversation piece. But anyone who supposed that Gummer was indifferent to the gospel of success, happy to give himself up fulltime to his other role as 'a Guardian of the Shrine of Our Lady of Walsingham', would be profoundly wrong. Gummer is ambitious before he is anything else.

He has a way of investing in any leader of the Conservative party the sort of devotion more properly channelled towards 'Our Lady of Walsingham'. It might be argued that anyone capable of worshipping stocks and stones might well be attracted by Edward Heath. This Gummer did as he worshipped the vision of Europe (naturally he was Chairman of Christians for Europe). In fairness, he was also a creditable, if ineffective, anti-Powellite, speaking up against the great deporter; but he was sufficient of a personal trusty to become a Vice-Chairman of his party at thirty-two. This enabled him to run around the country shouting that 'our destiny lies in Europe', that 'we must not be an offshore island' and the rest of the Euro-patter.

But the same Gummer is not only able to make a warm place for himself under the Thatcher sun but to feel the same excited delight at her existence. He is a species of drum majorette, readily transferable from the Bears to the Cowboys, but avoiding the Red Sox. The same promiscuous rapture is available for any aspect of Conservatism currently enjoying influence. As for Gummer denouncing something, it is quite special, like a small furry animal undergoing the ecstasy of a religious experience. When Greenwich Council took Nicholas Ridley to court for a slippery and tendentious leaflet defending the Poll Tax, Gummer was given a long session defending the official statement, in which he went off like a badly timed firework display on the glories of what he insistently called 'the Community Charge', raging like an operatic moth against the disgraceful and monstrous conduct of Labour councils everywhere.

The thought occurs that Gummer is without individual resilience. The most interesting figures at Westminster have an outlook of their own and make rough terms with the party which approximates nearest to it or gives least trouble. Such people are embarrassed by too much recitation of Conservative or Labour affiliation. But Gummer is a follower, needing in politics as in religion a hero and a group to identify with. To the person who less believes in a cause than he takes refuge in it, affirmation is correspondingly the most necessary thing.

Gummer thinks that by joining something – the Conservative party, Anglo-Catholicism, Europe – he *becomes* something. The analogy is with colouring books for children. Hence all this 'As a Christian I . . .' stuff, a conviction that the anaemic person of Gummer will suddenly flame up in cardinal's red or error-of-taste blue according to whether we are being a little Christian or a little Conservative that afternoon.

It isn't an accident that while any Tory grown-up loathes and tries to stay away from Harvey Thomas's fascist rallies – group rapture for the leader with lasers and electric organ – Gummer is deeply happy with them. He is in a group of the like-minded, offering uncritical praise to someone able to reward him, a synopsis of his life purpose.

One tries to be gentle and even affectionate towards Gummer, conscious that Sir Edward Du Cann, a man who normally expresses a balanced view by way of anointing its object with unrefined molasses, described Gummer as 'an inconsequential little creep who has never grown out of student politics'. He is better than that, being much less creep than compulsive follower and dependant. Whether he should be governing us as a Minister is more doubtful.

One is tempted to advocate Mikado-style punishment of such a paper flower opening only in the water of publicity. We might perhaps take his religious devotion seriously and send him into undated, meditative, silent retreat.

# CHAPTER 14

## Tam Dalyell

Politics is not, thank God, made up exclusively of the dark blue blur of smooth-shaven, Brut-fragrant aspiration, nor for that matter only of the zippered-windcheater, tufted-beard and open-shirt regiment of organised dissent. There are bits which stick out, unfixed and unfixable makers of trouble who hunt in no pack, whatever support they may temporarily gain for a cause.

It has been said of Tam Dalyell that he is the only member of the Campaign Group to own peacocks. Indeed socially he derives from a model of hereditary grandeur from which the Conservative party especially in Scotland, is trying frantically to escape. The Tories still suffer in Scotland from their past estrangement from practical business and professional people, something inflicted by the procession into seats progressively less safe of tongue-tied and unmeritable lairds educated beyond salvation at English public schools. Such lairdlings had been acceptable to the Scots only when Scotland provided the NCOs of empire. But in a country of natural levelling and republican sentiments the wee lords looked in our shrivelled latter days like so many toastmasters. The accents of Eton and Cambridge denied the tartan on the knee; the lace at the throat was soon joined by an electorate aiming at the same place. The owners of fine shoots in the kitsch and heather belt, they were brought down like grouse by voters in elections.

Such a man as Tam Dalyell, Edinburgh Academy, Eton and Kings' Cambridge, could have survived, as the Ancrams died like Jacobites around him, in only one place: the Labour party. Mr Dalywell is a miracle, though not one as narrowly British as we like to think. There have been red counts in Italy, socialist aristos like Graf Kessler in Germany and at the root of this tendency is the headless body of the Duc d'Orléans, Philippe Egalité, guillotined only for lapsing into regret at the excesses of a revolution he had ardently endorsed.

It would be a mistake to identify Tam Dalyell as being anything seriously to do with the ultra-left. Some fool did just that in one of those witless lists of dangerous reds which the Owen faction likes to produce near elections. He was listed as 'hard left' a statement as memorably stupid and wrong as the earlier list in another election which had accused Syd Weighell of communist sympathies. He must be the only member of the hard left to have been in favour of reprocessing nuclear waste on the north-west coast of Scotland, to support vivisection and to advocate a prohibition on a Militant Tendency candidate.

His views are like Oliver Cromwell's definition of land law, 'an ungodly jumble' but of his social position there can be no doubt whatever. Not far from Edinburgh stands a seventeenth-century mansion, The Binns, over whose not at all Adam mantelpiece hangs a vast and fearful-looking length of iron which was the sword, since only he at six foot ten could handle the thing, of Bluidie Dalyell. Now Bluidie Dalyell (also Tam), in the service of James Graham, Earl of Claverhouse, unimaginatively known as 'Bluidie Clavers', pursued the Covenanters, men who combined the outlook of Ian Paisley with that of the rabbis who throw stones at sabbath motorists in Israel, and did so with an agreeable ferocity. He was a blue-ribbon Tory who incidentally also beat up the Irish.

So devoted was this man to the memory of that dim, mendacious aesthete, Charles I, that after the king's execution he never again shaved his beard which, given his death in 1685, allowed for thirty-six years' growth. Such a luxuriance may have stood him in good stead among the boyars of the Streltsy in his years of service fighting for the Russians (he too might have got on a list of dangerous leftists except that the Russian gold this time came from Alexei Mihailovich Romanov, a well-known Tsar of all the Russias). In his later time as

Claverhouse's lieutenant, he helped smash the Covenanters and do his bit for the coming union by winning the battle of Rullion Green. An epithet was bestowed upon him by the text pounders of the kirk, which might cheerfully be echoed against his descendant today: 'The De'el and Dalyell begin wi' ain letter,/The De'el's nae guid, and Dalyell's nae better.' It says it all really.

Tam Dalyell has aristocratic credentials which outrun those of anyone in Tory politics. Even Lord Carrington goes back only to Pitt the Younger for his title and to a seventeenth-century grocer and banker for his family's start in the gentry. Compared with such sixth-baron *arrivistes*, Tam is actually *Sir* Thomas, seventeenth baronet, a title he disdains to use, and the thirty-first laird. If you go back far enough in a family of border-reivers or cattle-rustlers as they would have called them in South Dakota, it is possible to find Dalyells slipping across the border to steal from Ridleys, and Ridleys trying to hang Dalyells.

Having thus all the credentials in the world, he proceeded as he adopted socialism to obtain more of the newer sort by marrying Kathleen Wheatley, daughter of Lord Wheatley, Lord Justice Clerk and one of the most distinguished men in Scotland but also the grandson of John Wheatley, the father of council housing and easily the most effective Minister of the Macdonald Labour governments. But the Wheatleys are Roman Catholics and, even in the more liberal east of Scotland, only a man impervious to public opinion would cross that line while conducting a political career.

Tam began as a Tory at Cambridge, having been brought in by his friend John Biffen. But in the manner of the comrades who left the Communist party over Hungary, he was shocked out of Conservatism by Suez. That is instructive. The moral instinct, the literal insistence upon fair-dealing and truth-telling which is taught at the public schools but generally slid out of in the oiled-down world of Tory politics, is a simple absolute for the man. He tells the truth and could conceive of doing nothing else and despises, in the way only a socialist thirty-first laird can despise, anyone who tells anything else.

Dalyell's contempt for Thatcher is a thing which commands awe; the nostrils are distended, the lower lip extends à la Nye Bevan like a baroque curve; the lady is told, prior to Dalyell's latest expulsion, that she is a liar. Rather in the way of P. G. Wodehouse's observation that aunts aren't gentlemen, he once remarked, with all of POP gathered into the disdain, 'The Prime Minister, Mr Speaker, is a bounder.' Even in this age of sexual equality it doesn't sound quite right though one knows what he means.

He is not skilful in his moral onslaughts but he is unrelenting; they are coalhammer blows falling again and again. We shall never know for certain if Mrs Thatcher and her Ministers did coldbloodedly sink the *Belgrano* with huge casualties to scotch serious peace talks in the South Atlantic War. If true, that would be a piece of wickedness incapable of mitigation, or if there are other and better explanations for the attack on a ship outside the exclusion zone and moving farther away it is a matter of regret that we have not been told them. But it was Dalyell who, unskilfully but heroically, single-handed took up a charge from which official Labour wanted to stay safely remote and, at the cost of endless emotional stress, suspensions, uproar, much hatred from the Tories and few allies, made it again and again. When the full history comes to be written, the question is there, scored deep into the chronicle of current events and demanding a proper answer. Tam put it there.

If there is a purpose for backbenchers other than waiting for promotion or playing out time in the long evanescence after office, it surely lies in the making of trouble in the high manner of Frank Field. Alternately it can be rough trade, the not very articulate way of a calf butting an oak, in Solzhenitsyn's phrase. But either way it is the trouble which justifies the Member, and when it comes to trouble Dalyell hands out Hell and Maria.

In his gawky repetitive way, he has a certain moral imperiousness. He asks and asks; he finds truth wanting, so he breaks etiquette and received custom and shocks the company with straight charges of lying. The normal punches of working politics are pulled short of that and are often more effective for being so restrained, but Dalyell, a mattress stuffed with thistles, exists to torment. No one else has his nerve, his indifference to derision and the prevailing mood. Although he speaks of himself as 'a very, very assiduous constituency MP', he has nothing else of the politician about him. *Belgrano* is not a solitary break with the mainstream; he has given his life to dissent.

Scottish devolution is for the interim an undone conclusion, going through a posthumous phase until the right princess or frog unwisely kisses it. But it was yesterday's unanswerable certainty – all wisdom and Peter Jay were for it, who could be against it? The building which was to house the Scottish Parliament, the old Edinburgh high school, was already set aside; only the cranks on all sides resisted. From the Tory right there were Teddy Taylor and Iain Sproat, among the future Social Democrats there was the excellent George Cunningham, and there was Sir Thomas Dalyell of The Binns! He supported the Cunningham amendment which required a forty per cent vote in favour for a majority to register; he successfully opposed the use of national funds to finance the 'Yes' campaign. In all of this he was set against the conventional thinking of the decade. It was the way of the Labour right and of Mr Heath to value constitutional change. Arguably their passion for regionalism was partly a search for a therapeutic activity in the face of unsolved economic problems. Why else trouble the Welsh, who outside a few rather nasty country districts have never bothered with serious nationalism? But in the face of the SNP election victories and the odd, unlovable, menacing way in which they talked, the reaction had more to do with panic than therapy. Giving in to the Nats was second nature to those on both sides who had made names for themselves giving in to the trades unions. The entire episode was bad, cowardly, run-away politics cognate with a number of other shaming episodes – like secret talks with the IRA, like thirty per cent wage settlements, like the extension of the closed shop. Meddle-someness and wet-palmed fear combined to substitute schemes of concession and confection and to rationalise a retreat which some people had in their blood.

Dalyell loathed the surrender instinct. He was engaged in confronting the *Zeitgeist* and, though he could not know it, the *Zeitgeist* was about to be exorcised. He was joined at an opportune moment by the unsure Leader of the Opposition, persuaded that way by Teddy Taylor. Mrs Thatcher and Tam Dalyell have not often since been seen under the same colours. But, ironically, the defeat of devolutionism which allied them was also the end of passive politics, of government as the losing side conceding almost pre-emptively to pressure groups demanding in raucous voices what they then commonly got.

Thatcherism has degenerated at the end of this decade into bullying, secretive, winning-side government, and thoroughly detestable it is. But it is worth recalling what things Thatcher and her re-elections are a reaction against. Just as ironically, Tam made one of his great denunciations on the topic of the Zircon satellite and the invasion of BBC Scotland by policemen, precisely the sort of centralised authoritarianism which stands at an opposite pole from the trembling acquiescence of late Callaghanism. There is nothing to be said for either and Tam was against both.

But then being against things is second nature. It is totally stunning to allies when suddenly he is in favour of something. One's heart goes out to the Campaign Group – though not for long and not very sincerely, the Campaign Group being a bunch of sour-mouthed, froth-headed leftists of the sort which bring the term 'leftist' into disrepute. They were finally obliged to withdraw their slate nomination from Dalyell in Shadow Cabinet elections on the grounds that he had voted with them on only a quarter of all issues. What on earth else did they expect? On certain questions Tam could be mistaken for those upper-class rightwingers who have accidentally in a fit of adolescent enthusiasm ended in the wrong party, in the way of Reginald Paget or Woodrow Wyatt. Dalyell on nuclear power is very rightwing and evil indeed. He is for it, believes that the dangers are a conjuring of hysteria and that nuclear waste can also (in Scotland forsooth) be taken into one's processing stride. To combine this opinion with his belief that troops should be withdrawn from Northern Ireland (fifteen times more contentious in Scotland than in England) is not at all illogical. Both conclusions can be logically arrived at; but broadly speaking, people who want nuclear power stations are the same people who want 'union' and a continued military presence. People who want to be shot of troops in N. Ireland commonly want to be shot of nuclear power. Only Dalyell builds coalitions among his opinions.

His gaunt, frugal presence, tall, built at right angles from himself, his voice half quaver, half aristocratic summons, his odd, angular ways, are part of what used to be called a *persona*. Let us just call him a force, which is moral and not imaginable away from the constraints of Calvinism. It is honourable in the ways which public schools teach honour but assumes that they meant it.

It is also, despite the trappings of eccentricity, in a high degree rational. All those pieces of left and right opinion are entirely defendable in themselves, for his outlook is supremely eclectic. Tam Dalyell has picked and mixed, not ever for his own advantage or convenience, but for the merits which he perceived. But having grasped a conviction, he has never treated it relatively, never let English geniality get in the way of his iron-sided certainties. Those certainties have never enjoyed group endorsement, but he has a way of being rough and readily right. And Mrs Thatcher, who represents the most decisive turning away from the soft, defeatist mood of the seventies precisely as he rejected it, is the object of his unplumbed scorn over the *Belgrano*, over Westland, over Zircon and much more.

For all his discombobulated manner and solitary path, he is the upholder of scruple and honesty in politics. To be censured by him is something which can of course be brushed off, but in a longer context it may rank as a judgement. And one just wouldn't want, like Margaret Thatcher, to have been weighed by Tam and found so categorically wanting.

# CHAPTER 15

## *Michael Heseltine*

The pattern of politics is subordination. Though it is tempered for sure by disloyalty and daydreaming, and by the aspiration, among those thinking themselves fit for it, to enjoy the subordination of others.

The life work of Kenneth Baker is made up of cautious acceptance of any present bitter flavour in his mouth in the well shepherded hopes of ultimately enjoying the sweetest of all tastes. In this he is almost certainly wiser than Michael Heseltine, but in the process lacks his romantic king-over-the-water, blue-bonnets-for-me Jacobite appeal. And how well off he is without it.

What makes Heseltine different from the bland generality of politicians is his enjoyment of that difference. Even in his conforming days, he turned heads, drew attention to himself and stood apart. This was done not in the Peter Walker way, with a press conference to proclaim his wonderful new achievements, but existentially – by his sustained style, bounce and perpetual throbbing presence. Only Heseltine would have loaded up a charabanc of investment potential – executives, accountants, the cream of the entrepreneurial classes – to take them around Liverpool and be shocked. Whether, in the light of a tendency among the Liverpool workforce (the werkers!) to grind small any employer fool enough to hire them, he was doing anybody a favour is more questionable. It is not necessary to be very rightwing to consider that in view of the record of Mersey docks and the Speke motorworks, Merseyside deserves everything that has happened to it, as an area of outstanding employer avoidance.

But he exploded on to the question for which he had no direct responsibility, out of a measure of at least fifty per cent sincerity. Heseltine the wet, the public intervener who thinks something should be done and does it, is real. It may be dubious economics, but along with the ambition goes an honest belief in the paternal notion of government. He was at odds with the Prime Minister at all times and had the courage to do things which privately outraged her. In one sense he was wrong. The Thatcher stubbornness, allied with her failure to believe in the coming three million unemployment (nearly four when it did, despite rigging), has been validated by history. We got the unemployment, the world did not fall apart nor did the workers march on Westminster or even vote for Michael Foot; private wealth was not stripped from its guilty owners, nor were their heads stuck upon poles. Thatcher was right or at any rate right in inverted commas. The demands of workers crumbled with diminished expectations, unit labour costs fell, selectively and asymmetrically investment returned, there was growth, everything became wonderful.

Of course a formidable case can be mounted against the finance-heavy economy of Thatcherian Britain, so hungry for the manufacturing jobs which have gone that she operates as Japan's opportunity in the Common Market. There can be even more scepticism at the notion of our having intended what we did when we were stumbling from monetarism to cheap credit to the sterling crisis. However, to the extent that the wet position rested upon panic as well as sympathy the panic element has been exploded. From a narrowly Tory point of view we do not need to be one nation, provided that enough of the nation likes what it gets and votes Conservative.

But politics needs its element of romance and Heseltine, often in a preposterous way, has supplied it. He was playing romance when, in defiance of a small piece of Labour coerciveness, he seized the mace and waved it above his head. The flapdoodle of procedure deserves no special reverence; it doesn't greatly matter what happens to the bauble, but the event was a display of the central Heseltine flaw. He is a flashy, noisy exhibitionist without sufficient control of himself. There is a case, a stuffy one, for having excluded such a whirling dervish from the deliberative and executive high places of government. But to a degree, the Tories were grateful to have such a splash of primary colour on the ochres and olive drabs of the accountant-dark political sea. Life can't be all Norman Fowler.

For a long time they were very happy with what they had got. Heseltine's heterodoxy on policy has never prevented him from the most violent partisanship. Not for him the cool assessment of issues and the half-smiling dismissal of absurd conclusions which makes Sir Ian Gilmour so residual a Conservative and so formidable a Parliamentarian. Heseltine is a pathological Tory, at his gruesome best calling the shots of all the infamies in the rainbow. When the Sir Jasperish fit is on, he is inclined to indict the Labour party as a treasonable conspiracy. He can also be a perfectly dreadful patriot. His speech to the Conservative conference in 1984 ran with the blood of the Ardèche campaign, whose fortieth anniversary came that year. I have seen high-ranking Tories (Leon Brittan ironically for one, years before their conflict) laughing behind pillars in Blackpool at the raw prime fillet of Heseltine's rhetoric whenever he could get at the flag and the nation.

The contrast with Ian Gilmour is profoundly instructive. Despite their shared antipathy to most things that the Ice Queen represents, they are philosophical opposites. Gilmour is and has been since he edited the *Spectator* in its better days a Whig, a deep drinker at the fountain of enlightenment liberties, someone who knows his Entick *v*. Carrington and all those constitutional struggles and lawsuits which weakened the executive and asserted private liberties. He has the inheritance of Macaulay and thinks in optimistic terms of progress. Because he is an aristocrat, Sir Ian is seen as a paternalist, but what makes him a formidable and frankly contemptuous opponent of Mrs Thatcher is a sustaining, thought-out liberalism with which the old Tory party was reconcilable. Frankly, from such liberalism the 'Us' party of official secrets and stifled child benefits is alien. This is not the

Tory party which Sir Ian joined, and if he were starting again he wouldn't join it.

Vulgar nationalism and authoritarianism are not his thing. They are decidedly Heseltine's thing. The Heseltine of the Ardèche speech, the Heseltine of the defence of John Stanley over alleged inexactitudes on the *Belgrano*, the Heseltine of small arms issued to guards at Greenham Common and sending Sarah Tisdall to prison is, absolutely and in no uncertain terms, a vulgar nationalist and authoritarian. That is why Conservative conference loves him so much.

Paradoxically, it is why Mrs Thatcher holds him in shuddering irrational hatred. A thoughtful liberal with a distaste for flashy chandelier-swinging and 'God Save the Queen' on the electric organ is tribulation but no threat. A man given to playing all her own, most obvious C major tunes on a bugle, someone who can outswagger her, in whose throat a catch comes sweetly when he mentions the flag and its soldiers, who is as much at home among the blue ribbons and Harvey Thomas special effects as the circus princess herself, is a very terrible threat, at least to Mrs Thatcher's wrought and peculiar personality.

Rationally we should see Heseltine (and so should she) as the man who blew it, the high theatrical walker-out, through whose actions the stewing hatreds of a successful but bitterly unhappy government received an airing. On any logical count the man has put himself outside the company of those who serve and expect advancement. Only the inveterate enemies of the Ice Queen and those of a naturally buccaneering half-serious disposition would gather under his Jolly Roger of a standard. But who cares for rationality? She does fear him partly because he can be such a perfectly representative awful Tory, partly also because he has just that streak of gambling recklessness which she herself exercised against Edward Heath; though it is a wider and less wise element in his personality.

But she knows that while the conventional wets failed to remove her in 1981 out of a combination of diffidence, good manners and funk, Michael Ray Dibdin Heseltine is visited by none of those characteristics. He has the diffidence of a lady taking off her clothes for public entertainment and the rational timidity of Empedocles. The image of a stripper leaping naked into the crater of Etna to see what it was like seems about right.

That little torch of creative insanity makes him interesting, distinguishes him from the Tory generality and frightens the lady. He is also inclined to be obsessive. The Westland row was about nothing that really mattered, a preference for a European consortium or an American manufacturer. Admittedly Heseltine is cool to America (and correspondingly Euro-fervent), while the lady is rigid to attention when the band plays the 'Stars and Stripes' and treats the countries of the Monnet vision with a chill which makes the EC almost sympathetic.

But that is too rational an explanation. What we witnessed, what almost certainly persuaded Mrs Thatcher to leak the Solicitor General's opinion and then, before the cock crew, to speak eloquent untruth in the House and her teeth, was a naked power play, a bout of public-house elbow-wrestling. Both had to win, neither could countenance the relaxed grin and the observation, 'OK, you win that one.' It was a display of two-sided childishness, though the Heseltine camp not unreasonably argues that any sensible restraint on their side would have been followed by a briefing by Bernard Ingham suggesting that a new Defence Minister could be expected at the reshuffle. Mrs Thatcher had a very bad time, at least in part because the ordinary trust offered to more magnanimous Prime Ministers is never vested in her.

Heseltine at least is ungentlemanly enough and straightforwardly ambitious enough to have (almost certainly deliberately) cut his losses by jumping, unpushed and under lights. Accordingly, he is a political presence in opposition not someone deleted by pencil. Her misfortunes become his opportunities and, by extension, bad news for the Conservative government she heads and the country it governs is good news for him. Into such inversions can a patriot fall.

However, he knows that his strongest point is a constituency among the bullock multitude of party members who manage to think both him and her wonderful. He cannot therefore come out of the closet as the disloyalist he very reasonably is. There have accordingly been some atrocious displays of crude support for the government from our boy. They go down fine with the blue masses but evoke giggles among the sophisticated audience in the Commons. Yet it would be a mistake to discount the ability of Heseltine to turn a Tory audience on simply by looking it in the eye. There was more than a touch of the orgiastic about those hot soufflé numbers he used to give to conference with the hair getting in his eyes, the head tossing and all sorts of people coming over queer.

As a brutal and licentious colleague once put it of an ecstatic moment by the seaside, 'He's found the party's clitoris.' As a speaker to his own people he has a good deal of the experienced, sure-fingered lover, to whom nothing can be taught about foreplay. Correspondingly, among the whores and sophisticated nuns of Westminster the response was cool or at best one of professional esteem. The ladies as it were, were not for turning on.

Not that the Commons was ever a natural habitat for Heseltine. Notoriously as a Minister he would sweep masterfully in, deliver a speech and, ignoring or mistaking those he might meet, would sweep as masterfully out again. Guided by his very endearing former PPS and general lieutenant, Dr Keith Hampson, he is now making earnest endeavours to buy drinks and cups of tea and to help quite unimportant chaps on with their coats at night. The recollection of Mr Heath, for whom coffee mornings 'to meet Ted' were organised in his tenth and final year as party leader, had been salutary.

I once unkindly remarked that Heseltine was a fascist personality clad in liberal opinions. One outstanding press colleague, a strong supporter of the political left, argued early in the Westland dispute before the worst of the blood got on to the moon, that he would support Mrs Thatcher 'because she, with all her faults, was a democrat'.

Heseltine the populist, the man with the mace, the maker of the Ardèche speech; all these combine with Heseltine the shrugger-off of Parliament yet who, unlike Mrs Thatcher, has actually behaved with perfect constitutional rectitude and who hasn't lied to Parliament. They somehow attract to him an aura of Latin impatience with the forms. The whiff of piazza politics is there even if it is, as I believe, an essentially false scent; it is simply Heseltine's misfortune to attract unnecessary fastidiousness. But if he were a character in a cartoon, which he sometimes seems to be, he might well be called Rudolf Rabblefroth.

He is now perforce at one with Dr David Owen, a major talent, an out, a disruptive influence, a romantic figure, an ever more out-angled hustler, to whom the orthodox routes are closed. There is one possible way back apart from the catastrophe scenario: it is imaginable that a post-Thatcher government under, say, Baker might have a place in it for him, especially if the Tories faced grave problems and actively needed his high profile and concussive style of debate and if the lady could impose no discreet inhibitions upon her successor.

It is a stronger shot than Owen's hope of doing a late deal with Labour as the deliverer by endorsement of its ticket of responsibility, but as shots go it is a long one. The two men are obvious and natural allies – Owen is as much of a patriot if one with more restraint. This country as a notion sincerely moves him as it does Heseltine. Heseltine, the wet and public spender, would not be at odds with Owen's dedication to a highly geared public-sector National Health Service. He would be warmed by so unaccountant-like a concept. Both men have a profound, nostril-twitching aversion to any kind of far-left, pro-soviet or fun-revolutionary sort of politics. Both are natural armers, in distinguishable degrees, sceptical about Mr Gorbachev and what he means.

If it comes to that, they are neither of them excessively liberal or worked up about issues of freedom. Dr Owen made a cool, intelligent contribution to the campaign against the Official Secrets bill, but he hardly invested his heart. As for

Heseltine, locking people up for stepping out of line is second nature. Both men are to a degree soldiers manqué. They disagree a little about America, but broadly they are quite wonderfully alike. Party is of no account.

Here are two men, both oddly Welsh of sorts (Owen is of Welsh stock, brought up in Devon; Heseltine an Englishman from Swansea), whose brands of social generosity, military commitment and dislike of the hard left are as close as the traits of flamboyance, arrogance, recklessness, comb-wielding vanity, percussive candour and lack of pettiness, and make them temperamentally allied. Both are wrongly but understandably accused of Bonapartism and undemocratic instincts. Both are compelled to operate outside conventional party lines, punished by the conforming for having been such bad team players, such failures at the great obligation to be like Norman Fowler. They are natural kin, the party that can hold them both doesn't exist but they both belong inside it.

There are those of course for whom Heseltine is a sham, an operator, a piece of ferocious comic opera. Such critics would point out that the fervent militarist and taker of every available hard line did a short term on the barrack square before dreaming up the Parliamentary candidacy as a mechanism for avoiding National Service. The young Hesie put his name forward for an impossible seat in South Wales, sprang himself from the toils of obeying sergeants and keeping out Russians, to get on with the serious business of making money.

His very talents are held against him. He makes a good speech but – in the Commons or more especially at party conferences – it is a flashy affair pitched at stomachs untroubled by excess of patriotic *schmaltz*. He does a fair quantity of shouted heroics. The joke about his regular early afternoon slot at conference was that an elfin establishment would fix a clash with children's TV, the one part of the day *not* surrendered by the BBC to the conference, so that Rabble-froth's oration would give way to *Camberwick Green*, something altogether more wholesome. He is worryingly good, by the way, in entirely sham situations like fund-raising, where the sale of an article for fifty times its market value is part of the game. As auctioneer of a two-litre bottle of whisky, pattering and sham-sneering his way well into four figures, Heseltine will not be forgotten. It was a kind of parody of the own self of politics.

Even so, one can understand why he attracts devotion and a little awe. The manner in private for once justifies the cliché 'electric': to share a meal with him is like lunching with Lucifer. He is, oddly, more attractive when talking with a little healthy cynicism than in his public form, which is a degree too uplifted and ardent for a sunflecked future than most of us can altogether take. Heseltine assessing odds and chances matter of factly becomes attractive. Perhaps this is because raffish politics is altogether more attractive, not only than the brown-mouse politics of safe men (Gummer, Howard, Newton) but even more pleasant than the semi-tone sharp oratorio patriotism of his own official manner.

On the face of it, the odds against a return are long. While she lives, in power or able to influence it, he is damned black. But no likely successor feels the same fearful hatred of him and, since he is enormously popular with the party militias, his return under another Prime Minister is more likely than not. As for the possibility of Heseltine for the leadership – although I would have ruled it out as a daydream, considering how unlike the government norm of restraint and circumspection this semi-tropical figure has been – one begins to have second thoughts. Not only is he massively popular with the rank and file, his authoritarian sham-rightwing style speaks (very crudely) the language of leadership. All those volts which go out from him on the platform either make one laugh or feel oneself in the presence of a god. And as Hölderlin wrote: 'The voices of the gods are like fire' (*Wie Feur sind die Stimmen Gottes*).

Such excess would be seen off by conventional Conservatives in a normal year. But if the news continues bad, if the verdict of the Vale of Glamorgan and the Euro-elections finds expression again and again, and if the economic crisis and the political quarrel between Mrs Thatcher and her Chancellor deepen, we may not be talking conventional politics. In those circumstances the need arises for a distress candidate. Realistically, that is the only way for Heseltine to scale the top. But in such a crisis, which looks a better horse than anyone thought, the appeal of a flame-haired tempter with a massive degree of vulgar impact and the charisma of a small nuclear reaction becomes irresistible.

Somebody needs all the bad news for the Conservatives he can get his hands on.

# CHAPTER 16

# Donald Dewar

Donald Dewar will never be a popular national figure, he is far too good for that. One of the most underrated figures at Westminster, he is a man whose quality reveals itself over time.

To watch many politicians is to exhaust their substance and be disenchanted. Dewar, with his long, clumsy cudgel-shaped body and melancholy face, is the perfect antithesis of an advertising agency's notion of a public figure. The world is full of Boys from Brazil, to adopt Ira Levin's notion of cloned man, except that they are not plastic Hitlers, they are production-line Kennedys.

Dewar could never be a marcelled profile with the jellied ruggedness to sell aftershave. He is his own self, vulnerable, protected by a sharp, discriminating wit too subtle for groundlings, just as the face is distinct and absolute, a rejection of coiffuring and orthodontal Reecery. It is the knobbly, plain, intelligent face of an interesting man. He is almost as unamendable in his nature: very Scottish in some ways, but no part of the petty particularism which afflicts the Scots from time to time. He is part of a high-quality unofficial fraternity from Glasgow University which embraced such people as Dickson Mabon (now ruined by the Alliance), Donald MacCormick of *Newsnight* and, of course, John Smith.

They tended to win prizes for debating, indeed Dewar carried off the *Observer* mace for that indulgence. He has also been remarkably stable in his political views. Like his friends of that time, he is an old-style Gaitskellite who has been out of fashion and now observes his party effectively rejoining him, but he would never have been thinkable in the SDP. Quite apart from that organisation being unnecessary in Scotland where the far left never shone so bright, Dewar, without going grand opera about his loyalty like Signora Hattersley, is something of a trustee of the Labour party.

He is a good man ill-disposed to fashion. In Scottish terms, this means that he is unresponsive either to Scottish nationalism or to the call for illegal action against the Poll Tax. Both rejections, though absolutely sensible, encourage onslaught on a betrayer of Scotland. He will never choose to compete with the loud, street-corner populism of James Sillars and his Nats, but any idea of Dewar as a soft, clerical weedy type unequipped for the bunched knuckles of Glasgow's Jimmyish hard politics is immoderately mistaken.

Unusually, he combines a sensibility of mind with enjoyment of war. Unlike some individuals on the Labour right, he has been immune from any tinge of fashionable admiration for Thatcher and Thatcherism. His style towards the Tories is scornful and biting; he is what Hattersley might be without the self-love.

Yet Donald Dewar had been around for a long time. He came into Parliament in 1966 for the happy constituency of Aberdeen South, which in the past twenty-five years has been served by four very bright MPs (Dewar himself, Iain Sproat, Gerry Malone and now Frank Doran) and dispensed with three of them. When one thinks of places which endure the stodgy service of the same dullard for thirty years, the virtues of the marginal seat as a free market in talent are irresistible.

Not that it did Dewar any good. He spent eight years in the wilderness after 1970, only making his comeback with a by-election in Garscadden, one of the most melancholy and depressed parts of Glasgow, the slum of Drumchapel being the worst. He was elected to the Shadow Cabinet in 1984 and for as long as anyone can remember has been responsible, as lesser or greater Shadow, for Scottish Affairs. There are more grateful posts and some aspiring politicians, like Gordon Brown, have declined early offers of shadow junior appointments to stay away from the fifty-cockerel dunghill of Scottish politics.

It involves co-existence with drum-brained activists like Dennis Canavan, spying strangers when English Tories attend a Scottish debate, and with such embarrassments as the pitiful Ron Brown who brings out the Ludwig Wittgenstein in Canavan. It means dealing with the deep streak of meanness and vituperative ill-nature which runs through Scottish nationalism, a creature long thought dead until an unlikely princess in the form of the Honourable Nicholas Ridley bestowed a blood sample called the Poll Tax (Scotland) Act, transforming a dead Dracula into a live one. With characteristic forthrightness, on the night of Govan, with the Nats at their most cocksure and gloating, Dewar took them on frontally in the studios and, instead of flinching, started a counter-assault.

Labour is uneasily placed in Scotland. It is top party with forty-nine seats out of seventy-one, a degree of domination far exceeding Mrs Thatcher's highest hopes in a poll of Great Britain, but is trapped on the issue of identity. Given the fact of Union, Labour cannot influence all-Union policy as it affects Scotland, witness Mr Ridley's malevolent white-mouse-experimenting with a detested tax. But in the event of Scottish statehood, Labour would share the honours with the Nats in a problematic little country and have a touch above a quarter of the seats in the one which matters. Hatred of Scottish nationalism is arithmetical rationality for Labour. Attitudes to devolution, by contrast, turn upon whether one thinks of it as a step to separation or a substitution for it – the likely view these days. But with Mrs Thatcher (often in panic fright of Scottish nationalism) turning her face against devolution, Labour is left in the Wildean state of having position without the means to live up to it.

The Scots, with a perfect clarity of concentrated hatred, have fulfilled the fears Jim Prior had for the rest of the United Kingdom. Scotland has dumped the Conservatives in an accelerating way in three successive elections across the last ten years. The 'surprising resilience' in the face of towering unemployment, shown by the generality of the British, has no place north of the Tweed (it isn't all that marked north of Chester).

Consequently, Scotland swung steadily to Labour, which had stayed a good deal saner in Scotland than in the South in the mad days of 1980–1. The Tories are a marginal party edging into permanent third place. But Labour, led by Dewar in Scotland, cannot for constitutional reasons deliver. Donald Dewar can engage in rational debate with Malcolm Rifkind, he can throw his troops at the committee stages of bills affecting Scotland though there is, due to lack of Tory numbers, no *select* committee on Scotland. Dewar finds himself at the receiving end of charges about 'the feeble fifty' from Sillars, and all the miseries attendant upon minority status with majority support. Discontent with laws and a state of affairs brought about over Labour's protesting body led to a massive vote in Govan against Labour.

But it was also Dewar's misfortune to watch a local party, as was its right, choose instead of the clever, sensible candidate, Anne Maguire, whom *he* had wanted, a dull-witted local heavy with union connections. Robert Gillespie was in the same desolating category (to take examples from three other parties) of John Butcher at Crosby, Tony Cook at Darlington and Deirdre Wood at Greenwich, instantly eliminated on merit. In a general election a brass bollard with the party ticket will be elected. By-elections by contrast, being focused, unburdened with national considerations and thus dangerously democratic, require of a candidate talents approaching the upper edge of adequacy.

Everything said about Donald Dewar and the hole he finds himself in is rather dispiriting after the manner of a toned-down Apocalypse. He has one of the best minds in the House, he is very well liked and deserves to be; he works as hard and earnestly as an Opposition politician can (both at his brief and in Scotland itself). Against the exceptionally gifted Rifkind he more than holds his own. Yet things are awry and Dewar is placed to be blamed as the man in charge. Couple that with the misfortunes of his personal life – his wife long ago left him for Alexander Irvine, the man who would be Labour's Lord Chancellor – and there is about Donald Dewar in his doggedness something very sad. He lives alone in his flat in Scotland with his books and pictures, but lacks the warm private base for a public life. It shows on a face which is lined with as much melancholy as irony.

Yet doom is almost certainly overdone in this case. Dewar is hugely resilient; he came back to Parliament after eight years in the cold and did so at a time when the left was everywhere in the ascendant. He saw off his local leftists, having once in the sixties been a protégé and PPS of Tony Crosland. He clawed his way back in a Parliamentary party significantly more hostile, to make the Shadow Cabinet after another six years. His enemies are political rather than personal, adversaries rather than haters, and his judgement on Scotland will serve his party better than any other.

Devolution is to be supported, illegal action against the Poll Tax avoided. The experiences of the last ten years demonstrate what happens to acts of defiance in local government. A similar period indicates Scottish nationalism as having the quality of most infantile disorders. It looks more serious than it is and usually clears up eventually. But at the back of Dewar's mind must be the earlier by-election. The Nationalist cycle of resurgence may perhaps have begun again at Govan, but Dewar knows that the last cycle went into downswing for ten years at another interim contest – Glasgow Garscadden.

The early opinion polls in 1978 confirmed the conventional view that the seat made empty by the death of Willie Small would go to the SNP. They had a capable candidate with the un-Scottish name of Keith Bovey, who had fought the seat before and was prepared to fight it rough this time. In particular, he made a pitch at the Catholic vote (and the seat has a large Irish-originated element) by suddenly discovering 'the Child's Right to Life', the sort of thing which goes down in a big way with bright-eyed Republican Conservatives in America. In those days, of course, before James Sillars took it over and made it specifically socialist, the SNP was politically androgynous – leftwing when it suited, populist and rightwing at other times and places. Being in favour of the right to life under the eyes of the Monsignori was thought smart.

Labour in 1978 was apprehensive, fearful of Scottish nationalism, fearful of losing the seat and desperate for talent. Dewar had been balked of a return ticket several times in the early seventies (oddly foreshadowing the thin fortunes of the able Tory who had replaced him in 1970, Iain Sproat). Though still very active in the party, Dewar was directing his energies towards the prospective devolved assembly for which, remember, Edinburgh high school had been made ready. He had to be urged to return to put himself forward again for politics by friends, but his campaign, when it came, was widely considered outstanding.

He broke with the habit of pre-empting the Nats or flinching from them; he treated opportunistic anti-abortionism with a refusal to truckle. He argued intelligently and fiercely from the start, impressing onlookers, turning the election into a debate on Labour as it could be perceived under the Callaghan government. Since this all took place before the Fall, he was sustained by visits from such luminaries as Shirley Williams and David Owen. Like them, he was a committed supporter of Europe, not a fashionable or easy thing to be in Scotland at the time. In terms of political programmes, no great gulf will ever divide them from him, but in terms of personality there is a small ocean.

Donald Dewar has never been and is not today, 'an important person'. A central flaw in the SDP was that it gave the participants at the top their own theatre in which to dress up and cast themselves in important parts not being offered by the larger organisation. The petty squabbling which was to destroy such hopefulness in so short a time was apparent that morning when they brightly assembled at the Connaught Rooms for a press breakfast. The 'Gang of Four' sat on a raised dais above the seventeen or however many ordinary MPs who sat above the rest of us. Never mind ideology or even Labour party loyalty, one simply can't imagine Donald being so tragically self-important. Yet some of the success of the Garscadden campaign derived from the fact that he ran as the rightwing Labour Gaitskellite moderate he had been as an undergraduate – flight from which essential wisdom has almost cost the Labour party its place in serious politics.

When the result came he had done enough to hope for victory by a few hundred. The margin of four and a half thousand, stretched much further at the general election of 1979 and since, was a plain pointer to Scottish nationalism that it had passed highwater. The image of Dewar as a successful King Canute would not normally spring to mind, but if events are determined at all by individuals they surely were here.

The length of Cleopatra's nose (the best opinion has it that she was not a pretty lady, merely fascinating) is paralleled by the intelligence of a by-election candidate. Just as, if Tony Cook in Darlington had been competent and unflustered, the old Alliance parties might have broken the wall containing them instead of commencing their melancholy low withdrawing roar, so a Gillespie in Garscadden might have turned Scottish nationalism into an irresistible force (Gillespie in Govan has made it a public nuisance).

Donald Dewar is better placed than most to assert: 'Say not the struggle nought availeth.' Having stumbled once, he has had to struggle ever since and he has made rather a profession of struggling successfully. The solid Labour win in mid '89 at Glasgow Central suggests that Nationalism is spasmal. This is the perspective through which to view the current hallooing of the Scottish nationalists and the recurring pressure on Labour in Scotland.

Unlike some of his colleagues, Dewar did not respond to the waves of bad news; he is an excellent man to have around in times of low morale. In the good sense, if there is one, he is a party man – loyal, consistent, steady, unselfish, something of an anti-ego. He is in less need than many colleagues enduring the cold turkey of Opposition of a large motor car to be driven around in and brisk fond lackeys from the civil service to massage ministerial self-esteem.

Ironically, the formal rightwing group – Solidarity – of which he was a key member, has been dissolved precisely as the party has come round to positions on everything, even on defence, well to the right of it: a form of nervous humbug exactly reflecting the Labour party's crab-like personality. The aspiring element inside the PLP (to the extent that there has been anything worth aspiring to) all join the *Tribune* cap, once an honest bunch of leftists which has become an insurance policy. This is now an organisation so bogus that any public relations company would be proud to have set it up.

The strength of Dewar is strength. Despite the angularity, the anguished expression on a face lined like a map of Venice, he is remarkably steady, consistent and firm. It is not too much to say that if the Labour party after 1978 – both the parts which were to break off and the others who made feeble-spirited terms with the left until the train went off the line – had behaved like Donald Dewar it would have missed calamity. At no time was he going to leave the party he again represented in Parliament, and in no way was he going to pretend to be the leftwinger he was not. In the fullness of time the party, badly injured and perhaps broken, came back to a position centimetres away from the one always occupied by people like Dewar.

By that time the Dream Ticket had replaced the flight into outer space, the party had walked incanting three times around itself, the soft left had been invented and Mrs Thatcher had been queen for six or seven years. The stable core, of which Dewar is an exemplar, could see itself as exercising Frederick the Great's injunction, '*Durchhalten* – Hold through.'

In the era of destructive clowns like Ken Livingstone, borough councils in London roller-coastered by shrilling infantilists and the party covered by general intellectual ignominy, Dewar was part of the causeway linking Labour with normality. There is a risk that he may not get the thanks he deserves. He is well placed to be a scapegoat if the rabid voice of nationalism should be heard again. Not being a sexy figure like Sillars, he could be blamed for lacking charisma. Putting aside the thought that charisma belongs with cosmetic-finished political dolls, one would like to think that (like the wife contemplated by the Vicar of Wakefield) he has qualities which will last.

I think of him as the boy in glasses who surprises everyone in the playground by using his fists when attacked. We shall see him at it again soon, punching hard.

# CHAPTER 17

# Michael Howard

The very talented are often made up of a blend of an understanding which makes them attractive and a talent which draws them along the course of ambition.

In essentials Michael Howard is a likeable man. He sees jokes quickly, makes some himself, and the presence of a mind so quick is in itself pleasure enough to the onlooker. But against this must be set the problems of rising and a certain advocate's flexibility of soul.

The ostrich digestion makes disagreeable courses of action perfectly acceptable so long as they lead him upwards. Employment as the legislative manager of the Poll Tax is a case in point, a case in howling point. That tax will penalise families of modest income with a number of young adult members. Very much what the old left used to call 'a class law', it beamingly benefits the high-incomed with few dependants (with a little luck it will do the Tory party rather less good).

It goes beyond ending the assumption that rates should be a progressive tax, and will function in part as a redistribution mechanism in favour of the well-to-do. Howard has been grandly complacent about all possible iniquities and has acted as henchman to Nicholas Ridley's obscure notions of social revanchism – 'Why should a duke pay more than dustman?' – with perfect good humour.

Howard is a product of intelligence, passing exams and seeking advancement, a perfectly natural political course but one which in recent years has removed the gloss of disinterest in which normal political ambition once came cloaked. He is also a product of Cambridge conservatism, a strange phenomenon, attractive to talents which were fairly enlightened and socially negligible. It has stocked the Tory party with Lamonts, Mellors and young aspirants by the metric tonne, something to do – so it is reckoned – with the moral influence of the young Geoffrey Howe and his Bow Group in that university. Howard in his day has sat at the feet of Norman Lamont, whose brand of good-humoured scepticism about higher things plays a part in Howard. Except that the pupil seems to be a more systematic moral agnostic than his mentor. As the fetcher, carrier and draughtsman of Nicholas Ridley, he has been put ominously in the position of too keen henchman.

The bill is law and the ceiling has not yet fallen, but the Govan by-election in Scotland, where the Poll Tax exactions apply first, could be an indicator that Ridley and Howard may have brought off a piece of necromancy. Scottish nationalism, stopped, frustrated and marginalised in 1979 by a shrewd combination of Labour and Conservative anti-devolutionists, has sprung like any revenant from its repose. Devolution is back on the agenda; Scottish separatism is no longer a wild hypothesis. The arrogance of imposing the most extreme and eccentric Tory nostrums upon a province, sorry nation, where the Tory party at full stretch has twenty-one per cent of the vote and ten seats out of seventy-one, is characteristic of the government.

As a good hireling, Howard sleekly toiled through legislation, mocking the notion that it might be either unfair or unpopular, striking as he spoke some of the notes of an all-wise colonial administrator. His public manner, despite his personal good humour and lack of malice, is quite as irritating to those legislated for as the nobbish contempt of Ridley. It is perhaps Michael Howard's misfortune that he came into politics relatively late, in his mid-forties. There was no time to build up a private profile on the backbenches. Office had to come quickly or would never come. And since he has all the gifts of an intelligent work-despatching, legally proficient Minister, he rightly sought that advancement.

The opportunity to please came one afternoon when, to the dismay of many of their own side, the government chose to convert the receipts from council-house sales, which legally belonged to the local authorities, into frozen assets, thus turning the screw on the hated municipalities by means legal only because, in the teeth of natural justice, they had been passed by Parliament. Hostile speech followed hostile speech on the Tory side when suddenly up stood this polite Welsh lawyer to make a short, lucid, intelligent defence of the indefensible. The duty Whip scribbled excitedly in the little notebook which carries the day's comment on the herd, and within a few more weeks Howard had become a junior Minister.

With his talent and his office hunger, he is the perfect Thatcher executive. The question of being one of *us* does not arise. He works directly for *us*. *We* have hired him. But this was almost inevitable. He went to Cambridge a little behind the Howe and Biffen generation but with the Lamont, Peter Lloyd, Gummer, Ken Clarke congeries. He was a middle-class boy from a solid Labour hometown (Llanelli for Heaven's sake), and then only dabbling in post-graduate politics – two bashes at Edgehill Liverpool before twelve years of steady earning at the planning and employment bar – before surging late at Folkestone. There was lost time to make up and space to cover.

Another Fenland lion, Leon Brittan, as well as being a close and dear friend, was also his boss at the Trade Department as a battle-stained ex-Home Secretary when Howard battered his way loyally into his first job as Under-Secretary there. Everyone else from that Cambridge and Bow Group background had put together a dozen or so years of leisurely Parliamentary seniority during the time when Howard was a pleasant-faced man doing well out of the Okehampton by-pass enquiry.

He had been a loner at school: Llanelli Grammar. His father being a fairly successful outfitter, private education would have been possible but grammar school was preferred. He was even then a Tory – whether out of cussedness in a part of the principality where Labour rules like the Habsburgs or from his commercial background is not clear. Oddly, if ultimately unimportantly for someone very bright and Thatcherian in his diligence, he managed only a Lower Second in Economics and Law. His time as Chairman of the

Bow Group was thought of as liberal, and he did reproach the Heath government roundly enough to make an early head- line, for its less than perfect liberality towards distressed Asian immigrants from Uganda. He was also quite consist- ently tough as a young man on the trades unions, calling for an end to unemployment pay to strikers who, having free will, should choose to pay if they chose to strike. The two standpoints, on immigrants and unions, are straight Geoffrey Howe thinking – liberal both in classical economic terms and in terms of common-sense decency (there is a thesis waiting to be written on the influence of Sir Geoffrey over twenty-five years and another on the little noticed gulf separating his thinking from Mrs Thatcher's).*

But looking at Howard personally one strongly suspects an element of shyness, of which some traces remain. At Cam- bridge the heroic figure, the Kenneth Tynan of enlightened Conservatism, was the stylish, shadows-spurning, mildly phosphorescent Norman Lamont, whose best man Howard was. Beside this day-glo cavalier, Howard was stuck with the Ronald Reagan part of hero's best friend. There may also have been a touch of self-underesteem. He is a Lower Second with a first-class career.

But even now he is not a comfortable publicist. His political talents are either technical, like his grasp of detail for Japanese trade talks or his command of the Guinness brief, or they stem from the practice and habituation of argument in court. Between such skills and the assurance they build up and the natural self-confidence of a Clarke or Mellor there is at least a distinction worth making.

The one slightly sensational thing to happen to him before accelerated promotion in Parliament was marriage – not any marriage, but the role at thirty-four of fourth husband to Sandra Paul, a model, famous in her day, who had gone through husbands, including Robin Douglas-Home, the former Prime Minister's nephew, like a delightful Gulf

---

*We all have our moments of prophecy. This was written in the early spring of 1989.

hurricane desolating small towns in Louisiana. Ever an emotional man, he has got her average down and is still evidently happily married to the beautiful lady after fourteen years, a Pleistocene age in her terms, and has two children as well as a step-child as responsibility.

The husband of Sandra Paul and friend of Norman Lamont has his quiet triumphs in politics but there is no flash in his career. Indeed the abiding concern about this pleasant man is that there may be more anxiety in his personality than the barristerly suavity conveys, and that he will get it wrong precisely by the means through which he ascended – an excessive readiness to please. The professional advocate, like that serviceable obelisk, Sir Patrick Mayhew, does well enough in the professional mists of the law officers' department. Howard may go there at any time. He has brain enough to make Solicitor General something of an under-achievement (the job he would avoid, by flight if necessary, is Wales, the prospect of which induces amusing twitches of only half- mock horror).

But the rush to perform which served him well in respect of that opportune speech on frozen council-house sale receipts could rebound on a tougher issue. The municipalities, however wronged, are as friendless as the Cherokee in 1870. Doing them down earns no disapprobation. Other jobs, like supervising the Guinness events and throwing bricks at the Japanese over trade blockades, are blameless parts of the job. The Poll Tax, as suggested above, is another matter. It wasn't christened the Community Charge for nothing. It is a rule never to be neglected in politics that the prefacing of anything by the term 'community' implies its essential awfulness.

The potential for liberating new Conservative voters from, first, cash and then their recent allegiance seems to have made no impression upon Howard. He makes speeches and writes letters and articles for the press reasonably, even beautifully, pointing out how many poor people will benefit from the change of revenue selection. This means only that he concentrates his advocate's talents on the solitary person – what might be called tax and the single voter. This was not a line of argument with any appeal to those Conservative

Ministers who gave attention to the hypothesis of a Poll Tax in the past. Michael Heseltine speaks of it being in his and Tom King's time 'laughed out of court'.

The votes which will matter most to the Tories, because they are most precariously held or closely aspired to, are those of couples from or near the working class, people at the margin of party loyalty. The Tories have done well from such mobility. Nothing is better calculated to reverse it as tripled demands for payment dropping sweetly across the next two years first in Scotland (chippily unpleased with laboratory-mouse status), then in the rest of Britain. As the chief pleader for something rather likely to get everyone else unstuck, Howard is not only too much the hired voice, he is the over-zealous lieutenant. Machiavelli recounted the tale of one such, Messer Ramon D'Orco, a Spanish captain who, in the service of Cesare Borgia's campaign to secure the Romagna, was required to put pressure on the unresponsive city of Cesena. Messer Ramon, in Stalinist terms, overfulfilled his quota until the rage of the terrorised citizens and the disaffection of their neighbours persuaded Cesare that they had best be wooed back, something he did with the quartered body of Messer Ramon, left one night together with a note of apology in the main piazza of Cesena.

The excesses of Nicholas Ridley will not dominate Tory thinking for ever, nor will the strange needs of Mrs Thatcher to live up to an obscure rhetorical flourish about rates made in 1976. The busy executive of a psephicidal policy, which has slain votes like Holy Innocents, will himself do well to remain unchopped up and apologised for. The example of Messer Ramon should sit quietly on the shoulder of the member for Folkestone like a crow.

Come to think of it, the member for Folkestone has one sizeable black bird perched there which, unlike Poll-Tax retribution, he actively fears himself. The bird is called Folkestone. That unhappy port sits in the way of a development – the Channel Tunnel – so injurious to great parts of Kent that it ought to be called 'the community train link'. Simulations of a high-pitched shriek, like an Albert Hall full of over-wrought sopranos, have been played to audiences of militant local residents who clapped their hands over their ears. A number of otherwise motte-and-bailled Conservative constituencies along the resented route are heavily vulnerable. It is a matter of some chagrin to someone who waited until his forty-fourth year to enter Parliament, eschewing all marginals, to have a comfortable eleven thousand put to such risk. Howard has made his dislike of the project known but as a Minister he cannot, like other Kentish MPs, totally divorce himself from its unpopularity by direct campaigning. He has used surrogates. Leon Brittan, between his fall and resurrection, cheerfully shouldered this function for his old Cambridge friend. But Folkestone is simple bad luck. Howard just happened to be sitting there when this excavator came along and dumped earth on him.

Any unpopularity over the privatisation of water is personal responsibility. Again Howard finds himself chained to an oar in a ship navigated insouciantly towards the rocks by Nicholas Ridley. The turning of water from a utility into a metered equity is looked at with unease by very many Conservatives. As a candidate for privatisation, it comes a little way ahead in the good-sense stakes only of Wormwood Scrubs plc.

At the heart of the Minister's dilemma is the fact that the present water authorities are forbidden by the Treasury from raising money on the open market to reach higher Brussels-bidden standards of cleanliness. Also the state-operated water authorities in their last year were restricted to price control at a ceiling of ten per cent. Indeed private companies at this stage operated under statutory controls. As true privatisation loomed their (often French) equity holders pushed for and got notable price increases. West Kent with forty-two per cent was particularly notable but about a quarter of homes faced increases in the region of thirty per cent.

Quite simply, the privatisation of water, coming at the same time as insistence on higher hygiene standards, performed a service but exacted the full price and a profit for doing so. The general experience of privatisation with steel and gas had been of large numbers of happy first dabblers in the market. The experience of water was of bills and of the private sector being or looking (it hardly matters which) extortionate. The Minister attempted to restrain this by what he called moral suasion and his shadow, Jack Cunningham, called ineffective bluster. As Mrs Thatcher likes to say, 'You can't buck the market.'

A theoretical case could be constructed for importing profit, and its burden of price, into an artificially restricted utility. In fact, the government gave a fair impression; not of implacable insistence upon the market in spite of the outrage, but of not having seen the half-brick coming. No possible political sense could be made of replacing a state of easy content with the mood of householders in receipt of steeply hiked water bills.

It is the melancholy circumstances of Howard – whose own water board in Folkestone had a hand to play – that despite all his long hours of work (starting his working day at four-thirty, commonly closing at midnight or later) he had become directly identified with what Marilyn Monroe in *Some Like It Hot* called 'the fuzzy end of the lollipop'. Other, happier men got to privatise Amersham International or British Steel and did so to a soft cooing of village swallows rustling paper profits in deeper nests. Howard, having delivered one set of increased bills for the Poll Tax, was asked (very nicely) to make a second round very quickly but at formidable risk. A safe pair of hands, he was asked to field at silly mid-on.

He has few personal enemies, few who would rejoice at an early burn-up of talent advanced so far. (The sort of painful glee which met the involuntary immolation of John Moore would be heavily muted, a mere giggle at the graveside.) But having obtained early and accelerating advancement as probably the busiest and most widely active Minister of State – precisely because he is a serviceable advocate of ill-defined profile – so is he the man likeliest to accept suggestions that he should walk through fire and ice in very doubtful causes. He is indeed not disliked but, sufficiently burned or iced over, he will, as a senior water-drawer and wood-hewer receive sympathy and succour in the limited degree available to useful men used too far.

Having been brave to the point of foolhardiness and risked himself for dangerous government undertakings, he has great claims upon gratitude, something politics has always assayed at a pitiful discount. Even so, the lady does indeed owe him. But after so much fire something quieter – a law officership, even dull but soothing Wales – must have charms for one who, in Robert Frost's words, has endured six little terms of burning and six of ice.

# CHAPTER 18

## *David Owen*

The effective end of David Owen's political life is depressing. He was to have been so much; he has become next to nothing at all. Most of it is his own fault and yet when Owen talks of the impossibility of other people he may have almost as good a point as others have when they talk about the impossibility of David Owen.

The golden Owen ran from 1978 when he became Foreign Minister at an absurd age – thirty-nine – to 1987 when he picked a quarrel with the Liberals on terms which pre-ordained those who cherished him to cast a vote for his destruction. It was an intolerable situation involving a call for unity which Owen opposed and a majority of the old SDP wanted, but also *against* Owen which a majority did *not* want. Neither he nor his members seem quite to have understood what must happen when, like iceberg and Titanic, they first struck attitudes and charted courses.

But then historically Owen had done well out of defiance. Long ago, as a brand new MP of the '66 intake, he had cheeked Harold Wilson and got away with it. At a backbench meeting Wilson had pulled the leg of the new Member for some rightwing sentiment. Owen apparently accosted Wilson in a corridor and told him as day-old chick to ruling rooster that unless he, the Prime Minister, apologised to him the new Member, he would never speak to him again. It is not formally known what would happen to a Conservative newcomer who spoke in such terms to Mrs Margaret Thatcher (blessed be she): at a guess, something swift and terminal involving lasers.

Now Harold Wilson, who at this distance takes on a faint retrospective glow appropriate to the apostle of kindly despair, was some distance from the twitching imperiousness of the Ice Queen. Similarly the Labour party, unlike the castle of incremental deference across the road, is in its rough way a place for argument and no pulling of forelocks. But even so it took brass neck to behave like that and astonishing feebleness to respond as Wilson did. With the tragic timidity he was to lay clammily upon the age, Wilson bought this unnerving young man off with an offer a few days later of a PPS's job.

There is a saying among reactionary folk that a good flogging stops a good hanging. It could be argued that proper chastisement for Owen at that stage – a snarling reprimand from the Chief Whip, Ted Short, a chief warder who knew his business – might have cured the hubristic conceit which led him in summer 1987 to the political equivalent of a hanging: leadership of a groupuscule.

The very failure which Owen rightly perceived in Wilson's dealings with the left, a failure to stand up to them, was mirrored exquisitely in a disinclination to stand up to David Owen. Equally, Owen's own political personality, however right of centre it is in substance, is psychologically akin to that of the left. He has the aggression of the left and something of their fundamental indifference to rational calculation. They are fond of the word 'principled' and no one can fairly deny Owen, despite his mobility on the spectrum, a claim to principle. Like them he is a destroyer, like them he despises the petty men who play safe. Alas, they have a cave of votes to crawl back into after every election which rolls over Labour. The condition of warm, whimpering comfortable discontent is an indefinite option. By contrast, Owen is the first man since Asquith to have marginalised the mainstream!

After that boost, his career was orthodox but accelerated. He had the good fortune to work in the PPS job for Gerry Reynolds. Reynolds died in his early forties of cancer of the liver, but he was a funny, warm-hearted Labour moderate with more courage than commonly accompanies moderation. However, he lacked the prim élitism of the Gang of Four. He was cut down in the job of deputy Minister of Defence when promotion to the Cabinet was, in the view of the Prime

Minister, only one reshuffle away. Had Reynolds, who was of the age and seniority of Shirley Williams and Bill Rodgers, lived he would have had a chance of either stopping the split or of making it work.

From working with Reynolds on a tiny school desk which must have been hard on the ego, Owen progressed to Parliamentary Under-Secretary at Defence, which under the Healey reorganisation involved being Minister for the Navy. The affinity with Sir Joseph Porter in *HMS Pinafore* has its charms. While there Owen, who has Lloyd George's puritan Welsh instincts on drink allied to a medical degree, managed to abolish the grog ration. He then went to the DHSS to work a little uneasily with Barbara Castle, a noisily interminable woman who now seems as remote as Messalina, and in due course became Minister of Health though without Cabinet rank. As a qualified hospital doctor, he might have impressed colleagues as the sort of brilliant professional whom a party of the left should be able to attract (Mr Samuel Galbraith took up a frontbench posting in the present Opposition in less than twelve months after election in 1987, but then Mr Galbraith is a leading neuro-surgeon distinguished a little distance beyond the young houseman writing papers about beta-blockers).

The subsequent leap to the Foreign Office was like one of those desperate callings-up of a raw county batsman by the shattered selectors, a reflection as much upon circumstances as himself. It also reflected the smiling sun of Influence. Mr Peter Jay, the Prime Minister's then son-in-law, had added an eight-alpha First to his natural status as the son of a Cabinet Minister; he was incidentally Economics Editor of *The Times*. To be plain, Mr Jay, whose bad fairy had short-circuited much of this glory with an altitudinous view of the human race which amounted to a Godolphin Horn complex,* recognised some fearful distant kinship in the young Minister which made him, despite education only at Bradfield, an

---

*Godolphin Horn was nobly born
  And held the human race in scorn.

honorary Wykehamist. That was an awesome and terrible judgement which says everything. Herbert Wilson, Harold's excellent father, had remarked after heavy exposure to Jay's father Douglas, Hugh Gaitskell and Richard Crossman, that there could be no doubt about it, God had certainly been to Winchester.

Young Mr Jay who at all times displayed an inclination to legislate for the universe, decided that his friend Dr Owen was outstandingly able and lobbied his admiring father-in-law James Callaghan for radical advancement. Accordingly, Owen was snatched dashingly from the Club and Ground of Minister Outside the Cabinet to the first wicket spot for England of the Foreign Office. Here his attitude was a strange combination of seeming radicalism – creditably unpopular *on policy grounds* with the Tories over Rhodesia – and a private peremptoriness about which drivers and civil servants still speak.

There is talk about the fastest ever turnover in drivers, about private-office civil servants applying in bulk for transfer, about a cold, dismissive contempt of one not finding others worthy of contemplation. As a taxi-driver put it to me, 'I 'ad that Owen in the back once and I can tell you 'ee's not nice.' It should be said that with a wealth of such testimony, which widened to take in great parts of the Labour, Social Democratic and Liberal parties, there is the counter-voice of those who adore him. There has to be something here of Mr Geoffrey Boycott whose nervous breakdown-inducing qualities, to say nothing of a certain talent for running out his partners, Dr Owen evidently shares.

There is an interesting contrast with Mrs Thatcher, between whom and Owen great empathy exists. Mrs Thatcher – indescribably rude, hysterical and awful as she can be to her thwarting peers – always manages, if only by numbers, to behave in an exemplary way towards junior and subordinate staff. Owen can be superbly charming, intimating, as thoughtful intelligence to thoughtful intelligence, what ought to be done and speaking moreover with a gratifying candour. Most people dealing with him have at some stage briefly been drunk on Owen. It is a big personality with a commanding authority as surely as Geoffrey Boycott is a lot of runs and records, though Owen is nothing like so boring.

Most of politics is about rubbing along with other people. Owen, whatever his gifts, can charm or defoliate, but never rub along. That doesn't make him wrong. Indeed on a number of issues – Rhodesia, one-man-one-vote as an internal electoral system within the Labour party, insistence on a firm line on nuclear defence, the assumption that arm's-length association with the Liberals was infinitely preferable to union – he sounds like a man talking sense. But those are only the *issues*. Gilbert and Sullivan may have quarrelled about a carpet, but their real problem was that they couldn't stand the sight of each other. David Steel, who is shrewd in his lethargic way, didn't really doubt the electoral harm done by a fit of feebleness about nuclear defence. He wouldn't have pressed for union against Owen's wishes had he been on good terms with him. But he *wasn't* on good terms with him and neither was the Liberal party. Again, broadly speaking, Owen was right, not to be a booster patriot who loved the bomb, but to see the electoral death built into any ambiguity written into a joint platform to accommodate the soft-brained *Schwärmerei* of far too many Liberals.

It was to protect himself and ordinary God-fearing, office-pursuing politics from such carnivorous infantility that Steel had sought the alliance in earlier and happier times when the slow-motion low-thyroid personality of Roy Jenkins seemed to enthrone sense and good humour, if not effect. In so far as one can identify a root here, the mutual antipathy stemmed from Owen's contempt for compromise, something he had despised as a subordinate throughout the Wilsonzeit. This clashed jarringly with Steel's gifts of dexterous apathy which had so much in common in a minor key with Wilson himself. Owen at times gave the impression of making Steel his PPS. A more foolish arrogance towards a shrewd colleague capable of being hurt and of hurting back cannot be imagined. It was this policy of correcting the partner on camera and wearing him in the breast pocket: everything that

Dr Johnson meant by that description of his own adolescent arrogance – 'stark insensibility' – words which should be engraved where Dr Owen can see them.

It is an odd achievement to get the broad drift of ideas right and yet to so handle people that colleagues, who do not differ on those essentials, want you dead. Owen's position during the 1987 election was profoundly false. He seemed formidably strong, the dominant personality in a party attractive in style, weak in personnel. Actual defeat in the election, given the difficulties, should not have been a heavy blow. With twenty-three per cent of the action, this ought to have been good threshold politics. In fact, so many curdled hatreds co- existed under the dream topping that electoral armistice was the signal for open season with guns pointed inwards. It would have been possible to have held all the actual differences of policy, engaged in some serious public arguments, carried the day (since the arithmetic for winning defence arguments was there in the two parties) and then to have approached the entire issue of merger in a cool dispassionate light.

Owen might have played the post-election crisis long and by postponing a vote made sure of winning it, since the charm of unity turned upon a blind optimistic rush. Alternatively, he might have accepted the notion with all its problems and have written into the sovereign document both constitutional restraints on the Liberal instant membership, which was packing assemblies, and a strong preamble on defence. Either way he would have been involved in serious politics with an intact, if not perfectly united, centre grouping. Being of the sort of quality he is, he would probably have been leader anyway, however much some Liberals spat teeth at the prospect. Even without the leadership he would have commanded, dominated and vetoed things; and he would have been part of a grouping with seven million votes to be going on with, serious politics even without PR. For Owen, with all his impossible nature, has that tincture of the first-rate which no one seeking office in the new merged party has yet demonstrated.

Having next to no commonsense at all, he did none of these things. He forced a fast internal referendum, put his leadership at issue and offered a suicidal dare which was variously not believed or jumped at. On his own specifications, he was put into a long boat with a few chosen companions, a quantity of water and hard tack and invited to row to Australia – the exact condition, apart from its voluntary nature, of Captain William Bligh. David Steel hardly rates as Fletcher Christian, but the political prospects at the time of writing hardly offer the merged but cruelly exposed new party better prospects than the political equivalent of Pitcairn Island. As for Owen, he is adrift in an open boat.

Owen's disdain for the Liberals was well-founded. His belief that they had no coherent notion of policy, no leadership and a complacent desire not to get frighteningly closer to power and decision-making are probably all correct. His dislike of union was entirely reasonable; the notion that he was an effective leader and that nobody else in that company was remotely up to the job was, if anything, an understatement. The correctness of Owen on essentials is a poignant counterpoint to his inability to do the simple elementary things like being nice to people and staying politically alive. He is a major personality with enormous attractiveness and flair. The merged party is a big working base, a battalion capable of being taken somewhere. But the new party has no credible leader and Owen no credible party. The prospects that he and his former allies will shrivel apart where they might have prospered together are formidable.

Incidentally, it is a total fallacy to suppose that Owen alone might, like Enoch Powell, become a solitary force contributing seminal speeches which will fill the Chamber and the minds of his listeners. Owen lacks the necessary talent. Powell has a superb intelligence and is a fountain of provocative ideas, including some very silly ones. He has the interestingness of the thinking intelligence. Owen may have the panache of a squadron of cavalry, but beyond his specialist subject of health, he has nothing new to say and what he does say is marked by a ringing banality which sometimes suggests no very great loss has been sustained by politics in his fall.

Ideas and policy played, after all, only a limited role in the hatred which grew up between Owen and the Liberals. He is an old school Gaitskellite – hard on defence, pro-American, for the nuclear deterrent; this is reasonably good thinking and better than good politics with the electorate. A centre party unequivocally tough on defence would be a nightmare to the Tories.* The Liberals have a large wing which is compulsively soft-headed and declamatory on this issue. But there is a working majority of Liberals most of the time which can see that the Conservatives are good at newspaper propaganda and that if given an inch on defence, they will take an ell. Certainly with the Eastbourne vote the Liberals, in a moment of dereliction of mind, gave them a foot and a half.

There was nothing there that could not have been put right. The Liberal establishment was apologetic to Owen and wanted to accommodate him. But Owen will not settle for being right, he has also to be obeyed. The Liberals may be feeble and inadequate but it is not good politics to treat them as such. Owen's disdain reached out like a lethal cloud and affected most of those Liberals who on specifics actually agreed with him. An intense mutual loathing grew up, intensified by that other pact of hatred – the one subsisting between the Doctor and his former senior SDP colleagues, footling time-wasters who got in his clear-minded way. They also wanted union with the Liberals, partly as a means of protecting themselves from his imperium.

With a man for whom so many people are contemptible objects, there has to be something wrong! Owen had begun to cast himself in the role of *Menschenfeind*, hater of mankind, which, given his talent, charm and decent main purpose, truly is tragic. He is, in John Clare's words, 'the self-consumer of my woes', but he is also their creator. He had thrust the faltering Roy Jenkins aside; he now did as much to himself. He is the author of his own destruction, something for which he has a vortex-drawn talent. Neither mad nor bad, he is dangerous to know.

---

*Perhaps since Neil Kinnock's apostasy we have one.

However, it is not quite unthinkable that Owen may again hold high office. Despite proclaiming that he will never be a Tory, he has never promised not to serve in government with the Conservatives. He enjoys the admiration of Margaret Thatcher, who likes his anti-communist opinions and his affectation of decisiveness (actually, like her, he dithers all the time). A notorious window-shopper of men's looks, she enjoys his handsomeness. Margaret Thatcher has reached a stage of advanced arrogance seasoned with caprice, where the pleasure of affronting her despised colleagues by hiring an outsider would pleasingly proclaim the absolutism she yearns for. The hints have already been dropped in the treacle marsh of an interview with Brian Walden (she spoke of Owen there as a potential successor). More cautiously, a very intelligent Tory backbencher estimated that it is entirely sensible that she might put Owen in charge of the DHSS.

But Owen is not destined for the Conservative embrace. He surprised some people earlier this year by the warmth of his response to Neil Kinnock's long struggle with the left. And he talked about Labour again becoming fit to govern. The notion that he can help Labour with the middle-class vote and the anti-far-left vote by an apostolic nod sounds dafter than it is, but it is fairly far-fetched at that.

The idea that any one individual, however delicious in three-quarter profile and ringing in utterance, can swing an election is the height of dubiety. Enoch Powell and his loyal biographer, Dr Patrick Cosgrave, believed it of the February 1974 election; but they would do that, wouldn't they? Anyway, association with Powell and his passionate need to justify everything he ever did by back-rationalisation is a warning in itself. Realistically, David Owen, with all his gifts, now has nowhere to go. He left one party for good enough reasons, helped split a second in shared folly with others, and today commands a show so slight that it enters into no one's calculations. But there is a certain dignity in his coolly rejecting the Tory route.

It was thinkable: there is or has been Thatcherian goodwill. He could have been the perfect National Liberal, trading a hopeless party position for a modest quantum of office. He has been above that and has emulated none of the usual contrast figures – Joe Chamberlain or Enoch Powell. The Liberal party was saved in 1951 from merger with the Tories through the meek principle of Clement Davies, leader of its six MPs, who refused a Cabinet post from Churchill in return for bringing them on board. The Liberals lived to torment David Owen.

It is not the comparison Owen would have have sought, but it is an honourable one, and perhaps we shall see him ending his time in politics, on a diminuendo certainly, but with a sort of melancholy, doomed honour.

# CHAPTER 19

# Geoffrey Howe

An editor of mine, a few years back when Geoffrey Howe was already a part of the landscape, remarked on suggesting a piece, 'He reminds me of one of those rubber policemen whose bases are weighted so that however hard you knock them, they can't fall down.'

That seems about right but in the non-knocking-down resides a lot of virtue. Competence of course; Howe can imbibe legal and political paper with as little trouble as he can take on gin and tonic (and in an age of thin-lipped dietary rectitude how nice it is to have a plump politician who enjoys gin and tonic). But competence is, if not overrated, widely available. There are dozens of trim little executive talents in the House capable of swiftly despatching business. Wall-to-wall Norman Fowler is available at all leading stockists. Alone it does not account for Sir Geoffrey's agreeable particularity. Singularity of purpose without the usual heavy-breathing career obsessiveness has kept Howe available for all sorts of political purposes without visible stress since he started out as a founder of the Bow Group a surprising forty years ago.

Much, far too much, has been made of his Welshness, as if a man whose father was called Howe and whose mother Thomson had serious affinity with Daffyd ap Gwylim. He is a good deal less Welsh than the Duke of Wellington was Irish and as the Duke remarked, 'A man being born in a stable is not evidence of his being a horse.' He is, in fact, a white settler – Welsh the way Ian Smith is African only nicer and cleverer. Although there are Welsh ancestors, he is as utterly and comprehensively English (and southern middle-class English at that) in style as can reasonably be expected of any man.

He is admittedly one of several Tory politicians with remote proletarian syndicalist antecedents (the pitman father of Ken

Clarke and the strike-leading parent of Jack Weatherill spring to mind). A Howe grandparent was active among tinplaters in their struggles with the bosses long ago. But that merely underlines the elasticity and amenability of English middle-class society – not the gentry, another fish pie altogether.

But the charm of Geoffrey Howe, abetted by his wife, who is substantially significant in herself and not a woman's interest confection, resides in the fact that they represent the pleasant, good-humoured side of the successful middle classes. They are Surrey, not Essex. The money has been steadily earned rather than suddenly acquired. There is a good deal of conscience somewhere on the short spectrum between the Church of England and agnosticism, as well as the common-sense practicality of the educated first-class professional man.

Arthur Hugh Clough observed mockingly how pleasant it is to have money. But there is no charm in a truculent adherence to the rights and interests of the rich – something unpleasantly the case with the sleeker younger element assembling in a hawing double-breasted fuzz on the farthest backbenches. It is possible for a Tory to be something better.

Howe the Bow Grouper has always seemed to have been remote from the unpleasant side of the Conservative party, now heavily accentuated. Try to imagine *him* tolerating an eleven-minute ovation at Brighton or Blackpool. The bitter particularism and Tory triumphalism, which in the Prime Minister admits no merit or decent intentions behind any action of opponents, is very remote. He and Mrs Thatcher are of an age and shared the same political inheritance, having the social ladder they climbed very mildly shaken beneath them in the radical sixties. But whereas she appears to have felt threatened, to have seen The Party as a citadel and to have developed her own hot-lead response to all besiegers, Howe gives the impression of a man touched by panic at no time.

The contempt felt and privately expressed by Elspeth Howe for the Prime Minister may (a smidgeon of it) derive from ordinary woman and woman, ambitious wife and boss feelings. But smidgeon is all it is. Despite Geoffrey Howe's own dogged good humour and official loyalty, his wife only articulates a profound difference of outlook. The preposterous side of Mrs Thatcher – the ambulance-chasing, hushed voice thrilling-to-the-nation-at-the-bedside – would be fled by Howe and his wife for what it is: vulgar, unfeeling and egomaniacal.

Normally the wives and families of politicians are not worth writing about in the sense that they are not influences on events or character. One could never say this about either Mrs Thatcher or Geoffrey Howe. It *is* significant that Howe is married to a clever, sharp-minded woman who is the embodiment of a sort of Tory Fabianism. Having a voice like that in your head will offset any urge to go morally nap on the gilded age. Just as significantly, thirty-five years of marriage to a man pettishly reactionary, financially quick-minded, encyclopaedically philistine and closed to social sympathy of any kind has done a great deal to make Margaret Thatcher what she is. It is a small irony that while one Thatcher child should, with the help of graceless Harrow (that Romford among public schools), have developed into an heiress-catching spiv without any other visible talent, the only Howe anxieties over children have concerned a healthy idealistic leftwingery in his son Alec, whose relationship with CND was rather endearing.

But Howe was broadly with Mrs Thatcher on the central issue of policy. As Chancellor, though he made his full share of mistakes – overvaluation chief among them – Howe accepted at least the premises of a monetarist financial policy. In fairness, he did not advocate the terms of his own 1981 budget, the withdrawal of five billions from the economy. This was the insistent idea of Alan Walters who on his own account, aided by a rising civil servant with a wet finger held up to the wind, Peter Middleton, prevailed with the Prime Minister. Very painfully it helped reduce inflation, though at a gruesome price in Sunderland and all the other Sunderlands.

The stolid survivorism of Howe counts at times as a strike against him. His own advice was for a reduction of demand by no more than one and half billion at the outside. He was overruled; he stayed. He took his full share of the blame and the credit. Howe is too much of a regular, of a political steady, to contemplate resignation, too sensible and stable to enjoy the raging quarrels which are a staple to Mrs Thatcher. Yet his thinking was never so remote from hers on the economy as to make grand conflicts likely. He was on the record as an advocate of revolutionary tax cuts long before – in the days of Bow Group pamphlets. And tax cuts in 1981 seemed unimaginably remote unless very radical policies were undertaken. So one may charitably attribute an element of sceptical, wistful well-wishing in his response to the ideas of such a Marat of capitalism as Alan Walters. He was, far more than the wets, in favour of a vigorous market economy, and he was quite patient enough under fire to pursue the painful (and sometimes unnecessary) intermediary steps.

Ironically the Foreign Office, seen by some as a grand ceremonial mandarinate but which has evidently preoccupied and interested him, has also divided Howe far more sharply from the Prime Minister. Mrs Thatcher is absolutely and in no way any sort of racist, but she is at odds with a great part of the black and brown world for reasons which are perfectly good. Commonwealth Prime Ministers tend to a measure of empty talk which leaves your average European summit looking concise. They incline to an incoherent leftism which would try better patiences than Mrs Thatcher's. Howe has, and she has not, a tolerance for silliness in other people. He is, and she is not, a practitioner of orthodox diplomacy, recognising interests rather than moral avocations and, loosely guided by civilised standards, trying to follow those interests.

Howe has always been at home in patient, polite, stuffily kind relations with people. He discovered a genuine aptitude for diplomacy, talking softly, listening, suffering fools and those he disagreed with. The Foreign Office orthodoxies about which many of Mrs Thatcher's allies grow purple are more accessible to Howe. He is responsive to America, but not in a state of rapture; sincerely dislikes East European repression but has been able to take on the new climate without Cold War twitchings. He is not a natural for undying support of Israeli interests ahead of anyone else's. But of course he is, as Mrs Thatcher is not, 'a good European'. Not that he is blind, deaf and dumb in loyalty to the advanced thinking of the County of

Brabant. But he certainly does not share Mrs Thatcher's privately voiced opinion that the Roman Empire may have lasted for 1000 years but the Belgian Empire won't last twenty.

The Common Market is a bureaucracy built on free-market principles and Geoffrey Howe is a convert to the free market and a cradle bureaucrat. They were made for each other. European Ministerial meetings, apart from the nonsense of agriculture, are essentially eirenic gatherings if the Prime Minister is not part of the proceedings. Howe must find the dull, civil, decent company of his Dutch, German and Spanish counterparts wonderfully restful after long membership of the Thatcher Cabinet.

Naturally there have been stirrings against this steady orthodoxy. The atrocious David Hart, a slightly loopy entrepreneur of the sort often given houseroom by Thatcher in her compulsive distrust of colleagues and civil servants, has been openly advocating some sort of council of advisers – modelled on the United States of course, whence all blessings flow. If it existed, such a body would be more rightwing than the Foreign Office, uncritically pro-Israel, devoted to the United States, keen to help the Nicaraguan 'Contras', primitively anti-communist and anxious to keep the Cold War in its old soothing condition. It sounds exactly mad enough to have great appeal to our leader; I can see it happening if only out of spite.

This is written at a time when Howe is still Foreign Secretary, but when evident (and leaked) pressure is being put on him to accept a move to the Home Office.* It would be a demotion and is seen as such by Howe himself, even if sweetened by the offer of the deputy Premiership, a post withheld when it fell empty on the retirement of Lord Whitelaw. What is offered is honorific and phoney. If Howe takes it he will do so in the enraptured loyalty of a long-service rabbit whose relationship with the stoat has been described as a mixture of awe and dislike, but also from vague hopes of stray buses fulfilling his destiny.

But at least the possibility of his *not* taking it should be

---

*We now know what *did* happen. Here we see the options.

registered. If he is well-to-do in the standard Surrey lawyer's way, he is not rich by inheriting or property developing standards and, like Norman Tebbit, he has watched the really rich with some inquisitive fascination. Liked as he is, intelligent as he is, and with actual inclinations for work, he could command the bank of his choice and a quarter of a million's worth of directors' fees. Lady Howe is said to have commented on the family's relative modesty of income and would welcome an improvement. If he stays, he will be given a risible garland, a change of post which is a substantive demotion and serves Thatcher's convenience while doing nothing for himself.

The truth is that, badly as he wants to be Prime Minister, and good as he would be at it in a non-dynamic work-shifting good-tempered way, he won't get the job. She remains for many reasons including pure pleasure, but keeping out an orthodox, safe, serviceable but ultimately despised figure like Geoffrey Howe is high among them. Too cautious, he should have run for the leadership ahead of her candidacy in 1975 and he should retire and make money now. Otherwise he will be remembered entirely for his subordinate services.

Howe is just a little too well suited to subordination to hope for more. He lacks the gambler's touch, the instinct for rebellion which made her. He is not quite selfish enough to be a completely successful politician. His hard side only finds expression in the dogged promotion of hard policies, disemployment through deflation in the early eighties and the consignment of Hong Kong to China in anticipation of demand. The impression with many things Howe has done, right and wrong, successful and unsuccessful, has been of early reluctance and later dedication.

In the service of Mr Heath, being extremely loyal not to say keen, he not only devised the Industry Act as a bill-drafting Solicitor General, but was also an ardent pursuer of direct intervention in the market process. The image of Howe telephoning the Vicar of Trumpington to urge upon him the patriotic duty of not increasing his burial charges belongs in the anthologies.

Despite his intelligence and his own early sponsorship of ideas through the Bow Group, Howe has been too perfectly the high-level functionary, the brisk conductor of other people's business. In the opera of politics, as on the stage itself, the role of the notary, though indispensable, commonly falls to a second bass!

That very Industry Act was, of course, an education for Howe, not to say the rest of us. Its formula of registered and unregistered unions failed to take account of union solidarity and a mass boycott of the system. It was a very decent, fair-minded attempt to limit the unions without smashing them. Given wisdom, concession and reasonableness, it would have been the excellent, fair-minded thing which Howe and the Court's President John Donaldson intended. Given the blood-bolted rage of late unionism, it meant very ugly crowds stamping through the streets shouting 'Kill the Bill, Kill the Bill', and it meant a springboard for a dangerous clown, Arthur Scargill.

That was Howe harnessed to Edward Heath, trying reason and a rather scrupulous piece of law. After humiliation, he came back as the servant of Margaret Thatcher; the commanding mood was directed half-knowing, half-unsure, to the smashing of trades unions – by law and more effectively by tight money and a high pound. Half-knowing and half-unsure, Howe was part of a revenge. Yet he is unmalicious and happier at agreements and accords, but again he was the servant, this time the servant of the winning side. My own instinct is that Geoffrey Howe's course, for all his indestructibility, is almost run. The leadership dreams will be barred by an Elizabeth or at any rate a Violet Elizabeth, determined to live for ever. The Woolsack has been filled by a revolutionary Calvinist from the Highlands. It is Geoffrey Howe's tragedy to have become the William Whitelaw of his leader's third term – buffer, punch-bag, sounding board, hired human being. There are worse things, but Howe was always something better. He was right to want the Prime Ministership, wrong to suppose that merely being talented, hard-working, universally trusted and emotionally moored he had the necessary qualifications.

# CHAPTER 20

## Martin Flannery

There ought to be something terribly sad about Martin Henry Flannery. He keeps watch by the shrine of a losing side, a cause whose time has gone. He is faithful and honourable and deserving respect but it is impossible to like him.

He was described by Ferdinand Mount as 'the bottle-nosed ex-schoolmaster representing the constituency of envy malice and all uncharity'. That alas is it. Flannery spoils everything by being indescribably sour; he is resentment made flesh. He is also desperately predictable. As an old communist, he has the cassette quality of one reciting an approved truth. The speeches, though coherent, are strung-out clichés like a row of dim fairylights on a run-down prom.

Physically, he is a slightly tubby man with a pink face and a large nose, not bottle at all just something of a peninsula. There used to be a little sergeant's sort of moustache, extended for a while to join an intellectual's beard, which looked rather well but, in a moment of natural conservatism, the beard was shed to leave the correct line of the moustache in its leading role.

Although for half the time he can be genial and pleasant enough in a rasping way, it is the permanent pot-bubble of wrath that one notices. When it comes to anger, he goes into upper case and becomes very like Anger in a mediaeval morality play. He confronts the rip-off merchants of capitalist exploitation with the just anger and outrage of the affronted and disgusted workers who *will be heard*. 'Shall I slice it there, or would you like another half pound?' There are, of course, all sorts of ex-communists, including some of the most interesting and stimulating people around. Flannery just isn't one of them. And although he left the party in 1956 and has periodically included Soviet oppression in his anathemas, psychologically and temperamentally he is very much old-fashioned party. The cool open-minded intellectuality of the evolved CPGB would seem to him like iced buttermilk.

There are other bad influences. His roots are Irish and Catholic, hence a *tendresse* for the Republican cause, though he may just be attracted by little Brother Hatred. It is of course perfectly possible to be Catholic and liberal-minded or Irish and enlightened. But to make the shift from one or both to the CPGB of the thirties involves a double dose of perfect, incontrovertible truth, doing nothing for the digestion and less for breadth of mind.

Then again, he is a schoolmaster of the training-college-finished sort. That isn't his fault: university education for working-class boys in the North was miserably hard to come by in the late thirties when he was newly out of school. But the lack of it has narrowed him. He has inhabited a petty parish of seniority and properly marked registers, NUT meetings, endless little lectures and the narrow round of small business which constitutes the under-education provided for children in poorer schools in remote places.

Everything is wrong with British education, from Eton to Crookesmore Junior in Sheffield where Flannery was head-master. It actually does deserve a Marxist analysis, unjust and class-biassed as it is. The educational establishment actively dislikes a broad civilised culture, preferring its own fog of bossy jargon-obscured pedantry. The best schools are for the rich, the worst schools for the poor, while schoolmasters emerge either as cerebral footmen or battered drudges. Most of British education is life without oxygen.

If Flannery wanted to come out of all this as really anxious to change education out of sight he would have wide sympathy. But school-teaching, ill-paid and mind-stunting, naturally attract mediocrity, in Flannery's case dogmatic mediocrity, so that he emerges not as a reformer responsive to ideas but as a bundle of crude dull certainties and as the sum of all his wrongs. He is old left as Eric Heffer is, and though he lacks Heffer's hilarious self-importance it is equally difficult to take him very seriously. He was born in an age of, and in a region of, permanent embittered protest. He will be praised for never having changed, apart from his separation for the CP. But if this is fidelity to class and principle, one sees the point of betrayal.

Nothing does stay the same and those who remain in a condition of rigid, statuesque consistency end by looking anachronistic. Sheffield has plenty to be bitter about. Life in the steel mills was hard and bitter and is not made sweeter by their near dissolution into profitable slenderness. But to listen to Martin Flannery chuntering and droning about ancient iniquities is to understand the state of clenched inertia which kept steel unreformed, unproductive and under-invested for so long.

He expresses, does this schoolmaster in the schoolmaster's uniform of sports coat and flannels, the tribal resentment of the entrenched working class – what is called a 'raised' political consciousness, though it is raised into a condition of negation. But Flannery is also a tremendous reproach to the complacency of the Conservative establishment dominating Britain for most of this century. He expresses genuine class feeling unalloyed by mixing or mobility, narrowly confined into castellations of disdain and resentment. He is also the embattled, know-nothing aspect of the North, conscious of having been done down. He regards the workers as 'real people' and man in his mobile, aspiring modern condition as a yuppie or a seller-out.

It is not easy to imagine Flannery in modern Germany or any modern EC country. While he may have clung to adversarialism, the traditional Tories also liked it well enough as an expression of all being right with their world. Which world, if one thinks it out, bore an uncommon resemblance to Prospero's island. The fit and proper and God-designated filled their places. Smooth Jeeves-like servants and functionaries saw all things in order, and cleft within his tree and howling was Caliban.

The growing assumption about Britain, and in this Mrs Thatcher with all her livid defects is part of progress, is that everything is open to the fit and able without regard for origins. As a doctrine it needs some softening if it is not to turn into the democracy of opportunity embracing the South Bronx and White Plains. West Germany is a happier model. But Flannery exists in a world of 'hands' and masters, cavalry colonels and crushed workers, a world of fixed, unamendable class antagonism. He is political archaeology. But what does he tell us about the civilisation of class and subordination being dug up?

# CHAPTER 21

## *John Major*

John Major must be thoroughly weary of reading in profiles that his father was once a tightrope walker. No more to the point, Tom Major was also a soldier in the Brazilian army, a baseball player, the manager of a vaudeville company and sixty-six years old when his son John was born.

Even allowing for Mrs Thatcher's admirable devotion to social mobility, the current low price of baronets and Guards officers, Major of Brixton is a phenomenon. Yet the measure of the man is that the antecedents are not the aspect of him most talked about. The ascent has been so nearly vertical in recent years that roots in South London and Bohemia are upstaged.

One could take against the child Major. Like the boy Mellor, who seems to have been a Fauntleroid locust of office in the Tory youth organisation, he was shooting from the hip in the Tory cause in his early teens. He even took a soap-box around with him for better exposition to an ungrateful public. How these two have turned out the pleasant fellows they are and not admonitory deacons of the index finger Heaven knows and is grateful. There is incidentally a close acquaintance and considerable sympathy between them.

But the precise nature of Major's Toryism remains usefully imprecise. He cuts expenditure, of course, is a Treasury natural and scornful about the utility of money scattered. But he has seen poverty and been near enough to poverty, and nothing about the man suggests that anaesthesia of the spirit which sustains some Conservatives. His constituents were told at selection that he was against the death penalty and thus he remains.

As member for Huntingdon, Major is aptly placed. For even in the bleakest moment of the early eighties, it has been an important part of the East Anglian economic surge deriving from Cambridge technological spin-off and nearness to the deregulated ports facing Europe. He was an obscure man prospering in consort with his obscure but thriving constituency. He was first pointed out to me as someone to watch as long ago as 1981. To meet then he was as lucid, quiet and unspectacular as he remains. The self-importance which gathers around people with far slighter achievements has made no impression upon his nature.

The secret of Major's rise seems to divide into three causes. There is a genuine mathematical grasp to see him through Treasury work proficiently. But Peter Rees, an early Thatcher Chief Secretary, had that and nobody rated Peter Rees – indeed he was systematically disliked, a sort of Ridley without style. Then there is the shrewdness as a Whip: a man who so impresses as Treasury Whip that the Chancellor wants him for his own must have something. He was, after all, widely expected to become Chief Whip after his successful junior run at DHSS. This was his own expectation. But at Lawson's express request even this very high promotion was superseded.

Now a man who, in the uncovenanted crisis after the Brighton bomb, takes over the constituency duties of the injured Chief Whip is kind and shrewd in delightful proportions. The landscape painting and the case of claret which came from John Wakeham would be as nothing to the goodwill of someone whose goodwill was bankable.

The third and incalculable aspect of Major is a likeableness nowhere denied and very nearly universally applauded. Even Chris Patten has enemies of a purely political sort, people who dislike his point of view. Waldegrave and Mellor have enemies by the armful for being clever or combative, lordly or pushy. Major walks through life in a permanent haze of tickertape and rose petals.

It is not that he is anywhere supposed to be innocent or naïve. He is a banker with a talent for cutting public expenditure, not a combination of St Francis and Stan Laurel. Yet if one mentions his name anywhere in the Tory party, the fountains start playing and admiring things are said. The nearest to dissent came from a very alert Labour MP who declined to be impressed and defined him as 'the captain of the second team'. A great body of opinion has him as first team captain in waiting.

That Labour gruffness is significant. Extremely civil and rational in debate, he does turn a deliberately biting fire on the Opposition, especially its leader. This is good politics with colleagues and even better with Mrs Thatcher, whose unrelenting partisanship is one of the burdens of the age. And no one accuses him of being naïve.

The contrast which matters and tells most is with John Moore. Moore was early trumpeted as the anointed Thatcherian future leader. 'Golden boy', said one original-minded journalist. 'Crown Prince', said another. 'Dust and ashes', said events. But superficially they had a great deal in common. Both were poor boys who had made names and money on their own through their merits. Neither had been to university but neither was philistine. Both had a fair measure of charm. Both pleased Mrs Thatcher; both were delicately poised, ideologically close to her outlook but not clones. They were, as the cliché has it, 'examples of the classless talent flourishing in Thatcher's Britain'.

'Classless' is a facile word with a diversity of meanings. The self-made tend to have either aspirations or resentments or – and this was very much the case with Moore – to live with deep-seated unease. Eminence having been won by great effort, perpetual striving and busy activity would be essential if it was to be kept. Both Moore and Major worked at the Treasury: Moore as Financial Secretary, Major as Treasury Whip. Nigel Lawson grew increasingly aggravated by Moore's (unnecessary) promotion of Moore and his self-designation as 'Mr Privatisation'. And though no colleague can have worked harder, the relationship grew prickly and sour.

Major in a more junior post did his Sidney Godolphin bit ('Ah Mr Godolphin, never in the way and never *out of* the way!'), doing for the Treasury what the Treasury wanted done with a minimum of prompting, and understanding the department. Lawson, an exacting man, short on personal enthusiasms, was enthusiastic. Moore had Prime Ministerial admiration and the irritation and resentment of the man he had worked for; Major had the goodwill of both.

To take another example, Moore was to be shot down for forcing through a Social Security review to save money. The whole of Major's recent reputation derives from saving money and he is directly responsible for the freeze of child benefits, something Labour politicians denounce as bitterly in private as they do on parade. Yet Major has never been a target for such assault.

What truly divides them is the quality of serenity. John Moore is both a far abler and more likeable fellow than is suggested by his current depressing status of a toasted cherub lately in Hell. But his ineptitude as a politician owes a great deal to a lack of serenity. His disastrous compulsion to please the Prime Minister and to come running is not deference pure and simple but an oppressed need for approval. He has a restless uncertainty about himself which may explain the compounding of rotten luck which brought him struggling into the Commons on the day of that debate when he was quite seriously ill. A more relaxed, self-assured man would have postponed the fight until fit.

Incidentally, a formidable case can be made against Major as a cutting Chief Secretary: those freezings of benefits have in the expert view done real harm. The action itself reflects the passive greed of the middle class, happy to use benefits for pin money and extra holidays. Labour is thickheadedly universalist on the subject, on the reactionary Hattersley principle that anything habitually done is in a semi-divine condition of being all right.

A brave government would erect a ceiling at a generous point for benefits to stop or set up three or four decelerating increments. Major, as Chief Secretary, was rightly outraged at the waste but more shrewd than brave in his execution. Additional payments of £205 million were supposed to offset the freeze (though experts are sceptical about the targeting of this), and of that sum £130 million was already in the pipeline.

From an accountancy point of view, the Treasury is nicely up, but the iniquity of middle-class benefits has only been attenuated by inflation, something it shares with poor people's benefits which are elaborately and Heath Robinsonishly propped – wonderful politics but not really a triumph of good government.

However, as a piece of sheer skill, it illustrates why Major wins and Moore loses. Indeed, it was firmly rumoured that the Chief Secretary had spotted the trouble into which his colleague was running and had offered accommodations which Moore, in his desire to please Mrs Thatcher with radical savings, declined. As a spending Minister, Moore was apt to lurch between cuts one winter and urgent needs for more than he should expect the next, as he tries to compensate. To be fair, Major has not been tested as a spender, but his arithmetical and political grasp leave little expectation that he would open himself to any very damaging criticism.

Incidentally, he has the advantage that, unlike Moore, he performs very well in the Commons. Normally the manner is mild and rational but he can do the viperish bit when he thinks it useful. His dismissal of Neil Kinnock was corrosive: 'someone who will understand the economy in the year Donald Duck wins *Mastermind*'. Major then does well for a whole series of qualities which Moore doesn't have – serenity, self-confidence, an armoury of sharp Tebbit-and-tonic phrases, the lack of a burning need for Thatcher's smile, conceivably a better technical grasp, but above all a perfect relaxed belief in himself.

Both men are ambitious, intelligent, humane, fit for high office and, in the case of Moore, deserving an opportunity to get the ball out of the bunker. But Moore is breathless and surprised at himself in such eminence, even though his career as Chairman of Dean Whitter was more brilliant than Major's steady performance at Standard Chartered Bank. What he wants Moore wants too badly; he strives and is seen to strive. He advertises achievements better left for others to pick up and he risks being an anti-Godolphin – sometimes in the way, not always there when wanted. And he manages to be actively

‹›7‹›

disliked and envied beyond any actual faults. His rise caused enormous rage and his great stumble gave far too much pleasure.*

This is not meant cruelly, but the emblematic mark of Major's happier quality is shown in the activities of their wives. Sheila Moore, an American lady, writes books of a devotional nature about Mrs Thatcher. Norma Major has written a single, long-researched and well received life of Joan Sutherland. There is life away from politics.

Major has been a Whip, a junior Health Minister and then Chief Secretary to the Treasury. The practical record has been very good. At the Treasury he won brilliant opinions by turning his hotel bedroom at conference into what was called 'the slaughter house', as he worked his way remorselessly through colleagues and their demands, somehow making big savings without making enemies. The savings have been accomplished and the command of the Treasury has not been contested. He is now poised, as should hardly be the case for someone who entered Parliament ten years ago, to be discussed seriously as a rising Prime Minister. There are three big talents among the forty to fifty age group: Major, Malcolm Rifkind and Christopher Patten.

Although I believe that Patten will receive years of Cabinet seniority the day he enters that body, and although he has his own personal and ideological faction, he *has* been held back and he is sharply identified with the 'out' wing of the Tory party. Rifkind, probably the best intellect of the lot, is stuck with stroppy Scotland where Conservatism is better liked than bubonic plague but not entirely popular. He may also, disgracefully, have to struggle against an undercurrent of anti-Semitism unacknowledged in the Tory psyche. When a foolish backbencher, John Stokes, can say at the height of the Westland affair, *à propos* Leon Brittan, that 'what we want is a loud-voiced, red-faced Englishman in the post'; when 'Latvian' and 'Lithuanian' are code words; and when the

---

*His actual fall in July was received by one of my amiable wet friends with the crisp words – 'He deserves it!'

*Sunday Telegraph* thinks fit to ponder aloud about Mrs Thatcher's friendliness to Jews, civilised and liberal assumptions ought not to be made too lightly. Sadly, Major, who gets genuinely angry at all forms of racial prejudice, may unwillingly benefit from it. Mrs Thatcher's perfect indifference to all forms of race prejudice notwithstanding.

My own personal view is that the three of them have together enough ability, quality of mind and attractive character to set the Conservative party on a good course for the next twenty years. With ordinary luck, like Scotland not falling off the island, the three of them should be carving up the senior posts before very long. But undoubtedly Major has the lead at present; he is both in the Cabinet and in a job he can leave at any time.* He is with Thatcher on her key economic things but is not blood of her blood. He is, without having to calculate too minutely, Thatcherian enough for now and different and distanced enough for later.

Especially is he different from her in temperament. It is simply unimaginable to think of John Major throwing a tantrum about the Marxists of the EC. He would want to stop M. Delors but he would know how to do it politely.

Major is wonderfully placed to run without duplicity as change *and* continuity, as a non-twitching Thatcher, as free markets and tight money *and* a readiness to listen and spend temperately where the case is good. His cuts have all been done inside a general plan and as a subordinate. He would be more financially tight than Rifkind and much more so than Patten. But all three share a civilisation: the days of vulgar nationalism, Bernard Ingham briefings against colleagues, ever more manic security and the rule of the sleek assurance-propping admen in No 10 would all be over.

As a front-runner he is of course vulnerable. The turn of his ankle on an unseen tree root will have its joys for someone. But there is no crowd willing him to fall. All his life Major has been blessed with friendships which saw him on and up. There was Lord Barber, the former Chancellor, whose

*He did.

protégé he was at Standard Chartered; there was John Wakeham, and there was Nigel Lawson. Just as you commonly get the luck you deserve, so may friends be self-created. Yet never has he attracted a charge of toadying. He has considerable appeal to those who after Mrs Thatcher's fifteen rounds with the universe want tranquillity, but it will be a crisp cost-effective tranquillity; light years from the Macmillan-Baldwin cult of creative inertia, it will never be an excuse for dimly letting events govern men.

It may be that Major is the best synthesis of old Tory and new that we shall find, representative of no class or clique, but English and authentic without the awful formica-façaded finish of the boys in the button-down shirts running the account. In an age of charm schools and politicians taught to say, 'Have a nice day', he remains securely within the human race, one of *us* as it were.

The gift is one of doing the given job well, avoiding the ice-cool manner and sticking to room temperature, being neither chippy nor socially ascendant, avoiding quarrels with colleagues like death, and observing a consistent code of decency. Some advantage can be won by way of a short-cut in the short term by ingratiation, but it is noted as ingratiation. Trust percolates.

Occasionally the judgement is made of an ostensibly successful person, 'There's something wrong there' – witness Beatrice Webb's deathless comment on Oswald Mosley, 'Such perfection argues a rottenness somewhere.' The remark John Major attracts is that there is nothing wrong there. He is sane, balanced, thoroughly pleasant to know, shrewd this side of glinting calculation, willing even against Mrs Thatcher and as a junior to argue politely back and stay his ground.

He has no hang-ups, does no boasting and yet has few illusions. The schoolboy thrill at it all, so regularly and immaturely a sign of a rising politician, is simply absent. The best I can say is that Major is as good as he looks.

# CHAPTER 22

## *Roy Hattersley*

Roy Hattersley has been part of the political landscape since he entered Parliament in 1964. He is still a youngish man by the tolerant standards of politics, if not altogether a hopeful one.

Beyond any question he has high talents. No one who heard him floor Mrs Thatcher twice in a single week late in the summer of 1988 will have done so without wincing. A Tory would have done so because the right cross and the winding left to the ribs were so very good; a disliker of Hattersley because the fat man, *pace* King Duncan, still has so much talent in him; a steady Labour supporter because Neil Kinnock, though improving, never has consistently scored against her.

The material was the basic solid stuff which the excellent Dave Hill (who researches chiefly for Hattersley but is available to Kinnock) does so well. The difference was one of professional targeting. Hattersley asked a pointed question without flourishes and, finding the lady evasive, went back and back until she asked him to stop. Kinnock would have slipped in a performance of 'St Paul'. Yet despite such elegance and skill, it is doubtful if Hattersley rides very high. He has successfully rebuffed the candidacy of John Prescott for his post as deputy leader, and thoroughly disagreeable he made himself in the process, trusting that Mr Prescott would not wish to be humiliated by pressing the matter and swaggering through Blackpool as if the glory belonged to him personally, a demand for Roydie in person rather than an insistence on the status quo and no upsets.

It is Hattersley's talent to be admired and repellent at the same time. He has a sort of scornful insolence, very odd given his place in the political spectrum. He does not talk like a moderate man amenable to doubt and ambiguity, more like a believer spurning the unfaithful. Hattersley on the snub has to be seen: the lower lip juts out like a windowsill; the nostrils, always a touch porcine, distend; the voice, popping its 'p's, lisping slightly and more than slightly asthmatic, disposes of the intervener as a person not mistaken or silly, nor a good sort getting it wrong, but as someone not quite fit to be touched by human hand.

The Tories naturally loathe this approach and extend a dislike to Hattersley which would crinkle steel plate. Their experience is of being, if very lucky, only patronised, more commonly dismissed as lepers. There is an echo of sorts with one facet of Harold Wilson; essentially a very kind man who disliked causing hurt, Wilson was also preposterously alerted to danger and struck back with a self-protective sarcasm whose cruelty did not speak the man. But Wilson, not being malicious, could never keep it up. Hattersley can.

A great quality of politics, and what makes politicians broadly such an amiable and comfortable congregation of men, is its saving cynicism, the absence of zealous certainty and the persecuting or righteous impulse. From such good-natured indifferentism Hattersley is wholly free; he gets in a lot of despising. There is also a moody quality there, a tendency to be either euphorically up or non-communicatively and cataleptically down. It can lead him into displays of quite dazzling charm beyond the call of ordinary political wheel-oiling, and it can cause outbursts of unprovoked and uncovenanted rudeness calculated to make enemies of people who had planned to be no such thing. Such set-piece displays of Hattersley being irrationally unpleasant are not frequent but one is enough.

As for sanctimoniousness, he would make a very fair honorary Indian. That quality of finger-wagging, morality-invoking instant righteousness, requiring one merely to add hot water and serve – which shines through Lok Sabha politics from Krishna Menon to the puffy young Rajah himself – is on constant flow. Draught piety siphoned up from the keg is the Hattersley speciality. It flourished particularly, of course, in his great days of shadowing the Home Office. There is more fun in shadowing that department than running it. As an administrative bundle it is the old coelacanth, happiest in the hands of a Sidmouth or a Joynson-Hicks and dedicated to taking a spectator's attentive interest in avoidable disaster, witness the failure until too late to replace prison fabric and the complementary current apathy on AIDS. That tulip-shaped graph of prison population so grandly neglected at the start of one decade stands fair to be elegantly eliminated by a similar and balancing neglect of a prison plague which it declines to investigate until epidemic.

However that is the mere job. A shadow, especially a Labour shadow, can if such things excite him have a hundred fits, not only at the institutionalised negligence of the department but about 'racism'. Now there is, God knows, plenty of actual racial prejudice in existence, but it is the way of a certain sort of politician to grasp the issue as a two-handed battle-axe in the war of moral opportunity. Hattersley on this topic is in a permanent state of shame at the moral deficiency of other men. Liberal-minded Tory Home Secretaries who would be appalled to hurt minorities find themselves preached at as if they had been found writing things on walls.

Macaulay's remark about puritans' disapproval of the pleasure of bear-baiters deriving more from the cruelty than from the suffering of the animal has always struck me as doubtful thinking and cavalier morality. Pleasure from cruelty is quite evil enough to need no puritan conscience to take badly against it. Likewise racism is a very nasty thing, yet the satisfaction Hattersley derives from hating it somehow leaves him less attractive.

As he has laboured to tell the world profitably in a thousand articles for the *Listener* and *Punch*, Hattersley is a Northern lad, a Yorkshireman willing to bore for England on the topic. There is a school of thought, not least in Lancashire, which points out that any number of our leading murderers – like Peter Sutcliffe and Donald Nielsen together with most of the notable hangmen, not to mention Geoffrey Boycott, Michael

Parkinson and Arthur Scargill – all hail from a particular patch of South Yorkshire. For those who want to be thoroughly racist, it may be that heavy Viking settlement in this part of the world may have included a concentration of *berserkers*, the psychotic personalities picked out to fight without armour in the front line of battle and put due fear of death into the enemy. Hattersley himself, when he obtained a year's study at Harvard, was classified on his papers by the US immigration authorities as 'Hunnish'!

To dwell upon the racial characteristics of Hattersley would be speculative and unfair. What is not in dispute is that, despite his professional deftness in debate, his politician's fingertips and good intelligence, there is something old-fashioned about the man. He is not only moralistic but also heavily partisan, refusing all moral credit to opponents. This is old-fashioned on the Labour side, where defeat and a winnowing of past arrogance has produced the Bryan Gould style soft-voiced, rational discourse approach to politics, a profound improvement for any listener. Mrs Thatcher of course is thoroughly old-fashioned, oddly reminiscent of the old evangelical socialist. And for her the style works hideously well, but for a Tory to be like that – though there are now a host of inferior and cringing imitators – was a stroke of inadvertent genius.

In Hattersley the eyeball-rolling morality is simply a chapel staple, transferred to politics by Methodist-bred table-pounders long ago. It is the one authentic local Northern unmetropolitan thing about an otherwise worldly and rich London politician. It gives him some kinship with the old-time values and style of his leader – Neil Kinnock being a traditional South Wales, class-rooted socialist from before his time.

Hattersley also has roots and, despite the distressing way he has retailed them by the quarter pound, in many ways they are good roots. His mother Enid was, by the accounts of those who knew her, an exemplary local council leader of the sort which the left and Mrs Thatcher have conspired to replace and destroy. She sounds warm, brisk, mildly and necessarily bossy far below the Thatcher level of imperiousness, and generally sensible and moderate in a way not recently associated with local authorities, though the fashion is returning.

A shadow, if a soothing one, has to have been thrown on young Roy. It is rather as if Mark Thatcher with some talent and a lesser, nicer mother, had set out on a political career. Like Mark he is spoiled and wants his own way privately in a way not pleasant to see. The Hattersley private life, a conspicuous mess conducted for his own gratification over the heads of other people who have behaved astonishingly well towards him, is less that of a dumb ninny like the Prime Minister's son than of an artistic temperament declaring its genius and contempt for bourgeois values. Which would be fine if the man were not such a compulsive occupant of pulpits. Better read and with a far finer ear than the Prime Minister, Hattersley does not turn the stomach or set one laughing when he takes a high ethical line. But the drab gaberdine of transferred nonconformity, disagreeable in both of them, is also slightly outlandish as the costume of an amateur boulevardier.

However, politically Hattersley has made the essential right decisions for surviving in a hostile environment. He chose to stay with the Labour party despite his identification with its right wing, a sensible non-move at a time when the big gamble seemed to have better than even chances of coming off. He makes great and wearying play in his writings of Labour's role for him as home, church, mum and oxygen supply. This can be taken coolly, more than all of these it is his career; and under pressure he guessed right. Labour survives; the centralist bubble has blown.

But Labour today is not the hysterical lamp-standard-throwing scene of domestic tragedy of seven years ago. The existence of the SDP and the triumphs of the Amazon Queen have made possible the partial reconstruction of what is just beginning to be recognised as a moderate party of the centre left. It was long dogged by people you wouldn't want at your funeral, like that bubble of syndicalist dementia, Arthur Scargill, attended upon in the way of a babbling mute by Mr

Wedgwood Benn, long unable to extricate itself from a voter-unfriendly policy of unilateral nuclear defence, and led then by a leader, nice but incapable of winning an election. But it is now nevertheless a real and prospectively reasonable party, getting better rather than worse and with working hopes of ultimate resurrection.

Simply by being a mainline politician and a believer that something would turn up, Hattersley got it right. He has the standing of Mr Micawber in receipt of a small legacy. Yet at fifty-six, Hattersley has good reason to resent the folly of Labour's crazy fit and subsequent schism. It has put him in the wilderness for ten years, with another two, perhaps six, to go. In 1995, a good year for an Opposition breakthrough, Hattersley will be approaching his sixty-third birthday. For someone entering Parliament at thirty amid the drums and trumpets proclaiming Labour the natural party of government, it is a falling-out of the fates not be be mocked. He has done well to retain as much equanimity as he has, and was absolutely wise to diversify his life out of total politics into a notable second career as an entertaining journalist.

The wilderness succeeds years of patient assent, PPS, Parliamentary Secretary, Minister of State, finally and un-luckily Cabinet office with the high-aspiring but pathetic title of Secretary of State for Prices and Incomes. If there is one philosophic battle which has been won and upon which rational opinion on the left makes no serious contest, it is over the utility of government taking upon itself the power directly to regulate prices and incomes. Mr Lawson and his high-rise interest rates have taken their own knock to be sure. But nobody is going back to telling floods to desist. By the time he was through with that ungrateful employment under Jim Callaghan, Roy Hattersley had recognised as much and was passing great volumes of price rises as beyond the resources, even of Roy Hattersley, to stop.

This modest office was the reward of a sad encounter and unseemly submission in the days preceding James Callaghan's election as leader and Prime Minister. Hattersley had long advertised himself as a personal supporter of Anthony

Crosland. For reasons that must have seemed good the layer-waste of education was a hero to the younger man. Such sentiments had no appeal for Callaghan, a machine politician of compounded avuncularity, brutality and clarity of mind, who at that moment knew exactly what he wanted. Hattersley had been told that if he wanted advancement (and he did) there could be no messing about with votes for Crosland on the first ballot; it was Jim and a new job or not Jim and not a new job. Hattersley tried to explain as much to Crosland on the phone, in conjunction with a declaration of deathless adherence, to be told succinctly to 'fuck off'. Even so, between 1964 and 1979 Hattersley had seemed like a man going up, modestly but by no means inexorably, a stock better held than neglected and likely to appreciate.

In a sense he still rose in the thin, under-oxygenated air of Opposition, making terms with the creation of Robin Cook's skills as magic doll-maker: the great, new, irresistible leader Neil Kinnock. Defeat at the hands of Kinnock was so certain in advance that the conduct of an exemplary and uplifting campaign of disinterested lukewarm debate was made equally inevitable. The losers' clinch was frozen on stills for all time as the Dream Ticket.

Both men have behaved well towards each other in their time as leader and deputy leader – well rather than correctly. Kinnock has his warm side, Hattersley is a three times circumspect realist. But it is odd, when waves began to hit Kinnock for a run of erratic and lopsided leadership – splendid in terms of courage, deficient and unimpactive against the Queen of Sorrows – that none of the extensive speculation about alternative and better leaderships which began in 1988, as Kinnock held three defence policies in ten days, contained a moment's thought of Hattersley for leader!

There was no reason on paper why he should not be so considered. He has been more solicitous of the left's sensibilities than John Smith, yet Mr Smith's name before his illness had been mentioned all the time, sometimes on the left. Admittedly, Hattersley had not had much of a time shadowing the Treasury, a job he had insisted upon with more status-consciousness than sense; but competence has never been of the political essence and he was by this time back at the ethical coalface doing his unbeatable decency and multi-racialism routine. Hattersley wasn't considered because he is old, known, used, superfluous politics. That is cruelly put, but simple truth. He has passed the point at which things, given normal luck, go on getting better, and is lodged where he must defend what he has and hope to stay there a little while. The present tense is a state of aspiration.

It is not that Hattersley is not intelligent, wittily professional, up to most of the political functions and much more polished than Neil Kinnock. Time passes and loyalties disperse. As Mark Antony put it, and Tony Crosland might have:

> Those that spanielled me do now discandy
> And pour their sweetness into Caesar

No one is being particularly base, they are recognising – as Hattersley did with Crosland – that the future does not that way lie and accommodating themselves accordingly.

Hattersley in many respects possessed superior talents to Kinnock. He had, and deservedly, a superiority of experience at the time of their mild contest, in terms of Ministerial office and important shadow jobs stretching back to 1967. Kinnock, for reasons of combined past radical outlook and a touch of indolence, had had a few months as a PPS and a single Shadow job to his name. For what it was worth (nothing) he was not then a member of the Privy Council. But losing to Kinnock could be put down to the need for choosing a man with leftwing fittings, the House with Pink Shutters as it were. As the Kinnock leadership ran into trouble for unrelated reasons, none of the objections of 1981 applied, yet Hattersley was not the subject of anyone's thought. Instead, he found himself the object of a rescue campaign *by* Kinnock.

And would the Prescott *défi* even have been made if Hattersley had been thought well of? It would never have been launched against a Smith or even a more ideologically provocative Gould occupying the deputy leadership. It was

Hattersley's misfortune, securely as the machine was to protect him, that Prescott's personal dislike, a happy two-way process nurtured between rough worker and polished-uppered *flâneur*, was accelerated by the notion of a Hattersley who was not really rated.

As a presence he survives still – intelligent, amusing, good enough to injure the Prime Minister in debate but subtly relegated and far too shrewd not to understand the fact of relegation. He would be loyal anyway and has no motive for being anything else. He may indeed still be able to influence Kinnock in minor ways, since the steady undemanding partnership between them has been as easy as the one inside the former Alliance was nightmarish. Accordingly, he is slipping imperceptibly and ahead of his time into the ways of elder statesmanship. Conceivably Mrs Thatcher in her demotion of Geoffrey Howe to the floor leadership has indicated Hattersley's destiny.

Which is not to suppose that he is through with politics, interesting and original editor though he might yet make. He will stick around for a while because it is the work he knows, the familiar, pleasing routine, and because in all the flannel about roots and love for the party there is an element of truth. Hattersley belongs to the Labour party even though it will never belong to him.

# CHAPTER 23

## *David Mellor*

One should beware of stereotypes. Early impressions of David Mellor proclaimed a rising, clever, smoothly successful lawyer-politician of the obvious unendearing sort.

I put myself into judgement very early and quite wrongly with the observation that Mellor was as attractive as a mouthful of Brylcreem. It just ain't so. I know the anti-Mellor arguments backwards. They are not without grains of truth – pompous, too clever, an acquired taste, hooked on publicity. The things said against Mellor are superficial, two and two adding up to five and a half. I am prejudiced by friendship, but have found the taste entirely worth acquiring.

The impressive thing about Mellor in the last couple of years has been an impulse to speak his mind which has not advanced his career. The episode in Israel involved him in publicly rebuking an army officer for the treatment of Arab protesters (only a few days later we saw on TV an Arab having his arm deliberately broken as a punishment by members of that not always very enlightened army). It was not calculated to do him any good in a government whose Prime Minister, for reasons of sympathy and Cold War purposes, maintains a strong attachment to the Israeli state. Information received says that her response was one of rage.

It was a Foreign Office view to be sure, but no merely ambitious politician in *this* government who happened to be posted to the Foreign Office would make the mistake of seeing its point of view. Mrs Thatcher is a lady of obsessive hatreds and one of the things she hates obsessively is the Foreign Office. It is conciliatory where she would use broken bottles; it is European where she is a Little Englander and America Firster. (Truly to plumb the Prime Minister's commitments you must watch her standing to attention, right hand over heart, as the Stars and Stripes is raised.)

The FO sees an Arab cause where she empathises, not very critically, with the Israelis; it has a vein of melancholy relativism where she sees truth painted in primary colours. If it were practical, as in the way of our lost civilised television, to bring the whole thing to an end by getting a pet capitalist to preside over the FO's break-up and dispersal to contractors, the chance would be snatched at. No merely smart Minister at the Foreign Office would publicly identify himself with the department's unforgiven attempt to understand the world.

Yet Mellor is smart and successful and rising fast (on his third Ministry of State at forty). He is a classic case of the new tendency (showing now on the Labour side as well) for the able not to be left around mellowing like vintages but to go into important jobs in their thirties. He has already been a junior Minister, then Minister of State at the Home Office and Minister of State at the FO. He is now, as number two to Kenneth Clarke, in a make-or-break job with a heavy share of responsibility for holding the weakest point in the Tory line. That job is not made easier because both men have to reconcile the weakness of the Tory position in the public eye, according to every poll on the subject, with the requirements of the Treasury and the intentions of the Prime Minister.

Clarke and Mellor did not invent the Health and Medicines Bill with its glaucoma-inducing, jolly little charges, but they were stuck with having to defend it. Also, they are under pressure from the Treasury cast of mind which made such demands and whose appetite grew on John Moore's submission to them. On this topic, both were aggressively in support of the party's correct and unpopular line. Very wrongly from his own point of view, Mellor in his wind-up speech on the night of two miserable majorities (sixteen for teeth, eight for eyesight) made a tactless joke at the expense of his tormentor, the curly, bearded upholder of Bow Group values, Jerry Hayes. Now Hayes, though essentially a de-

lightful youth, can be infuriating when his boyish exuber-
ance exuberates. But at the back of that incident, which
might be called an endorsement for irony, is probably something altogether deeper.

Much more than most ambitious Ministers of State doing
well and coming to terms with Mrs Thatcher as an extension
of destiny, Mellor is an uneasy, unresolved old liberal. The
'L' word has become almost as damning within the Tory
party as in Mr Bush's kinder, gentler, destitution-approving
republic. Peace has been made by all the old One Nation
people, with greater or less enthusiasm, with the new illiber-
alism. Douglas Hurd was ready to admit the Goths, with
their wall-to-wall quiz shows and draught inanity, to the
inner citadel of broadcasting. John Moore, overfulfilling his
quota, tried to re-jig Social Security the Treasury way and
stumbled into a preserve of middle-class savers able to
contact their MPs and, in the process, did himself an irrepar-
able injury.

The norm is conformity and Mellor conforms with the best
of them. But his heart isn't comprehensively in it. His attack
on Jerry Hayes, for all that he is much more successful, was
touched by an envy of Hayes's skylarking clear conscience
and ability to have fun making war on the Treasury's least
charming undertakings.

Occasionally, one encounters in politics people whose
abilities far outrun their talent to please. Mellor, who is
strong on publicity and likes the cameras the way other
people are said euphemistically to like a drink, has no
diffidence problem (he is dangerously articulate), but he
does manage to understate his merits. The image of ambitious abrasion comes over, and does so in the way of all half-
truths – claiming the entire field. The contrasted merit is not
the reasonably obvious grasp of detail nor the high intelligence. As much is conceded by opponents. What is missed is
the unease of a quick mind wedded to a natural liberality,
someone not properly at ease with the facile absolutes of the
present 'Stack it high, sell it off, look after yourself buddy'
Thatcherian imperception.

He knows enough to know that it is crude and has a core of class war and golf-club thinking behind the serious economic case it can make, that it is more successful-seeming than successful. He is also, despite the enjoyment of low-flying planes over Colombian poppy fields, the attendance of highly intelligent civil servants as his graceful entourage and the enormous pleasures of being a Minister, quite capable of stepping back a pace and asking himself if he wants it at any price.

In fairness, personalities and styles within the government probably have more adverse effect on him than actual ideology. His natural model is Christopher Patten, much more readily identified as a voice of doubt within the triumph. But his high culture, a genuine and ardent preoccupation with music which keeps Schubert on the official car radio, Peter Frankl on the Foreign Office guest list, and the Latvian conductor Mariss Janssons as a personal friend, is more important than it might seem.

As with Imperial China, the tastes of the Emperor are readily copied and the tastes of this she-Emperor constitute a perfect Egdon Heath of the senses, closed to music and literature, preoccupied only with official papers, relaxing with a comforting re-read of an author like Frederick Forsyth – better not read at all but shot full of all the approved paranoid war-next-Sunday opinions. Mrs Thatcher's main cultural activity appears to involve feeling underneath the bed for an assurance that the reds are still there. Mellor loves the Russian composers, Liszt, Mozart and other fripperies. Because he has a very quick mind and is an efficient hand at administration, he is able to make himself time to have a mental life away from politics. Denis Healey, who always took a similar attitude, likes to speak of having a hinterland. The culture is not a lacquer nor a gentlemanly accomplishment; it runs a hard race against the natural ambition of a very talented publicity-shrewd politician and staves off boiled-eyed preoccupation with the office.

Yet the beginnings of Mellor's career were classic – not to say parodistic – models of busy advancement. He filled every

office available for filling within the Young Conservatives and
joined the vast army of Conservative talent – Patten, Lamont,
Clarke, Brittan and the rest – being assembled at Cambridge,
which has looked at times like the Detroit of the Tory party.
He was a candidate at twenty-six and a Member of Parliament
at thirty. And indeed he always had fun with publicity. Mellor
against drugs was Mellor flying over those Colombian narcotic
fields and getting enough prime time to make enemies among
other Ministers of State to last for a career. Occasionally the
publicity was inadvertent, as when he took a group of fellow
MPs to watch his local football team, Fulham. It was the week
when Edward Du Cann, a man who brought tone to the office
of first footman, had to some mirth advocated a pledge of
loyalty. Mellor's remark when a Manchester City fullback put
the ball in his own net was widely reported: 'Well done, lad.
Du Cann would be proud of you.'

He has had his self-serving moments. The quite unfair
remark about Brylcreem was prompted by a rather awful
conference speech but, to paraphrase Dr Johnson on lapid-
ary inscriptions, at Conservative party conference a man is
not on oath. It brings out the worst in everybody. But if you
have abilities and no other advantage, ambition follows
logically. Mellor, who is the child of a remote part of the West
of England – Wareham in Dorset – the son of a schoolteacher,
with no connections, no useful circles of allies, has made his
way in the fashion of meritocrats, discovering that he was
able, discovering also that sequences of modulated notes
ravish the ear, and choosing his own intense culture.

Such a transformation is common enough now, but it is the
first time for the person involved and everything is done by
oneself alone. This can make for the aggressive self-suffic-
iency of Mrs Thatcher's most dedicated followers and it will
scar even the most sensitive with resentments and a need to
push and perform.

What is attractive about David Mellor (never 'Dave' by the
way, despite Auberon Waugh's best frantic efforts, to anyone
who knows him) is that he has been through this tunnel at
speed but has also matured quickly into a premature scepti-

cism about the glory of it all. He is beginning to function as a reflective intelligence rather than a merely aspiring one. His worst fault – and it could be fatal if he is not careful – is the besetting sin of all the examination-clever, that as his mind runs very quickly and a point is seized he can convey boredom or irritation with the less clever. The greatest art of politics concerns the simulation of that perplexity common to the rest of us. Intelligence is not a felony in politics but too much of it too apparent can be a serious misdemeanour.

But he is in charge under Ken Clarke of a department which requires all of that intelligence. It also requires funds to function properly, which makes it the representative spending Ministry. It is the natural focus for some of the more effective Opposition thinking. The general tightening up of the Opposition performance has been out-performed by the rational severity of Robin Cook. The strength of the Opposition case here is that the National Health Service is, of all Labour creations, the most enduringly popular. It is something Labour did and ought to have done and it won't go away. It is also very expensive and grows more expensive by annual increments.

Even if the government were not in love with privatisation, with all things American and with spare money for tax cuts, it would worry about the cost of the NHS. But Clarke and Mellor have the inestimable advantage of having watched John Moore attempt to oblige the Treasury and die with that terrible silence of Conservative displeasure behind him. They may make a great issue of fighting the more unreasonable (COHSE) nurses, but they combine as old-style spending Ministers able and willing to fight the Treasury when it thinks of a number and divides it in two. Never mind their own old Bow Group principles, it is not even good politics to make submission in the manner of John Moore, who seems to have been marked 'Tear along the dotted line'.

The Ministers of State under Mrs Thatcher have been compared to civil servants, so strong is their party's hold on power. They await the exigencies of promotion or passing over in a spirit of fellow feeling with the real civil servants who accompany them on the next escalator. But, despite the homogenising tendencies of a rather boring degree of success, they are blessedly variable – twitchy finger-drumming Waldegrave; John Patten genially cynical beyond his years; Chris Patten perfecting a sort of hilarious melancholy; Mellor doing the high-octane performer's bit and being drawn by an undertow of convictions to speak with more candour than we expect. They are a bundle of talents waiting the disposition of this god or the next one.

Mellor will probably do best in a competition of pure skill and felicity – disembodied merit as it were. He is part of an élite and élites are not loved. The politician is too young, accomplished and promotional to be naturally popular, though privately he deserves the affection of his friends. The gap between private and public liking is divided by a ravine and the bridge is rickety. There is enough simple merit to see him through, but he lives with the abiding problem that this same talent also focuses resentment.

The undercurrent of doubt and conscience require to be remembered along with the public performance. They are the part of him which has the highest claim to esteem.

# CHAPTER 24

## *Adam Ingram*

The office of Parliamentary Private Secretary is an uncertain one. Sometimes it goes to limited dull men, eminently to be trusted but not to be taken as heavyweights. Sometimes it comes to the young, very bright and hopeful, getting a first sniff of the inside of office which they aspire to occupy.

In the case of a PPS for a leader, the recent record is not brilliant. Archie Hamilton is a capable chap but one can't see him much above the rank of Minister of State. Both Ian Gow and John Stanley have goodish abilities vitiated in very different ways by a streak of absurdity. Sir Fergus Montgomery is a sort of non-resurrectable policital mummy, a dim provincial semi-articulated loyalist. On the Labour side John Evans is a good Northern hardman from Jarrow, just below the top rank but nobody's nonentity, a very useful lieutenant indeed. Kevin Barron, charmed easily from the mumbling embrace of Dennis Skinner, is a sort of working-class Fergus Montgomery. Not quick on the uptake in a job which is either chief of intelligence or bag carrier, he rapidly found his level at the manual end of the scale.

The new PPS Adam Ingram has indeed to carry bags; it goes with the job, but he is emerging as a remarkable influence in his own right. Sensibly loyal to Mr Kinnock, but in a grown-up, non-deferential way, he seems able to reach the leader as faithful expresser of reservations. As part of the outstanding raft of Scottish talent which came in 1987, he is very well wired into a key section of the working party which includes some of Neil Kinnock's most sardonic critics. He is both bridge to and insurance against any major source of doubt.

Ingram is thus very new but he was into a Whip's job within months (one of the pleasures of membership of a party doing badly is that talent is swiftly articulated into a function, witness the irresistible rise of Tony Blair). As a Whip he entered an office which had won no credit on the Labour side for a long time. The Tory Whips office, with the exception of occasional hired thugs like David Lightbown, is a sophisticated place run by subtly genial people like John Wakeham or genial but effective bosses like David Waddington. Talent like that of John Major goes through it to the Cabinet, subtle and amusing players of genteel dirty tricks like Tristan Garrel-Jones linger like students of Machiavelli unwilling to adjourn.

By contrast the Labour Whips office is run either by excellent but depressed men like Michael Cocks, by brutes of the Bob Mellish stamp, or by uncomprehending cronies like Derek Foster. Partly this is a result of Labour being the party of rebellion rather than hierarchy, partly the hangover from the annihilatory razzle of the late seventies. Whatever the reason, talent goes as readily into the Labour Whips office as it does to posts covering defence.

The decision of so intelligent a man as Adam Ingram to become a Whip was a brilliant example of buying at the bottom of the market. He made his name very quickly by unrelenting energy and inventiveness. The idea of the Whip as sleepy apathetic onlooker was replaced by a scurry around the committees, close liaison with shadow ministers working those committees and a string of suggestions on new lines of attack. The great strength of Ingram is his optimistic interest in what is being done and his belief that it can be done well if only somebody bothers to do it better. He was the perfect antidote to the lethargic defeatism which was the mark of Labour Whips for much of the last Parliament.

Compliments are not distributed broadcast at Westminster, certainly not upon bustling newcomers. But two of the wisest old hands separately described him as a future Chief Whip. The idea of this job, so long either a breaker of good men or an accommodater of dullards, being run by a restless intelligence comprehensively indisposed to being broken, recalled the great days when Ted Short carried the stick and John Silkin gave out the cups of coffee.

Removal to the Private Office of the leader was a promotion made at a low point in Mr Kinnock's fortunes. Its effect shouldn't be overstated. The recent revival in the Kinnock performance, the rediscovery of wit, the briefer, more impactive speeches and the attempt to see more of colleagues are ultimately his own decisions and Neil Kinnock is entitled to credit for an excellent self-retrieval job.

But while one should not see Ingram remotely as Svengali over so strong-minded and often tetchy a leader as Kinnock, if a sensible, common-sensical realist who speaks plain terms and doesn't lack courage is put down in such a key spot, and if the changes begin to take place, one is entitled to draw mild conclusions.* Ingram is credited with setting up at an Italian restaurant the dinner at which carefully chosen colleagues were encouraged to speak their minds about the various difficulties the leader was facing. A dedicated Italophile, Ingram seems to have trusted in the disinhibiting effect of decent quantities of Chianti.

Broadly, the message put often enough before – about long questions, lack of a light touch (for which Kinnock actually has great aptitude) and the failure to mingle with the troops – came in a clean but friendly way into the open. The points were, if one likes, obvious and they have been voiced before. But they are also essential and they had never carried. It seems to have been a case of what oft was said but ne'er so well expressed. This was political diplomacy of a high order: whether *propter hoc* or not, Neil Kinnock is talking to his party more easily, and questions are down to forty per cent of length, with notable and injurious effect upon the Prime Minister. Incidentally, the egg-and-cheese speech on the episode of Edwina the Girl Scout and the reply to the budget were excellent examples of the old, funny, unmalicious Kinnock of earlier days.

Ingram himself is a good example of Labour's modern realism. Like many Scots, he was caught badly on the wrong foot by the 1983 election when he fought the safe Tory seat of

---

*Credit also belongs with Bruce Grocott, a freelance verbal intelligence close to Kinnock.

Strathkelvin and Bearsden (the Ruislip of Glasgow, it has now fallen to the surgeon Sam Galbraith). Scotland had endured none of the factionalist trauma of Greater London. In spite of good performances in Scotland, the overall result came, he says, like lightning. Ingram's response was to say: 'Very well, if what is needed is a machine politician I'm happy.'

As indeed he is. He has run East Kilbride as council Chairman, as hammer of the Trots, and tolerates no self-indulgence. And he is temperamentally at odds with the sort of role-playing and exhibitionism which became a substitute for working politics between 1979 and the great Bournemouth assault on Militant Tendency.

Ingram is representative of the high-quality Scottish intake – Henry Macleish, Sam Galbraith, Calum MacDonald, Alistair Darling and a cast of thousands. But he is probably its most comprehensively working-class member (and the quality of such ex-workers has been very mixed in recent years). But he is light years away from the union or council heavy, whisky-misted and articulating few words and fewer ideas.

He is very bright indeed, ideally able to reach out to different talents from different backgrounds and get best use out of them for the party. He is a natural Whip of a very high order. Come the day, if the day should come, when offices are at the disposal of a Labour Prime Minister, there is no reason why Adam Ingram should not be seen as a prospective occupant of No 12 Downing Street.

He needs (and he knows it) to beware a besetting sin of impatience and reflexive hardness: 'Och, Adam would pick a fight in an empty room' was a fair point against him. But effectively he is, to draw a metaphor from retailing, someone who has found a hole in the market and sought to fill it. Labour's shameful indifference to the Whips' office should have been remedied by the election to it of the excellent Jeffrey Rooker. But, given that Rooker – another combative fellow and one with a good deal less tact – was resented for his brusque, independent ways and evident failure to listen affably to light minds, that race was never on.

Ingram has Rooker's record to beware and he is of course absurdly new and likely to accumulate resentment as he busies himself. But not being an intellectual, merely an intelligence, even with his fighting edge he may make fewer enemies. Certainly he has identified that hole, as certainly he is doing shrewd persuasive work as his leader's man at hand. He is at least as good as Ian Gow, who rose fast to important office for as long as he personally wished. But given Labour's needs and his own clear direction he should go further. He is a self-acknowledged machine politician in a party which used to be rather good at them, but which is still recovering from a messianic tantrum and a riot of abstract theorising.

Above all, he is a dynamic part of the essential optimism of the new intake who are distinguishable from older hands by a sustained belief that life is not necessarily a comfortable condition of steady jobbing defeat and that Labour has both the talent and the duty to be something more than a conspiracy of inadequacy. At times he has functioned as the shop steward of the intake. Energy and optimism have been unlikely stocks on the political market of the Labour party, but they show every sign at present of looking up no end.

# CHAPTER 25

## *Christopher Patten*

Too much adulation is bad for the character. It doesn't do too much for writing either. One wants to avoid giving a syrupy Sauterne flavour to political comment. But adulation of a very extensive nature seems to have done no harm at all to the intransigent good nature of Christopher Patten, so there are no excuses for souring one's sentiments.

People in politics adore the futile but delightful game of the succession, not to say the next succession but one. And while the more farsighted of the company advert to first Major and then Rifkind, whose chances are closer, it is startling to hear Patten being talked about in much the same breath. Talked of, that is, for the next succession but one if things move quickly, but also for the next if the lady were to bless us with another five years of her fingernail-across-blackboard presence.

Patten is extraordinary among outer-rank Ministers in already having his own identifiable faction or party. To a degree this reflects his under-promotion. Patten was an intelligent presence known widely in politics before he entered the House. He has been a Thatcher speechwriter, (though one wouldn't think it to listen to her) since the seventies; he has committed no gaffes and no indiscretions, though calling my friend Dr Madsen Pirie a 'fruitcake' must have been fun. Given his own steadily liberal, humane and Keynesian inclinations, he has managed to be Mrs Thatcher's loyal servant without ever turning his coat or sweetening his way to court. A secure, confident Prime Minister, which Mrs Thatcher (as the clatter of forte pedals and the yanked-out bombard stop makes clear) is not, would have been able to accommodate a first-class talent, a popular and civilly dissenting figure, cheerfully into the Cabinet. For ironically, by every account, Mrs Thatcher actively likes Patten. It would be hard to see how she couldn't. He has a light, humorous touch, an excellent intelligence and although ambitious, as he should be, he is the least furtive, eye-swivelling or career-crafting of politicians. She likes him enough to want his company and his work on her speeches. But promotion is limping a good four years behind merit, which means a full twelve years behind the schedule too long allotted to Lord Young.

Pope, speaking of Addison's collection of thin-talented cronies, alluded to the Grand Turk or Sultan when he observed in 'The Epistle to Dr Arbuthnot': 'Bear like the Turk, no brother near the throne.' Patten has escaped the bowstring so far, but he has kicked his heels in lesser subordinate offices. His latest post, Overseas Development – in a government notoriously disinclined to throw money at anything, never mind foreigners who would only keep it in the bath – engages his humanitarian instincts within the narrow budget permitted but not his energies. There is in that office only so much you can do ; the heads of able and active Ministers quickly bang against the ceiling. A year or so back the friends of Patten were reporting him mildly fed up at perpetual subordination and not inclined to outlive another reshuffle without the prize of the Cabinet.

Writing before that reshuffle, I would expect him to come through this time, partly because it is talked of and because such hints are presumably destined for the Prime Minister's hearing. Mrs Thatcher is not long on either gratitude or imagination and her record on personnel is grotesque, studded with handsome props of men equipped to sell Conservatism 60p off in Chelmsford market, but she intensely dislikes waste and, up to a point, she dislikes embarrassment. The departure of first-class talent and a major player in the popularity table would involve rather too much of both. In a gush of late gratitude, a promotion long lost under a cushion or sat on by the cat will be graciously bestowed.*

Ironically, she once sacked him – from his post as head of research at Central Office. This was in 1978 when the Thatcher

---

*All this came about.

camp was struggling to substitute its own infrastructure, and compulsive intriguers like Airey Neave had a whole new cause to occupy them : the purging of enemies. The innermost Thatcherites tend to think in terms of enemies. Patten, selected by Ian Gilmour to serve Heath – a former member of Heath's Cabinet Office and personal assistant to the party Chairman – had the qualifications to interest any committee of public safety.

It was open to Patten to sulk with the outs and hope for a return, to join the SDP which would start up in 1981 early and late enough in his own career both to start again and come home laden. He could also have come, with a twitch of the bottom and a pleading look in the eye, to ask nicely to snuggle near to power.

That after all was the course taken by Selwyn Gummer, a Heath follower so devout that he had even married into the office – his bride, Penny, being Heath's secretary. The actual course taken, giving the loyalty which a reasonable leader is owed while speaking his own mind where issues mattered to him, has looked good. But a long tract of Patten's career was a moonscape. Deleted from Central Office in 1978 amid the usual confetti-shower of humbug, his election in 1979 was followed by a four-year wait for junior office, a normal run for a good if initially unknown new Member. But Patten was very well known, on and off a part of the Smith Square machine (and highly applauded and liked) since 1966. His namesake, John Patten, also a liberal though a coolly adaptive one who had not yet in his Oxford base made a national reputation, was given a job the first of all the intake in 1981.

When Christopher Patten, after a couple of PPS jobs, finally made it to minor Ministerial office, he was given, surely not accidentally, the exact same job with the same function : lightning-conducting token Roman Catholic junior Minister in Northern Ireland ! In the meantime his patrons had all gone. After Heath, Ian Gilmour – most thoughtful and stylish of wets – had gone down in the September Massacres ; Norman St John Stevas whose PPS he had been had fallen earlier, the pioneer Thatcher victim and hideously grateful.

Happily the Patten model of functional, non-sulking loyalty, amended by thoughtful remarks in print, left him clearly defined. And blessedly, unlike the bulk of the wets, he did not talk the dismal code language of 'Disraeli' and 'one nation', though the expression 'dogmatism' has slipped through his lips.

An article in one of the Sunday colour supplements gave a very good idea of the essential Patten: dislike of greed in its frilled shirt-front and household drinks bar Essex manifestations were at the heart of it. He doesn't believe, and never has, in the inviolability of the market as a solution for all problems and likes even less the caste of flashy philistinism which accompanies market triumphalism. There is a streak of unsnobbish aestheticism in the self-distancing from the dry right of someone who can quote Cavafy and Larkin. Quite how he and Alfred Sherman, a first draft of the new right, ever worked together on Mrs Thatcher's speeches remains a major miracle. The fact that so few of those discourses emerged not merely as camels but two-headed camels is more surprising. Yet interestingly Sherman, who has charitable instincts towards wets the way the Ayatollah Khomeini had ecumenical leanings, speaks affectionately of Patten.

The other instructive comment in that article concerned the Labour party. It was written at that party's lowest, least hopeful historic point. The black-leather boys were on the doors at conference; Wedgwood Benn was up and running and thought likely to win; all the virtuosi of class and race war were on song; the centre Alliance was looking golden. Chris Patten observed that most of the blood spilt in Labour's career was its own, that it was the home of much that was most generous, warm and decent in British life as well as an element of the base. It was a kind and truthful observation, the sort of cross-party scrupulous perception which goes beyond civility to understanding; and his instinct at that low point that Labour would come out of the dark wood has been proved true.

Patten is inadvertently different from the bulk of the Tory left. He has not fallen back on mantras, resentments and toasts across the water. He has gone on thinking (though he is not a fountain of new ideas), but by way of response to things actually happening, not to accommodate the leader's correct line. His outburst on 'a yob society' came from very deep within him and poses questions for the narrowly economic-minded ascendancy to which it is not responsive; an under-educated, raucous, mutually indifferent nation, a people which has become what the Russians call *ney kulturni* which means something profoundly more than not having a taste for Mozart. He is profoundly at odds with Loadsamoney.

Although he is too sardonic and funny to enjoy moralising, he is a moralist, a distinction always to be made. He is a special kind of continental thing, a liberal Catholic, much more a Christian Democrat than a Tory. Hardly ever, except for an uncharacteristically pompous attack on Neil Kinnock's innocent little joke about Mrs Thatcher as 'the immaculate misconception', does he go on about religion. Taking it seriously, he flinches from self-anointing fits of *Gummererei*.

The Christian Democratic tradition, deliberately fostered in Germany, Belgium and Holland to be at a mighty distance from the clerico-fascism of Dolfuss, Fey, Monsignor Tiso and for that matter Hilaire Belloc, is long on involvement in the workplace and on the social consequences of economic acts. In the European Parliament it has been consciously at a distance from the Tories, even though that contingent is less than Thatcherish. This is Christian Democracy at its North European high point of course. The Italian version is a criminal conspiracy using rosaries like bicycle chains. In the world of Marcinkius and Forlani the occasional man of high complex scruple like Virginio Rognoni is more isolated than Christopher Patten is among the developers in ruffled shirts.

There has to be a major change in British and Conservative politics before long. Ten years of Thatcher have passed, but there was more than a touch of sourness on the tongue at the celebrations. The actual triumphs have a brass-through-polish look as the economy begins to overheat. Much more important, the Prime Minister's eternal insecurity shows through in ever less measured assaults on the ear. Lawson's policy has let her down, now we are a grandmother, she feels like a tigress 'and you know the tigress is more, well, better than the male'. All this and a war with the Europeans about matters as disparate as the social dimension, anti-smoking warnings and a wicked subsidy to help us learn foreign languages. The slightly cracked quality is in evidence and a Thatcherian succession is nowhere in place. (Mr Major may be seen in that light but he is hardly her colour.)

For this reason Christopher Patten is likely to become an enormously important figure. As I argued initially, he will on entering the Cabinet, under Mrs Thatcher or her successor, gain a number of credited years of seniority. He will be without personal enemies. His combination of complex conscience and eirenic gaiety are at polar extremes from her mixture of *schreyvogel* public address and Mark's-mum slipperiness. If he had been in the Cabinet as early as Rifkind or Major – proper subjects for comparison – we would indeed be thinking about a possible succession. He is that good and that attractive. As it is, one is definitely looking forward in a couple of years to one of the three sweet jobs fatuously known as 'the great offices of state'.

Patten at the Home Office given any civility at the top, say in a Baker Cabinet, is a real prospect. With Rifkind, if Scotland is not shot from beneath him, and Major, Patten will be part of the triumvirate likely to dominate the Tory party for at least the next fifteen years. They will be a subtle but sufficient counterpose to ten-plus years of fierce-purposed *katzenjammer*. One can only marvel at the ability of the Tory party to be so diverse and to contain such contradictions and such talent.

It would be crazy to say more, but from outside the Cabinet as I write he is weighed with its possible future leaders and counted with them, not a negligible performance.

# CHAPTER 26

# Gerald Kaufman

There are lots of Gerald Kaufman stories, like the one about Joe Haines (in the days when both men worked in the viperous outer office of Harold Wilson) hearing some ingratiating remark and throwing a book at Kaufman's head with the observation 'creep'.

Then there is the account of Lord St John of Fawley, the Conservative party's answer to golden syrup wih double cream, refusing to be interviewed by a TV company in Kaufman's intolerable presence. He was finally prevailed upon to do so at the opposite end of a studio, sitting with his back to the hated object, talking by monitor screen in argument with a man twenty yards away, as if in another city.

All this proves of course is that Kaufman is hated by Joe Haines and little Stevas, two sub-operatic personalities set with sharpened stakes like siege pits. But then Kaufman, though nearer the human mainstream than either, is a bit like that himself. However, the thing that matters about him is intelligence and a certain disengaged clarity of mind.

For all his long devotion to the Labour party, he is very good at standing back and judging it diagnostically, sometimes in the way of a Recorder recommending borstal training. (As Kaufman himself, a notable finick of other men's copy, would be the first to point out, we no longer have that useful resource, but it has the right anachronistic ring for Labour.) As the world well knows, it was Kaufman who coined the remark about the 1983 manifesto, a froth of Footish plans to put the universe back into good socialist order, as 'the longest suicide note ever penned'. The Kaufman of that time was limitlessly pessimistic. He prophesied to friends that Labour would lose that election and the next, proving himself exact even in the rhetoric of exasperation.

He is capable of equal, and creditable, detachment in other involvements beside that of Labour. He is Jewish, proud of it and very amusing about home life in Leeds during his boyhood. But Kaufman, the good democrat, wrote about Israel (in the short, arresting book he produced after touring the country) without a scrap of illusion concerning the rightwing, racially bigotted, unlovable place – the Hassidic Rhodesia – it has become. Even among his own people, *Mapainiks*, gathered in liberal German style at a classical concert, he ruthlessly caught the sense of isolation, a slightly less acute version of a liberal gathering in South Africa.

Kaufman can't be fooled; but that is at least partly because of a masochistic streak in his nature which counts the teeth of gift horses and dislikes paradises whether they belong to fools or not. That makes him a perfectly attuned collaborator to Labour leadership trying to reform a party spongy of heart and discombobulated of brain.

The work he has done in drafting Labour out of its unilateralism has of course created the predictable anguish from distressed leftists and, even more predictably, has started a low, primitive chorus from the ranks of the damned in the Conservative press: 'Will Kinnock Press the Button?', 'Kinnock has sold his Soul for Votes' and so on. But the surgery at the time of writing looks clean and likely to heal. Kaufman at all times maintained a sharp understanding of the implications of a resumed multilateralism in the circumstances where the Soviet initiatives and needs convert that term into literally meaning 'many sided disarmament' and not, as Mrs Thatcher would like, a warm and unbudged status quo.

Kaufman is unlikely to flounder, in the way of many of his colleagues including Kinnock, because he hasn't read or thought a problem through. Never does he rely upon facile words as a substitute for reading and facts. Unlike many such colleagues he is unlikely ever to substitute wishful thinking for rational expectations. But this clarity, this remorseless intelligence, does not make for easy relations. Not cut out for clubbability, he avoids the club.

One is occasionally tempted to see Bryan Gould, with his late arrival and swift assumption of responsibilities, as the man from Coopers and Lybrands seconded to produce a report for an ailing company. But Gould is a warm, surprisingly talkative fellow, happy in his colleagues' company and despite the gold-starred Oxford bit, not remotely aloof. Kaufman, for all his sincerely intended assertions of his Labour devotion and his fair claim to life-long party roots, is much nearer to the reporting specialist's role (and politically most at ease when he acknowledges the fact). He is one of those clever people, not truly happy, despite the effort made, in the company of the not clever. Foolishness directly affects him; he can of course suppress annoyance and contempt, but annoyance and contempt govern his attitudes from their hiding places.

Interestingly, this disdain spills on to people few others would think deserved it. Douglas Hurd for example – not perhaps the Immanuel Kant of the Conservative party but on most counts a pretty decent and highly cultivated mind, if given to the self-assuaging passivity of the higher civil servant he really is – rates on the Kaufman esteem chart as a dull, second-rate, lazy bureaucrat. It is a judgement which for unforgiving ferocity can be replicated all round the political forum.

Kaufman's judgement is like a very bright, penetrating light which misleads by giving unreal prominence to quite minor blemishes. Hurd can be lazy, but only in the wise way of a man not prepared to become a drudge in the office when the world is such an attractive place. One can very well see him skipping a few points in the brief in a light-hearted cavalier way. This can lead, during debate with a human laser, to embarrassments but it can also lead that adversary into contemptuous assumptions which are wrong.

Perhaps he developed this characteristic from years spent as a journalist. Few politicians have jumped over the gallery balustrade, but those who do often come as doubters of the goodness of human nature. Probably the worst thing about Kaufman is a compulsive critical impulse. This leads him in debate not to distinguish big issues from little ones and drives him to flurries of obnoxious point-scoring which do nothing for his side of the argument. He is an adversarialist by personal disposition. His natural moderation in the Labour spectrum (and he has been decently consistent over the years) does not produce the relaxed conversational approach to the other side which makes for easy co-existence.

Quite good-natured Tory Ministers are disconcerted to find themselves facing Fouquier-Tinville on charges of being enemies of the human race and not very bright with it. As well as finding out error, he is something of a trigger-happy moralist; this however suits Labour well since a sense of being morally one-up is fairly general in that party, a nonconformist personality quirk it shares, much as both may hate the association, with Mrs Thatcher.

As long as Kaufman's softly bitter, fastidious and distancing style is addressed to the official enemy, it does very well. But the potential for savage rifts with colleagues has been there. One suspects that his correct but formal relations with colleagues stems from his understanding of this, and he has shrewdly defined himself into the most useful role. He is grateful to Neil Kinnock for personal kindness and appreciation of his worth, and has set his mind to being the leader's loyal and constructive colleague without being closely attached.

Perhaps the ill-natured and feuding history of the Wilson entourage was a lesson in itself: a body of mutually malevolent aspirers to the leader's love and favour, frustrated assassins obliged to stab with cork-tipped daggers, made for a sour climate of disappointment.

Kaufman made his way to high ratings in the Shadow Cabinet elections not by cozening friendship in the smoking room but, in a dark time for the party, by being extremely strong in debate, reliable in all his work and self-evidently a complete professional. The Parliamentary party's attitude could best be summed up in the word 'gratitude'. A natural combatant who might have been readily tempted to internal squabbles, he has disciplined himself, turning his face and his blade outwards. Personally very bleak in his hopes for Labour until quite recently, he could not bear to do a job less than well and by sheer proficiency plus a wise investment of his harshest side towards the government, he was offering, at Labour's low point, one of the very few consistently high-quality performances on the frontbench.

The Shadow Cabinet put together in the last three or so years is rightly admired and with Cook, Brown, Blair, Gould and Cunningham is stronger than the government. But in the mid-eighties, with Hattersley a flickering and variable light and people of the quality of Gwynneth Dunwoody actually shadowing Secretaries of State, Kaufman and John Smith carried a great burden. Indeed they took on an aspect of Horatius and his comrades.

Labour is back on its feet, but it would do well to remember that certain key people – of whom Kaufman was eminently one – saw it through a dark defile in which it could have vanished. Gerald Kaufman guards his privacy. He is a man of high enthusiastic culture (as a bachelor he can afford to attend music festivals the rest of us can only read about). At the worst period he found some solace in quick but worthwhile book-writing – about Israel and about his passion for the cinema. He has also made a brilliant sideline of his journalism which has benefited from the breadth and catholicity of his interests. The concerts and the cultivation provided a base from which a lonely solitary figure could commute to the party, doing a fine job for it precisely because his mind rather than his strongest emotion was engaged.

He has worked out his own function, maximised what he could do best and avoided the travails into which his sharp-edged personality could have stumbled. Lucid as ever in the business of self-management, he has been almost as detached as in his diagnosis of his party. He is a link connecting Labour's sane past with its hopeful future. Given the crevasse which had to be crossed, gratitude to this fierce, amusing, derisive and faintly unlikely man is the least that is owed.

# CHAPTER 27

## Nicholas Ridley

There is frequent and rather pat explanation given for the truculent and sour nature of the Hon. Nicholas Ridley, a man whose bitter, but also rather self-pitying, style is untouched by any sweetening good humour. It lies, they say, in that preposterous little abbreviated honorific, 'Hon.'

Like the Redesdale sisters chronicled by Jessica Mitford, Ridley is the superfluous non-inheriting issue of aristocracy. To devotees of social order, the social lute-tuners on the court columns of most papers and all parts of both *Telegraph*s, he is the Honourable Nicholas Ridley, a younger son of the last Viscount Ridley and brother of the present title-holder. Such people are, at least grammatically 'to be honoured' by the rest of us, something we must try to remember.

The little drawback in life of missing the coronet – not altogether to be compared with the tribulations of people on family income supplement – is said to have embittered him. The consolations drawn by Wordsworth, also a Conservative of sorts, from the comparative social chances of the leech-gatherer have not been apparent to Ridley. If this theory, which one hears commonly, is true, then the man has been engaged in a lifelong sulk.

Ridley has nothing to sulk about. He was blessed with more substantial gifts than aristocracy and the Caste High School, Eton. The unhappy man has a first-class degree from Cambridge in engineering. The same unhappy man has a talent in watercolours which, along with that of the former Law Lord, Lord Pearce, is esteemed at the very top of non-professional attainment. His other external interest – gardening – has produced, with the purloined help of a minor diversion from the Windrush, an outstandingly beautiful water garden in his Gloucestershire home.

Yet the entire Ridley style in life is one of sourness and resentment and it has made him something of a bad angel to the Prime Minister. Her harsh and insensitive instincts are encouraged by his resentments. Most of the gentry element in the Tory party, while seeing that Number One gets his tax cut and is generally looked after, reckon to afford a certain social geniality. Ridley responds, according to his local paper in Cirencester, with that observation, 'Why should a duke pay more [in rates] than a dustman?'

The most obvious answer to that is likely to be given (is perhaps, after the Vale of Glamorgan, already *being* given) in crude electoral language. But it would have been answered by the Whitelaw school of obligement in terms of political good manners. Ridley prides himself on being an enemy of cant. It is then fascinating to hear him using the prime cant word of the decade 'community', as cover for the brute truth embodied in a name which goes back at least to the fourteenth century. Whether Wat Tyler would have known his dustman's place and gladly paid his Poll Tax in the early days of Richard II if it had been called a Community Charge is a nice point. There were no communications consultants in the late fourteenth century.

However only Ridley, of all Mrs Thatcher's Ministers, would gladly have embraced a flat-rate tax with its chances of offending people and turning off the electorate – in the way of a small boy at the zoo pushing a stick through the cage of a mangy but irked leopard, to see precisely what it might do.

Ridley's time in politics has been marked by a similar cavalier approach to people better conciliated and issues more wisely foreseen. He was that junior Minister charged with handling the unpleasing Argentine government when the Falkland Islands were issue number thirty-seven on the government's list of priorities. It was open to the Foreign Office junior to impress upon the Argentinians the government's regard for the interests of the islanders ('The interests of the Islanders are paramount.' Mrs Margaret Thatcher *passim*). Clear, unequivocal speech, however linked with willingness to negotiate, ought to have been enough to forewarn the generals from illegal and adventurist excursions. Their invasion, when it came, was an extraordinary act explicable only in terms of perfect conviction of British indifference.

Given the conspiracy of suppression which surrounds the convenience and ineptitudes of British politicians, we may never know precisely what Ridley said to the Argentinians. But we know his nature. It is not long on consideration for unimportant people standing in the way of his ease. There appeared in the pages of *The Times*, always sensitive to the requirements of Ministers, an article on the Falklands entitled 'These Paltry Islands'. Ridley's closest personal friend, Jock Bruce-Gardyne, would always refer to the Falklanders with lordly distaste as 'the Sheepshaggers'. It isn't difficult, given the sequence of events, to imagine the Argentinian military drawing conclusions proved false by subsequent events, after taking in the ripe flavour of the frugal semi-nob, fearing expense and spurning colonials with the end of a ferrule.

There was everything to be said for firm clear words and the effective discouragement of illegal action, a course easily available to us. There was something, in an unattractive way, to be said for a cool and sustained policy of abandonment to the wretched generals of an expensive, little-valued territory, providing that the Falklanders were compensated. There was nothing at all to be said for talking loose and acting firm, for negligently encouraging acts which had to be undone by huge logistics, high heroism, great cost and extensive loss of life.

Ridley may have reflected government (certainly Foreign Office) thinking before public opinion and the Tory backbenches blew up on it. But a role in starting an eminently avoidable war and bringing about a shoddy political triumph at the cost of so many interred bodies, mutilated faces and traumatised lives, might have induced a period of humility and quietness in any Minister responsible. However, humility is not Ridley's way. Guilt is for weaklings and losers and his sour, selfish personality revolts against admitting fault. The gravest of all sins for such people is the sin of admission.

'Never apologise', says the maxim, 'never explain.' Ridley is not a Balliol man for nothing.

His earlier career (and he has been in the Commons for half his sixty years, entering in 1959) was not marked by success. There was a brief period of political intimacy with Edward Heath during the phase of Selsdon Man, when Heath was excited by his ruthless instincts and desire for efficiency. He delighted, said a socialist commentator of the time, in the views of 'Nicky'. It didn't last and Ridley went to early redundancy, but not before he had been directly involved in the Industry Bill, an ill-advised portmanteau commitment to intervention and possible subsidy conceived out of Heath's calamitous panic and fear of the unemployment to which the next Tory government would respond more robustly. The entire business flew in the teeth of Ridley's convictions (he was a dry before the word was coined, a taker of the Treasury view at its most desiccated, a friend of Jock Bruce-Gardyne's) yet he proceeded to handle the Heath bill in all its open-bowelled panic. It didn't save him from the pains of a reshuffle and he returned to the backbenches. But he was an early conspirer against Heath even when enjoying office, and indeed the Ridley home was a frequent base for operations.

Even so, his career proceeded quite slowly since he had few friends and did nothing to increase his amiability quotient. He had been a Minister of State (at Industry) before his temporary fall in 1972. He became again a Minister of State at the Foreign Office – not dazzling promotion especially as he had plotted ardently against Edward Heath and subsequently *for* Margaret Thatcher from an early hour. However, his ability to survive mistakes which would have been death to less happy men easily outweighed the moderation of his advancement and he duly became Financial Secretary, Secretary for Transport and then for the Environment. Ted's Nicky became Margaret's Nicky without ever having been the well-beloved of anyone unimportant.

There is nothing discreditable in working against a government you disagree with, nothing wrong in embracing a strict, dry, monetarist view of the economy. But Ridley was a happy conspirator, investing an element of malice in his dissent from Heath as he made his flat available to the cabal. And as for dry economics, they can be either an abstract piece of thinking – a harsh course deemed necessary for good reason – or they can be most attractive in their very painfulness.

In this sense someone like Keith Joseph, who was absurdly and venomously attacked from the left, was a classic illustration of a humane, kind, readily distressable man reaching conclusions involving hard answers for reasons of intellect and arithmetic. In the process he lent the entire classical liberal cause lustre, for despite the eccentricities Joseph's humanity is self-evident.

Ridley, by contrast, a mismatch with all forms of political good nature, was psychologically made for the pains of tight money and high unemployment. An Etonian with a Wyke-hamist personality, not only did he elevate cold rationality, he added a sort of snarling gusto of his own. Ridley could take a lot of other people's suffering. The man who can make a joke about the open bows of the Zeebrugge ferry has something missing: good manners certainly, a sense of what is fitting indeed but also, and most important, regret or sympathy for fellow human beings.

Ridley's rightwing politics are thus an extension of his personality not, as with Joseph, a product of cerebration which goes against the grain of the personality. This is actually rather important since the validity of free-market thinking *is* affected by the motives which cause it to be adopted. The impulse to privatise water and to impose the Poll Tax certainly would never have come from ordinary, soft-centred, public-minded politicians like William White-law and Peter Walker. But I can't see dries-by-conviction who are also benign by nature – such people as Joseph and John Biffen – ever starting up initiatives which were at the outer rim of their ideological thinking, not central to recovery and likely to involve a bitter row with the citizenry. For such enterprises they lack the malice. All his political life the Hon. Nicholas Ridley has never gone short of that commodity.

Consequently the course taken by Margaret Thatcher, who for all the circus heroics is liable to influences, has been affected by the withdrawal of Willie Whitelaw from her shoulder and the advancement of Ridley to an eminence within government which only Margaret Thatcher would have dreamed of giving him. Like her, he is brave in a crass, fight-picking way; like her, he is socially blind without any discernible downward-directed sympathies and, as roughly speaking she is not, Ridley is malicious. There is in him no end of Achitophel:

> In power unpleased impatient of disgrace
> A fiery soul, which working out its way
> Fretted the pigmy body to decay . . .
> Pleased with the danger, when the waves went high
> He sought the storms; but for a calm unfit,
> Would steer too near the sands to boast his wit.

Ridley represents the sort of personality which flourishes under late Thatcherism. Because he is intelligent and competent in office, which for men of her colour with a degree of seniority is a rare thing, he has been able to rise steadily. But running alongside the doctrinaire free marketeer is the displaced aristocrat: 'Why should a duke pay more than a dustman?'

The combination is odd and explosive. Most nobs have a softening agent, either a wise apprehension of what comes from pushing that stick through the bars of the public cage or, quite commonly, a genuine sense of their own luck and a concomitant need to be nice to people. Ridley is not happy without high waves and it is at least arguable that under his influence, that of 'a daring pilot in extremity', the boat has indeed come too near the sands.

If the Tories have begun to suffer the kind of defeat where votes are not just withheld in protest but actually, as at the Vale of Glamorgan, go bodily over to Labour, then its new, combative, opinion-deriding outlook has responsibility. The corpse in the library at the Vale was actually the Health Service. But the source of the new save-and-destroy impulse towards Health is not Kenneth Clarke, its executant, but Margaret Thatcher. Like Prometheus, Mrs Thatcher is now unbound; Thatcherism in her days of assured ascendancy comes through no pastel filter. The instinct which pushed through the Poll Tax and privatised water (along with electricity) is her aggressive, aggrandising, statute-book-filling urge to glory. And the voices at her ear are either those of henchmen of her spirit like Mr Parkinson of those who, like Ridley, feel that the revolution is thirsty for more blood.

The single most destructive policy so far wasn't of his fashioning, but the endless nagging of successive Health Ministers to come up with hard little rationalisings untroubled by what the public felt reflects the Thatcher and Ridley overview, pride modified by wrath. It is not good politics.

But we have yet to see the effect on the electorate of Ridley's personal contribution: the Poll Tax. This more or less loony idea, all rational arithmetic but likely to be hugely expensive to collect, falling with succinct severity upon poorer more populous families and removing the rough sympathetic supposition that people in large houses would be best able to pay, is perfect designer class war.

We can only guess what will happen; some people of course will not pay it and a series of unedifying court cases will follow in which the government might, just might, look vindictive. Frank Field, who always treats the government with perfect fairness and who admires much of the mainstream free-market approach, describes the Poll Tax as a future parent of homeless youngsters. The Scots give evidence of loathing the idea so much that Malcolm Rifkind, saddled with supervision of the laboratory mouse, is now dropping heavy hints about the need for the Tories in Scotland to rethink generally. The idea, snatched at after an Adam Smith Institute pamphleteer, Douglas Mason, had mooted it, has been described by the former Environment Secretary Michael Heseltine as something his team simply laughed out of court when it was put to them. Electorally, there is a body of white-collar new Conservative opinion which has done very nicely but which has grown-up children at home in its low-rated, recently purchased, former council house. A fight picked here does not seem like self-interest.

It should be added that not all of Ridley's failures derive from his rage at mankind. The *misanthrope* is supplemented by the *klutz*. His Water bill has, to the joy of Dr Cunningham and the Labour side, been coming apart: badly prepared, wrong about its internal costs and a general slatternly mess. But the rush to the Poll Tax is part of this sloppy precipitation as well as an expression of the Ridley quarrelsomeness.

However, the scope of his troublemaking hardly stops here. Ridley, the Secretary for the Environment with the cigarette tab dangling from his nether lip, is after all the man currently showing warmth to developers in Southern England of the sort who would link Henley and Thame with bricks. England is a small country with a demographic shift from North to South. There is a real problem, genuine pressure for occupation, pitted against a green belt policy which is credible only if it makes no concession and arouses no nibbling expectations. Ridley's motive here need not be simply his usual 'To hell with you' cavalier's shrug of contempt, not that it is lacking. There would be trouble whatever happened.

The risk of letting the green England of our affections die half a grain a day – or rather quicker as the fanciers of prime development spots receive understanding hearings from the Department of the Environment – makes trouble for the government among its own people. It is an instance, if it happens, of the government misguidedly fighting someone their own size. And thus government, which has already taken a mandatory count of eight from the Kent lobby against the cheap and unpleasant options for the Channel Tunnel, will not push for a Brazilian reputation in the trans-urban dwellings among the trees and fields of people who very commonly vote Conservative.

It was again sloppiness and not at all dishonesty which led Ridley to deride NIMBIES (people who said, 'Not in My Backyard' to all development), when he had registered his own successful objection to building plans injurious to his own handsome view in Gloucestershire.

Against all this, Michael Heseltine, member for Henley, fellow garden fanatic and succinct follower of the country Tory pulse, has found territory on which to do himself nothing but good with almost everyone except the developers and Downing Street. Probably at this fence, Mrs Thatcher with a still sufficient bump of circumspection under the coronation robes, will do the pulling back herself.

Mrs Thatcher does not fight her own people; her expeditious conversion to the Green cause, which was put through like a diploma from an Alabama degree mill, makes that clear. The thought, even notionally, of disaffected people in three-hundred-thousand-pound houses would be enough, without the thought that the natural beneficiary from such a conflict would be Michael Heseltine. Hatred and deep apprehension of Heseltine run through the Prime Minister like an underground river. 'Nicky' will be forgiven most things and encouraged in most of his schemes, but proposals tending to give a handle to 'that man' will be stopped.

There is a 'Ridley for the Exchequer' school, basing itself on his paper intelligence and standing at court. But it looks less and less likely. Lawson is needed to occupy a hole of his own digging and anyway controversy which can be indulged in lesser departments has the potential for detonation in the edgy and febrile world of the exchanges. Lawson is not a tactful man, but compared with Ridley he is a combination of Coolidge and the Buddha. One can perfectly imagine Ridley saying that sensible people would be getting out of sterling.

He will soldier on for a while, but if the weather deteriorates, if Labour goes on winning by-elections and if the Poll Tax is half the public charmer one expects, Ridley acquires most of the value of a negotiable intercontinental missile. His deletion from the government becomes a useful psychological gesture as the advertising agents, with their morticians' paint-boxes, set to work on the caring, presentable face of Conservatism. Ridley is either an act of defiance or he is a risk waiting for elimination. Trade may be less explosive an employment, and as someone especially close to the Prime Minister he could count on a token of her especial esteem, unlikely to be shown either Lawson or Howe on departure. She hasn't made any new hereditary viscounts for some time. What a pleasant way out of a difficult moment. What asymmetrical solution to Ridley's abiding misfortune.

# CHAPTER 28

# Richard Shepherd

The life of a backbencher is a melancholy thing. It was characteristically offensive of Douglas Hogg, custodian of the family charm, to say that it was merely an interlude before one's promotion to office. But, although sweeping, that was not broadly untrue.

Government backbenchers divide into groups: the new and aspiring for whom office is a possibility; those either long passed-over, for whom all hope except a small chivalric particle is denied; and those repulsed from the upper or lower walls of the Castle Despond of preferment. These are men bitter or philosophic according to personality, but without illusion and only occasionally able to submerge talent and frustration in the chairmanship of one of Parliament's interesting but unsatisfactory committees.

The aspirers have a function, and act to win office, whether by useful displays of intelligence in debate (intelligence not being required by any government of its members on standing committees, merely votes) or by displays of ingratiation. The losers and non-starters have their campaign medals to take care of. The House in such cases serves as an access point for additional outside remuneration, together with the mild residual esteem attaching to legislators. In the catchphrase of the day, the Commons is an eco-system, with its predators, scavengers and sources of animal protein.

The idea of the independent Member whose personal significance subordinates his function as the Member of a political party is naïve, unrealistic, out-of-date if it ever had validity, and occasionally fulfilled! It is a little easier for the Member of an Opposition party to be a major independent force, significantly easier for a Labour or centrist Member. For a Conservative it is very hard indeed. (The term 'Whips' derives from whippers-in, and whippers-in control packs of dogs.) For a Conservative in one of the long ages of Conservative government the role of backbench independant approaches impossibility. There is then all the more reason to rejoice at the existence of Richard Shepherd.

The sponsor of a bill to reform the Official Secrets Acts, the biting, impassioned opponent of the government's illiberal substitute, and the steady, fearless opponent of the authoritarianism dear to the Prime Minister, he is the man nobody saw coming. Politically, Shepherd was identified as being on the right (though we should know how meaningless such characterisations can be). He was known as a successful entrepreneur (Shepherd's excellent supermarkets), as a dedicated and intelligent critic of the EC and member of the European Reform Group of Conservative MPs.

Although Mrs Thatcher is no friend of the Common Market, overt antipathy to it is considered bad politics and wins no promotions. This has something to do with personalities. Teddy Taylor, founder of the ERG, an old-fashioned likeable Scottish populist who deserved office, was sniffed to death by Lord Whitelaw and compounded things by the candid singularity of his zeal on the topic. Jonathan Aitken, thought possessed of every gift in a young politician, made a private and personal enemy of Mrs Thatcher thereby, while Antony Marlow affected overmuch the style of a Captain of the Freikorps.

By associating with this group, whose best friend in government was John Biffen – a discriminating form of doom – Richard Shepherd was doing himself no possible sort of good with the Whips. If he had wanted to be part of the scamper on the official stairway he had only to go unofficial with his Euro-coolness, say that he was of course *devoted* to Teddy Taylor but, and make a great play of his own genuine grocering success as an excuse to orate about the work ethic, standing, as it were, on one of his own orange boxes. In that eventuality the glories of being a PPS, a junior Whip and all that lies beyond could have been his.

The compelling thing about Shepherd is that such speculation seriously intended would be pure insult to the man. He is genuinely, and not by way of consolation, indifferent to the small pleasures of office. He has always done everything for himself. Like quite a few Tories these days, he has no inherited wealth. His father was an airline steward, something which gave him a single privilege: cheap or free travel all over the world as a student, something he delighted in. The later business success – a small chain of very good, well-sited, pleasant supermarkets started with a single shop in Earl's Court and a bank loan when he was a recent graduate of LSE – was everything this government at its sensible best would approve of.

Business success tends either to make a Rotarian or a free-market bore of a man. Shepherd is indeed (unboringly) free market in his outlook. But where businessmen in politics are either narrowly functional or scared of the clever people who are *real* politicians, he is fiercely and seriously engaged. There are two or three issues which matter to him far beyond the game of politics or the pursuit of office. One is an old-fashioned nationalism. He has a high regard for the Union, something normally made most of by the reactionary mannerists of the post-Powellian group – Budgen, Stanbrook and friends. But as a consequence of this nationalism he holds the intrusive powers of the EC and all its insidious institutions in contempt. This brings him happily into the ERG. He had been Teddy Taylor's associate before entering Parliament.

Taylor is now a director of Shepherd's company and influence appears to flow two ways. One can't quite see Teddy on his own making a major issue of official secrets, but the comradeship of one campaign spreads to another. Teddy Taylor made himself the voice of passionate reservation, if that is possible, over Europe, and Shepherd was his disciple. But Shepherd is a classical liberal in respect of personal liberty as much as supply and demand. Nationalism and systematic liberalism do not normally mix but they do here.

The group as a whole is affected. On freedom and secrets Shepherd is the motor and Taylor is drawn in as are other unlikely figures such as Tony Marlow. Almost by inadvertence and certainly through no self-serving purpose, a formidable dissentient group has formed at this point. The adherence of Rupert Allason, a young but intelligent and very well briefed security specialist (otherwise Nigel West, the critical historian of the spy business), and Jonathan Aitken, a self-exiled, derisive, verbally subtle member of the Beaverbrook connection, has made an enormous difference.

They were joined in the January debate on the committee stage by Steve Norris, newly returned for Epping, somebody very significant in his own right. For Norris is not tinged by any sort of eccentricity, if one discounts an undergraduate whirl with the future Edwina Currie. He is an orthodox talent – a bluff, sharp-minded businessman with a line in self-deprecatory cracks about 'scrap dealers like me'. The Whips esteem him; he is a head to be hunted, a candidate for natural elevation, yet Norris is prepared, on the issue of Security Service secrecy, to pick a fight with his own promising destiny.

Shepherd cannot take (and would not want to) all the credit for other people's stands. Yet he raised the standard on this issue. He meticulously argued the case with a speech on that Friday in 1988 when his private bill came forward which deserves a place in any anthology of Parliamentary debate. It was against that bill that Mrs Thatcher incredibly ordered a three-line Whip, something without precedent for a private member's measure. Richard Shepherd had in his quiet way become a catalyst.

The government, originally happy to do nothing, was roused into a fit of petulant dragonising with a measure of its own, actually more repressive and despotic than the nonsense of 1911 and without the excuse of war panic. Intelligent and very disparate Conservatives threw themselves into that battle on the same side. (Sir Ian Gilmour took his incongrous place beside the European Reform Group with a couple of wickedly sardonic contributions.) Single-handed, Shepherd made a moral test of the government and of certain individual members.

It is simply no longer possible to argue, even with rabbinical refinement, that Mrs Thatcher is not authoritarian by nature. Her glass-shattering imperiousness was roused. Incidentally, in the early days of Shepherd's bill, he was given an audience with the Prime Minister in an attempt to have him back down. He was, remember, an admirer. He wanted very much the economic free-market side of this government's programme. He might perhaps have been open to a softening and sweetening process.

No one quite knows what happened, but the strongest impression exists that he walked into the full anvil chorus of Mrs Thatcher's personality, an onslaught of brazen bullying, possible only to a fully aroused scold. He appears to have come away bitterly enlightened and unlikely to call himself a Thatcherite again.

At the same time, a long process was begun which brought security secrecy and freedom to the forefront of debate in practical, untheoretical terms. Odd alliances were formed in Parliament. The SLD and Labour parties were compelled to think hard about issues which did not naturally preoccupy them (Labour's own authoritarian compulsions were given a healthy kick), and certain politicians – notably the Home Secretary of the day, Douglas Hurd – would never again look quite as good as they did.

Mr Hurd's sad role as the settler for the least bad terms he could get, in the form of a ferocious bill of which Lords Sidmouth and Castlereagh would have been proud, made a dreadful mess of his claims to liberalism. Circumstances brought out the fourteen-year bureaucrat, in his own phrase, in full court plumage. He was obliged to defend the abolition of the public interest defence, his deputy compelled to say that 'quite rightly' would someone be liable to prosecution if they revealed that they had been burgled or phone-tapped by MI5 since the protection of a complaint to a tribunal had been provided.

The stark division between the attractive liberalism of Conservative economic policy and the hysterical Bourbon-nery, the mood of Naples in 1840, apparent in its approach to authority was bathed in light. In the short term, Shepherd may feel bleakly that he has conjured up demons. In fact, he has surely started a debate which must eventually be resolved the other way. Government has retreated into a position so objectionable that even quite Conservative newspapers are at odds with it. There are some grounds for thinking that Browning's optimism has its place:

Never dreamed, though right were worsted, wrong would
    triumph,
Held we fall to rise, are baffled to fight better,
Sleep to wake.

These were momentous issues for a quiet, previously little noticed backbencher to have aroused.

Personally he has paid a price but made a reputation. The price lies in the free flow of *ad hominem* malice which comes from loyal sources. A newspaper profile of Shepherd alluded to unsuccessful attempts made to attach a homosexual label, as if that mattered. Failing that, the next under-the-arm thrust suggested that such was the man's fanaticism that he was clearly 'sublimating'. He is vulnerable only in the sense that he has minor unimportant idiosyncrasies of speech, for example a voice which cracks in the upper register. Also, despite a very robust independent personality, he *looks* frail, with his slightly clumsy build and faint look of Tintin. It is also considered in some Tory circles to be bad form to mind anything overmuch and the whole point of Shepherd is that his actions are founded upon a deep sense of outrage. He minds very much indeed, and thank God somebody does.

Governments are not naturally truthful and this one, taking its cue from the heroine of Westland, is less scrupulous than most. The pressure upon a sustained critic of a government position is always heavy. Otherwise orthodox Tories like Jill Knight and Michael Mates were coolly and efficiently voted down for party offices for taking contrary lines on medical tests and the Poll Tax. Shepherd, prizing no such thing, and hardly to be denied what he did not seek, has to face attempts at marginalisation, and little slanders. Quite whether the authorities in their rage will try to play the association card and seek to be rid of him altogether waits to be seen. But they are capable of it.

A minor embarrassment is that in the period since the second reading of his own bill he has become something of a hero to the Opposition parties. They have sensibly tried to avoid presenting a poisoned garland, but it is not possible to hold back admiration altogether. In fact, together with Frank Field on the Labour side, Shepherd must be counted as a Parliamentary independent. Both men vote for their party most of the time, but where rational convictions or passionately held belief intervene, they break ranks without hesitation. Field's estrangement is of a slightly different order, relates in part to constituency pressures and involves less frequent public clashes with the official line, but it runs quite as deep. Both men are doing what we have supposed Parliament to be for. Their contribution is made in spite, frequently in the teeth, of the Whips. Yet a case could be made that they are the two most valuable individual members of Parliament.

Conscience plays a part in their role, but in Shepherd's case he is saying on secrecy what a firm majority of Conservatives would say in a perfectly free debate with all pressures withdrawn. The institutional Conservative party has been ordered to vote for an hysterical nonsense, for the legalising of illegal acts if committed by a privileged group. The hypnosis and amnesia of Parliamentary life do their work. The institutional Conservative party votes for this with a readiness which suggests that if pressed to vote for the slaughter of the firstborn they would provide a majority at least at second reading.

What Richard Shepherd may never be forgiven is the degree to which he has asked his party clear questions and obliged it, given its present nature, to give disgraceful answers. He has done the worst thing possible: put them in the wrong.

# CHAPTER 29

# David Steel

David Steel is a hard man to get right. Someone easily underestimated and overestimated, he was treated for years with hovering respect and latterly, not least by this writer, with exasperated dismissiveness. 'I wanted much. I began much, but the gale of the world carried away me and my work.' The noble words of the Serbian Chetnik leader, Draza Mihailovic, describe Steel's career well enough.

The historical fact that Mihailovic was shortly afterwards taken to a high-class golf course and shot by a communist firing squad for his failure to manage the middle ground between left and right goes beyond the lesser misfortunes of Steel's career.

He has become remarkably equable on retirement from the Liberal leadership. That party has a gift for malign squabbling, so many intensely disagreeable personalities – Alexander Carlile, Michael Meadowcroft when he was around, at an absurd level Cyril Smith – together with better and otherwise interesting people like Simon Hughes and David Alton, who have it in them to be unbelievably silly. With such personalities and the self-devouring bitterness of his former deputy, Alan Beith, Steel could think himself well out of the job.

To the Liberal party and its expanded successor party (the one with the impossible name) applies exquisitely Parkinson's Law: that work expands to fill the space provided for its performance. The Liberals, as I reflexively call them, having no power or prospect of it and being barred by the vanity and Pleistocene immobility of Labour (and themselves) from striking the rational deal which would do them both a favour, must spend great quantities of time examining their policies in minute detail simply to seem active.

Indeed as the Tories, in insolent occupancy, grow increasingly peremptory, clicking their fingers seigneurially at the legislative process, dispensing with consultation, White Paper procedure and free speech, so the Liberals seem to be making up for it privately by ever more consultative reflection on their own small actions. The Liberals couldn't eat a salad without a consultation paper on the lettuce industry.

Because it is a small party and a cosy one, bitterness has the dimension of domestic tragedy. A single destructive crank counts for something in a Parliamentary party of fifteen to twenty. One cannot see the Tories setting aside time at their conference to celebrate the reconciliation of Geoffrey Dickens if he had absented himself and sulked away from Parliament for a while. But the Liberals did exactly that to celebrate a return of Cyril Smith, against which they might more wisely have held a service of intercession. Because the Liberal party is so querulous and contains such a quota of over-profiled cranks, part of the appeal of David Steel was his sanity and normality.

Such was the despair in the party when the previous leader, Jeremy Thorpe, crashed infamously out of politics by way of the criminal courts that they begged the leader of ten years earlier, Joseph Grimond, not just to chair the party in the interim but to re-assume the leadership. Thorpe, remember, left the High Court acquitted with the warm encouragement of a typical High Court judge and with no other stain on his character. An exciting, witty, dazzling, flashy sort of politician, catching the eye and putting up a delightful façade, might, with his alleged conspiracy involving a gaming-machine manufacturer and other odd company, have wrecked his party. He was, although acquitted, universally seen (not least by his constituents) as unfit to continue in politics.

But the Liberals are incapable of falling clean over. Their style is that of the toy policeman with the lead weighting at the base. Too keen on the *game* of politics to despair, they bounce back after every *bouleversement*; too obviously made of rubber and lead, they find measurable progress hard to make. But David Steel, the son of missionaries to Africa, the son not just of the manse but of applied political Calvinism, was a necessary chemical opposite. In fact, it would be easy to overstate the pious and moralistic side of Steel. He is privately a pleasantly dry and humorous man to talk to; there is a thorough composed quality of steady decency which makes the devotion of men like Menzies Campbell easy to understand.

He is not in any way a prig. And that word 'dour' so overused by the cliché-tossers of Scots politics in need of an adjective, has little application here. Certainly not in a lifetime would he ever be called flashy. But Steel is an instinctualist, trusting affinities with other people, friendship and indeed opportunity, not abstract convictions. What he absolutely is not is a dedicated eyesight-endangering, paper-eating work mill. The observation is intended as pure praise. The boringness which politicians endure and ultimately enforce in their own characters by the devouring and writing of pamphlets, the Green Paper mill and general Fabianitis, is a source of dismay to those who want to enjoy politics.

Even so, while one sympathises with the instinct which makes both Steel and Neil Kinnock eschew the plantation labours at detail which have made Margaret a dull girl, nonchalance is a risky business. Also none of his beliefs is ardently held. Steel's political baggage is the standard sixties-plus consensual package, obtainable from every good retailer in the High Street. He is a European and makes all the necessary affirming noises, but he is hardly a *dévot* in the way of Tory activists like Linda Chalker or Hugh Dykes let alone Mr Heath, let alone for that matter Roy Jenkins. He would vote the neo-Keynesian way over public spending but without either the fervour or the reading that Ian Gilmour puts into the same cause. He tagged happily behind Labour's fondness for incomes and prices policies, or was it prices and incomes? He may or may not believe in the private Liberal thing about site valuation.

But nothing is taken up as a matter of desperate urgency. It is a strike against both him and Bob MacLennan that when the Shepherd bill to reform the Official Secrets Acts, an issue which is logically at the centre of any halfway thought-out liberal or Liberal philosophy, was proceeding, neither could contribute to the debate because the dreary politicking of the fusion struggle had taken MacLennan to Sheffield for one party meeting and Steel to Glasgow for another. The pettifoggeries of factional struggle took over from the sort of issue which politics exists to fight. In MacLennan, who probably believes and minds too much for his own good, this was an aberration. For Steel it was natural; ideas do not excite him.

This is not a drawback in the world of television. Nobody watches the screen to hear percentiles or an explanation of the sheepmeat régime. The thing actually registering, the nature of the man behind the coloured shadow, was very well received across his twelve or so years in the job. All Scots start with an advantage if they bother to be nice to the English, since there is a bias in their favour south of the border which must distress nationalists.

The English esteem the Scots for their seriousness. They drink a serious alcohol, they practise arguably the most intellectually impressive religion anywhere available in their elevated mainstream Calvinism; they have the best doctors, lawyers, scientists and economists, or seem to; and they do feral street violence better than anyone except the Irish and the Lebanese. If one of them turns from all these many concerns and talks to us courteously in a soft Edinburgh accent, we are flattered and pleased.

Quite apart from which, Steel's brand of vague goodwill is fine with the English, who like nothing hard and sharp but delight to hear fairness and decency praised regularly in the way of a secular liturgy. Weighed down by his party, oppressed by his allies, not very hot in the Commons which found him cloudy and glutinous like blancmange, Steel got beautifully on to the national wavelength. He had the style and limitations of a perfect GP right down to the accent; and everyone knew quite well that there was no serious risk of his being allowed to operate. Accordingly he was for long stretches the most popular, because the least demanding, politician in the country.

Steel is actually quite lazy and one is never quite sure listening to him where laziness ends and agnosticism begins. His speeches on tour are perfunctory and limp. In 1983, an age before the despair of the last election occurred, his battlebus tour of the West Country had a quality of somnambulation about it. Steel had the same speech to make from the articulated bus platform whenever we found parking in Totnes or Winchester. He would then go and meet the public, always cutting a crescent through the crowd, literally propped from behind (defended against assassination?) by the busy Lord Chitnis. There was no energy in it, no driving purpose.

This is a product perhaps of other weaknesses, such as the lack of a strong debating style, but he has never yet seemed to me stirred to animation by any cause. When his political career as leader was coming to an end four years later, a tour in South Scotland, his own territory, was even more markedly inanimate. He recited a formula in a dull voice for the shortest possible time. Even the eve-of-poll meeting I heard was a thin *kaddish* of unfelt hope that things might be better than they looked. It was all very understandable, but not long on the indomitable side. The energy which he would summon to precipitate all sides into eighteen months' manic destructive activity immediately *after* the campaign would have been better pointed at the Tories before it.

He was a victim, one of many, of David Owen's electric-scythe personality. He had been, as the world knows, ruinously belittled by *Spitting Image*, as the pencil in Owen's breast pocket. He had been corrected in the studio by Owen about defence policy. There was a general madness about on that campaign. Yet political professionalism requires a measure of stupid courage against odds. The winners look back on their Athelnys and Valley Forges in the knowledge that they kept their nerve. What might be called the successful losers die with the *Revenge*.

Steel, not Sir Richard Grenville's type, faced war neither by running away nor by doing anything heroic. He reminds one of some of those American Civil War generals on the Union side with a tendency to overrate Confederate strength and a taste for elaborately executed, time-consuming and conflict-avoiding manoeuvres. He brought to electoral struggle the gloomy scepticism of General George Maclellan.

Yet as a strategic thinker for his party, Steel was usually apt and right. Perhaps 'thinker' is too grandiose a word. His instincts were straightforwardly sensible. He rightly grasped that going forward was conditional upon association with another force, and was helped by his friendship with Roy Jenkins. The scheme he devised was to fail but was still original, disruptive political activity.

In principle, an alliance of the centre aimed against Mrs Thatcher's forty-two per cent absolutism and the Labour party's heavy class- and interest-weighting, has enormous attractiveness. It fell down over two things: the need under first-past-the-post rules to perform so much better than very well merely to register impact, and the genius of most of the dominant personalities – Mrs Williams, Owen, Bill Rodgers and Jenkins – for running a positive soap opera of antipathies and conspiracies. To preach moderation and practise *fronde* induces schizoid characteristics.

But this is hardly Steel's fault. He had the understanding and the courage (a different thing from the stamina he lacks) to push his party towards alliance. He had the same instinct back in 1976 when the Lib-Lab Pact came into existence to keep the Callaghan government above the water. It might be that the very pessimism which makes him such a poor campaigner informed his long-term approach with a degree of realism. There is a profound impulse in small groups towards particularist retreat, the inverted triumphalism of strict and particular brethren, the satisfaction of being right in exile, of eschewing compromise and even more so its fruits of serious expansion in order to maintain the perfection of the cloister.

In fact, the impulse towards such self-sequestering was grossly inflated by the noisy talent for publicity of the group of Northern councillors around Michael Meadowcroft and Tony Greaves. Good old-fashioned cranks anxious for a puddle in which to shimmer, they were systematically overweighted in everyone's mind – Steel's and also Owen's – by their alliance with the amorphous trend to near-unilateralism on defence. That Greaves-Meadowcroft group was fiercely beaten up when it tried to resist the vote for unification at the special Blackpool conference in 1988, as it had been in Llandudno when the *alliance* with the SDP had been voted in. Sixteen to one was the vote the first time and it might have been salutary for both Steel, dreading his loons, and Owen, over-angry with inevitable nonsenses on defence, to have kept that ratio in mind.

But the ability of resolute minorities with political flair to bullfrog themselves by propaganda and by coat-tailing additional causes exaggerated both the strength of the left in the Liberal party and that of homespun, ginger-bearded West Riding super-particularism.

The sad thing for Steel was that he sought escape from one sort of conflict – the one natural to his own chronically tolerant argumentative party – to encounter another: the private will to squabble among prickly ex-Ministers from government and a big party, watching one another like a scorpions' reunion.

For Steel had never been a happy Liberal. If he didn't in so many words actually dislike his party, he was not an enthusiast for its company. Increasingly, he flinched away from broad party company at conferences and other gatherings, taking refuge (just as Neil Kinnock did for some time) in acceptable private company. There was reason enough in some of the shrill nonsenses of those conferences. A leader faced with the trombonings of unreal people like Claire Brooks, the latest unreadable sludge from the Association of Municipal Councillors, the running jumping and standing-still qualities of that sweetly demented hamster, Simon Hughes, had good reason to lock himself in a hotel bedroom to scream in greater comfort.

But any man who has got away from all this to meet the Jenkins-against-Owen rage is entitled to his share of *anomie*. Steel would have quite liked to have been a conventional politician in a decent-sized party. Whatever instinct led him as a very young man into Liberalism was at least subconsciously regretted. He is not eccentric. The Liberals, if not compulsorily eccentric themselves, are uncommonly tolerant of personalities in need of a plain van and restraint. He must have felt, as the war of the former Ministers raged self-importantly about him, that he had escaped from one ward into another.

This was not broadly the way of the two parties in the constituencies, who regularly seemed better able to get on, do deals and live together than either the conference folk or the great ones. The attitude of many ward-stampers towards their leading figures was like the embarrassment of mature-minded children at their overwrought and rather shaming parents.

It goes a long way to explaining the state of battered acquiescence in which he fought the two elections waged by the Alliance. It does something to make sense of his sudden precipitancy on the morning after defeat in June 1987 when he sent the pistol-to-head missive to Owen. 'Unite or die' was effectively the slogan. It ran clean against the entire form book of all the races run by David Martin Scott Steel. It was passionate as he is not. It was a bridge-burning gamble, and he dislikes gambling. It was done at least partly in rage, and the sin of wrath holds very little equity in Steel. The situation actually required total immobility and a skilful ducking below the parapet until time lapsed and the Tories made mistakes, something which is second nature to Steel. Instead, he conjured up eighteen months of useless activity at the intersection of a sniper's cross hairs.

The only consistency of the entire episode is that the move followed up (drastically) his deep convictions about unity. Now conviction for Steel, who is masterfully apathetic about policy, is confined to political mechanics. PR matters in the way Europe and the economy never can, because of its direct relevance to seats in Parliament. The achievement of unity had become a similar means to the end of lifting Liberalism out of the chuntering margins.

Something else: the entire centre-left for a decade and a half, since the collapse of Mr Heath's Selsdonism in the face of union power, had been devoted to mechanical changes (constitutional reforms like devolution and, worse, regionalism, as well as PR) precisely because the economy and the handling of unions had defeated them. Any fool can juggle counties and declare a new administrative area, but the thing has not been done because it was needed but rather as a twiddle upon legislative worry beads. Mechanical or structural reforms had their full element of escapism from the first miners' strike onwards.

Belief in the health of unity without reflection on what or whom was being united blinded Steel to the psychology of the people all around him, the deafening screams of the unwilling, the bewilderment of the ground forces in the constituencies at contradictory orders, and of course the awful folly of exposing the flammable personality of David Owen to the steady flame of the unification. The failure was grievous and it was a failure on Steel's own ground, on the area of tinkering mechanics which he knew and liked best.

The retreat of Steel himself, making way for another leader, was not as grievous a blow to him as the harm done to a new party at once assembled and shattered by the year and a half of raw, unrefined personality-conflict, the tossing of tantrums, the endless meetings boring even to politicians except Liberals and Social Democrats and the display of emotional frailty and simple incompetence; fifteen years of adverse publicity stuffed into eighteen months!

The leadership was not dear to David Steel by this time. Nobody lasts much over ten years as leader of that party. Jo Grimond with his usual wisdom set himself ten years and got out in 1968. He has been in major credit with all observers ever since as the wise old boy who isn't leading the Liberals. (The wisdom and the eschewal of leadership were seen as much the same thing.)

Arguably, Steel, who strikes me as a happier man doing the elegant traveller's job of Foreign Affairs, watching Paddy Ashdown's gallant but over-urgent exertions, and quietly accumulating at fifty-one the first undercoat of elder statesmanship, has found a happy berth.

The leader of the political centre grouping is in much the

same position as the Speaker or the Archbishop of Canterbury. Like them he is blamed by cantankerous leaderwriters for not providing 'decisive leadership' or vigorous discipline when in fact it is the function of all three to avoid anything so damned silly. It was only when David Steel broke with the habit of twelve years and offered leadership almost provocatively decisive, and an encounter with his difficult ally less like discipline than a meeting of seconds, that he inflicted almost terminal harm – on his own party and the prospective merger partner. Only that rubber-policeman aspect of old-time Liberalism will save them from so much incendiary vigour. The man who had elevated diffidence into high art leapt on to a white horse, only to come down rather anti-climactically on its other side.

None of which late unwisdom detracts from Steel's essential sense and attractiveness. He is a reasonable, good-mannered, sympathetic presence; conventional moderate politics pleasantly and quietly advocated. He has always been liked and the public were right to like him. But if he escaped the firing squad, the self-judgement of Mihailovic returns: the gale of the world carried him and his work away. Except that this was a gale of pettifogging irreconcilability among politicians incapable of commonsense and silence.

# CHAPTER 30

## *John Prescott*

The Labour party at the top is highly educated and securely middle class. North Oxford would be, indeed is, entirely at ease with Bryan Gould, Gordon Brown, Tony Blair, John Smith, Jack Straw and Gerald Kaufman. For the most part they know their Mozart, never split an infinitive and – in a nice, sports-jacketed, democratic way – know about starting with the outer forks of a table setting. Bryan Gould is even expert on the Burgundy no one can any longer afford.

This is inevitable and something to be relaxed about. One of the very few foolish things George Orwell ever did was to drink tea from a saucer out of solidarity, in the proletarian fever of the thirties. No social betrayal is involved in douce manners and indeed, since the rise of the working-class Tories – Tebbit, Major, Moore and Parkinson, not to mention the grandson of a Communist party member (David Davis) and the great-grandson of Tom Mann (Nicholas Bennett) – something has gone out of the effortless superiority of the Tory party. As it bore a fair resemblance to the easeful death contemplated by Keats, they may be the stronger for it. However the impression lingers, especially when the gently bred and sweetly spoken Tony Blair is in debate against Cecil Parkinson (a social re-spray with a special-offer accent), that Labour is actually slumming.

The beauty of John Prescott is that he is Labour's only frontbench link with the working class. Some might urge Neil Kinnock himself. But Mr Kinnock is Welsh, and the Welsh, for all their coal mines and socialism, have never been convincingly working class in the heavy, inarticulate all-suffering way of English workers – too much education and articulacy, no class system worth worrying about, no betters to be respectful towards or bitter about (all of which incidentally makes Roy Jenkins even more remarkable).

Prescott however is the authentic thing and he has all the marks of English social division upon him. The old eleven-plus was a wretched one-off test of ability for little-motivated children from homes with no educational background and was itself hugely variable from authority to authority. Failing it is not remarkable in an inherently intelligent working-class boy, but such failing had a way of indicating the high-flying fork of life and the low-trudging one.

Accordingly, by making that initial stumble, Prescott condemned himself to a different route and, when a high place was finally achieved by natural ability, to a lasting unease. It is generally seen as amusing that his time as a ship's steward should have been commemorated by the words, 'Hey Giovanni, mine's a Scotch, see what my friend will have.' The author of this playful remark, the Honourable Nicholas Soames, is actually an endearing, good-natured and widely popular fellow, in whom most of the Whiggish good humour of the Churchills has been deposited. But only in England of the European countries (and one does mean England) could anything so awful have been said. Nick Soames would die before he joked in that way about a black man or a Jew. And remarks about ex-waiters are if possible more common among his popular democratic working-class-representing Labour colleagues. The unspoken message is, 'What is somebody like *you* doing here?'

Thus, if it is objected that John Prescott is chippy (and by God he is) then he has something to be chippy about. Yet the actual record is impressive. He may have failed eleven-plus but having progressed from Ruskin to Hull University, he took a degree (and passed first time, he might be inclined to remember in view of his leader's troubles at Cardiff) and moved briskly on.

Inside the Seaman's Union he had been a follower of the radical Jim Slater, so oddly characterised by Harold Wilson in the late sixties as part of 'a tightly knit group of politically motivated men'. The opponents of a bought-and-sold company-deferential union leadership, they were naturally agents of Moscow. But Prescott benefited from the hostility of the NUS leadership, which was delighted to provide scholarship openings to take a radical opponent out of the struggle. Ruskin College, Oxford, which he values as the great liberating experience of his life, followed. An attractive aspect of John Prescott is the pleasure he took in that education and, as he says himself, the other pleasure of realising that he *had* abilities and was not the dull heavy he had been cast for in life. His actual record, though fast-rising, was based on exile. He was an early participant in European politics, going to the Council of Europe in 1972 for three years then being nominated to the Strasbourg Parliament and serving for three years (until 1979) as leader of the Labour delegation, as it then was.

The wicked thought offers itself that Prescott has a way of being sent to distant places by people who can't stand the sight of him, but he has always put the exile to excellent account. He has the rare distinction among politicians dazzled by high rewards of having turned down a firm offer of a European Commissionership. Friends calculated that over two terms, which would have been likely given that it assured opponents of eight Prescott-less years, he would have netted well over £400,000. Rejection should fairly be seen as both puritanical, in the bitter self-denying way of his friend Dennis Skinner (who thinks himself corrupted by the acceptance of a cup of tea), and ambitious self-assurance. Europe is a soft landing on a mattress stuffed with fiduciary issue, but you have to fall off the Parliamentary ledge to have entitlement.

The Skinner link is interesting, for the two have shared a roof in their London accommodation. Skinner, also a product of Ruskin, is both random wit with his halting-prose blunderbuss, and single-purposed leftwing conscience. He is also capable of delivering the Campaign Group vote in PLP elections! Genuinely, he despises most of Parliamentary politics as a corrupt farce, giving a memorable put-down to the late affable, tainted Reginald Maudling.

Maudling, a fat, florid man accustomed to the sort of short living absurdly called 'good', was sounding off perfectly correctly about the inefficiency of British manufacturers and the workforce within them. 'It takes a German worker less than a day to make a car,' he said, 'whereas the British worker will take three and a quarter days.' ''Ow long would it tek you ter mek one, fats?' asked Skinner, winning the argument in a very Labour party way by an appeal to morality and against the person, while being thickheadedly in the wrong on the issue.

Being Skinner, a sort of pit-village St Just, is all very well if you are content to stay Skinner and let sour, laconic rectitude be its own reward. But Prescott wants no such thing. He is decently ambitious, has put together an intelligent and full *curriculum vitae* and has a fairly settled place in the Shadow Cabinet. But in the process he emphasised a leftwingness which is emotionally truthful but ultimately misleading about his outlook.

Because of his links to the NUS (a battered union which these days has an honourable but inept leadership and is a hideous loser) and to one of the least attractive of all Mrs Thatcher's friends in business – the sleek, gemstone-hard and exquisitely wired-up Jeffrey Stirling – he is closer to the directly confrontational side of union politics. But Prescott is not a union reactionary, anxious to prop inefficient practices for the indefinite future. He is probably as realistic about unit costs and jobs as the most formally educated of his frontbench colleagues. For all the dourness and despite the binding links with the unions, he prizes rationality.

But if an image of him as union heavy and male battle-axe has established itself the fault is partly his own. He was until recently quite absurdly rough and rude in his dealings with the press. Too much of 'Yer what, yer fucker?' can induce in journalists the judgement that he is Skinner without the charm. Being ourselves nicely brought up and having a fair simulation of education, we can be very cutting about people who trample our sensibilities, swear at us and rather come the stage proletarian. There is great truth in the observation of Dr Fagin of Llanabba School in Evelyn Waugh's *Decline and Fall*, that 'There must be whisky for the press.' Otherwise, he said, 'the pictures of sportsday in the paper could be very embarrassing'.

For a long time Prescott bullied and shouted in situations where he was perfectly equipped to talk quietly and well. Dismissal of him as a resentful thug was as natural as it was wrong. However he is a great one for learning his way out of mistakes. Circumstances involving shadowed departments have turned him into something of a regular on *Newsnight* and the style has changed out of recognition. Any roughness now is of the affable sort. He reasons instead of asserting or knocking down, and has generally adapted to a civil style. Finally, the private warmth and decency are coming through. No one listening only for the last two or three years would slot him into the stereotype of crude union bodyguard.

The quarrel *not* mended is the one with his leader. Both received bad advice about the other. Prescott was encouraged in bitterness, Kinnock in unmagnanimous contempt. The qualities of courage and battle which have made Kinnock a good leader against enemies have made him a poor concili-ator of critics. When Prescott, contemplating a candidacy for the deputy leadership, was persuaded it would be a mistake and pulled out, a good reaction would have been one of generosity and thanks, sincerity being no precondition of such sentiments. Instead concession was treated as surrender and scornfully dismissed with the side of the shoe.

Foolishly snubbed, he as foolishly plunged back into conflict a year on and fought a candidacy against the deputy leader which should never have been launched and which, if I know anything about Labour, will not be forgiven. Though the end the second time round was fairly graceful on all sides, if the picking up of the bits of flung crockery ever can be graceful.

In part that candidacy derived from an antipathy towards Roy Hattersley. A decade or more ago, Prescott, using his knowledge of the sea and the international fishing industry and his status at the European Parliament, cheekily but also rather brilliantly put together with Icelandic representatives a set of concessions and terms in the Cod War which went below British offers and expectations. They were rejected furiously by the then Minister of State, one Hattersley, singing the correct Foreign Office tune, as improper, unauthorised and unacceptable. When terms were in due course reached by the authorised and proper channels, they were of course inferior. Between a man of obsessive rough authenticity and one more felicitous but a systematic sham – a mighty flaw around which substance has been tastefully arranged – there is a gap of mutual disdain which it would be a pity to bridge.

Attempts by the leadership to put Prescott into some apt diminishing shadow have been disappointed lately. Transport, where he had been before, was meant as both demotion and railway siding. The succession of Kings Cross, Lockerbie and a tube strike – to say nothing of the quavering administration of Prescott's social opposite number, the tremulous Guinness heir and Mustique holidaymaker, Paul Channon – has kept Transport resolutely on camera. The trains have been running pretty smoothly out of that siding, almost on the hour; the Opposition job is well enough done. The man himself is a worker who will never be caught under-read for a debate. There are people – the fervent and dim Michael Meacher and the sloppily bonhomous Frank Dobson – who do not fit in a modern-minded Labour frontbench. Prescott, on intelligence and serious purpose, emphatically does.

His disputes are two-way affairs in terms of blame; his harsh abrupt ways are heavily amended. Indeed with Kinnock making a presentation to the Tories of his own inelastic temper on the *World at One*, Prescott looks almost genteel. It is important that a substantial, honest, closely applying representative of the class which created the Labour party should be integrated into the group. If he needs to keep up his night-school studies of tolerance and maintain his recent recognition that civility is not a betrayal of the workers, so do other people in the Shadow Cabinet need to stretch out a friendly hand. Sensitivity is an odd word to use about a politician, but it is the core of Prescott's character. Always having had to struggle, he needs more than most to be appreciated and valued. He is an asset to Labour if a rough-edged one, but he has been in too many disputes and been too often grumblingly at odds to have many kind things said about him by colleagues. Interestingly, he will talk about people as different from himself as John Smith and Bryan Gould with candid admiration.

It would be great wisdom on all sides if the resentments and condescensions could be traded in. His fault is one typical of the historic Labour party, maybe of Northern English workers themselves: a kind of dour distrustfulness and scepticism. But he learns and adapts, and a party primarily of the workers would be ill-advised to fall out with the only man in its ranks who has been mocked for his origins.

# CHAPTER 31

# John Stanley

Of all the short lives of this account that of John Stanley is perhaps the saddest. He was a zealot, a believer, a follower of Mrs Thatcher so comprehensive that he once let fall the involuntary *double entendre*, 'This country doesn't *deserve* Margaret Thatcher', a proposition to which many non- believers felt able to drink.

Yet Mr Stanley had become Sir John at forty-six, as comprehensive a sign of political death as an entry in the book of remembrance is for the real thing. Knighthoods are awarded in science only to eminent scientists, in the army and the civil service only to those attaining very high posts, and in business only to those able to afford the most bountiful liberality towards the Conservative party. In politics on the Tory side, they are given either as acknowledgement of failure, deletion from minor office or long, blameless loyal under-attainment on the backbenches. The use of the honorific form of address as the small change of Whips' patronage, as a long-service medal, as an order for inglorious mutes, is a continuing comfortable scandal.

Sir Alec Cairncross and Sir James Black are marks of deserved esteem; Sir John Stanley is a plastic handshake, a perfunctory gift at quietus. He was left with few mourners, many deriders and wide relief.

Yet Stanley was not only a hardworking and earnest Minister, he is probably the father of the government's best idea and least questioned achievement. He is the most likely onlie begetter of the great council house sale which has done so much to seduce authentic proletarians into becoming trainee Alf Robertses; a stake in the country having proved a stake in the heart of municipal bounty and authority.

There are other claimants. Mr Peter Walker – denounced by his predecessor in Wales, Lord Crickhowell, as a 'trumpeter' – believes that, like so many good things, council houses for sale flow from the mind of Peter Walker. This is one of those paternity cases where the candidates positively queue up demanding an affiliation order.

But John Stanley carried out the bulk of the work and is entitled to his credit. It was a superbly effective idea, an apparent indication of a liberal market conservatism which would let people get on with their own lives as citizens rather than dependants. Neither by personality nor by the rest of his authoritarian instincts was Stanley able to live up to it.

In any other politician such a palpable hit would have meant urgent murmurings about Bloggs's turn for the Cabinet. The doors of Transport, Energy and Northern Ireland, those increments of office, would have stood open. But Stanley is the victim of his style. He has a mannered deliberation which invites mockery, a sort of prissiness perhaps derived from his time as a schoolmaster. His whole manner evokes the footman, not the magisterial statue in livery rebuking the social deficiencies of guests by his marble perfection but the running, fetching and carrying sort.

Dedication to the leader works politically only if it is of the rough, unmannerly gut-slitting sort. Both Norman Tebbit and Bernard Ingham, to name two partisan politicians, have played the role of ruffian on the stair. Their loyalty was expressed in the form of a series of serious abrasions and grievous bodily hurts. No serious gang is complete without a Big Louis character of the sort best played by Herbert Lom (with whom Mr Tebbit has affinities) to say 'Shall I do him over, boss?'

All Mr Stanley could offer by way of rough treatment was to squeak at somebody. It left him looking like a less lovable

Gummer; to Mr Tebbit's Rottweiler he was a querulous Pom. Even so, he was entirely 'one of us'; he believed in the Thatcher thing. He had been her PPS, though he never achieved the theatrical high point in that office of Mr Ian Gow who alone can give sycophancy class. He had more than a touch of the lady's contempt for opposition as enemy, criticism as war and Conservative doubt as treason. He had all the littleness necessary for ascent but he did not ascend.

The truth is that it was never possible to take Stanley seriously. His brush with the Commons over the *Belgrano* produced a measure of shabby theatre from Michael Heseltine at his most melodramatic, Fireforefiddle the Fiend of the Fell; and of course Mr Ponting, went to court if not to the jail that had been intended. The precise truth of that episode remains murky, but Stanley hardly emerged looking more attractive.

What was interesting was the obvious relish of Heseltine for the defence for, interestingly, Stanley was a sincere loyalist to two people who enjoyed the tranquil diplomatic accord of two stoats in a sack. Heseltine is aware that Stanley is sometimes absurd and has cheerfully laughed at him, but his affection is deep and unaffected. 'John' to him is a dedicated worker, good office professional and unswerving loyalist. The attraction for Stanley must have been not to the warm and sympathetic side of Heseltine, the social softliner, but Heseltine the Argentine general; as a pair they would look quite well on the balcony of the Casa Rosada.

If there should be life in Heseltine's political career and the polls still smile at him, then Stanley, knighthood notwithstanding, would resume political life. My guess for Heseltine is neither death nor glory, leadership nor immolation, but Home Secretary to Kenneth Baker. In which case Stanley would stand a very good chance of lesser Cabinet office on the love-me-love-my-buddy basis.

The story is everywhere related of Stanley in his MOD days trapped in one of those antiquarian cage lifts favoured by the departments, demanding in the usual imperious tones that his important work be brought to him while he was held captive, and of Heseltine coming to the banisters to join the mockery; even so the affection and, more important, the gratitude remain, which may tell us more about the master than the man.

Stanley, loyal and snappish, was made for canine metaphor, so far does the Minister recall Shakespeare's observation: 'A dog's obeyed in office.' Many people have felt that most kinds of dog were fine by them but that they drew a line at John Stanley.

The poor man has erected paranoia into an art form. In the process he has gone beyond derision to something close to hatred.

A cruel remark from his time in Northern Ireland asked why his guards were changed so frequently and gave the reply, to minimise the risk of their doing a Mrs Gandhi and shooting their charge out of hand.

Stanley is without humour, sense of proportion, tolerance, good nature or the capacity to see any merit in an opponent. In a strong personality such astigmatic singularity of vision can be a fearful asset. In a man essentially silly, high-pitched in speech, with real hair which looks like a wig, desperately proud of office, 'man, poor man dressed in a little brief authority', it is calamitous.

But the House of Commons, little as this government cares for it, is a great finder-out of human nature. A good administrator with a flawed personality goes a long way in any non-answerable form of government (and Stanley would have fitted sweetly on to a party praesidium in Czechoslovakia or East Germany). But even so diminished a Parliament as the one of recent years – a John Bull printing outfit in the hands of the Whips – will discover a man's foolish vanity if he stands long enough at the despatch box being foolish and vain. By the end of his time Stanley had probably more enemies on the Tory side than in the Opposition. In a less serious way he attracted the sort of *sotto voce* esteem now given to Nicholas Ridley.

The Tories are a fine filter of their own talents. They can spot a conman, which Stanley certainly was not, and they know who is standing on tiptoe to be seen above the despatch box, very much his problem. Office is much bobbed and dipped to because office is a strong currency. But office never hid a fool from his honourable friends who, in the way of honour and friendship, identified a sweating, diligent useful buffoon, the sum of whose industrious parts was weighed down for ever by his preposterous whole.

# CHAPTER 32

## Peter Walker

The first remarkable thing about Peter Walker is his astonishing stamina. He first burst in upon us in 1960 when the *Sunday Express* and *Daily Express* (Lord Beaverbrook being still alive) made, in advance of his election, a great drum-rolling of the wonderful young man who would be representing Worcester after the by-election (by-elections were like that in those days before Orpington).

He was of course fervently against the loony nonsense of joining this foreign thing, the Common Market or whatever it was called. Partly because he was in partnership in the City with David Moate, whose younger brother Roger would become one of the Commons' staunchest anti-Europeans, Walker's conversion to an equally fervent devotion *to* Europe gave him for a while the reputation of careerist and turncoat.

That, unconsciously, has influenced commentators in their view of Walker. But after fourteen years of systematic sustained, non-coming to the heel of Mrs Thatcher, it can no longer be entertained. Whatever his faults, Mr Walker is entitled to be looked upon as a man of principle. He was in particular Mr Heath's personal and particular disciple. Somewhere along the road from Lord Beaverbrook's esteem he fell in with Mr Heath, then in transit between the chores of the Whips' office to the glory of 'getting into Europe'.

Sincerely and totally, Walker bought the Heath package and the Heath candidacy. For fifteen years he was closely and directly involved with the crumbly intransigence, the incoherent advocate and fool to himself. Walker was essentially a practical man, not a thinker or an ideologist. But not being a cheap opportunist either, he sincerely wanted something to believe in. Europe has been called 'Ted's only idea so he has to believe in it.' Walker didn't resist the brief flirtation with the Selsdon man free-market approach, but he put all his heart and energies into Heath's reflationary job-buying phase. He will probably die for that principle, having assaulted Mrs Thatcher's single-truth, shining-path notions of government perhaps pre-emptively in April; and the Bernard Ingham Hang-a-gram was threatening the despatch of 'dead wood' within a week.

But before that moment Walker was unlike other Tory liberals in his ability somehow to serve, dissent and carry on in a private tower from which he hung a different flag. Normally the options have been to submit or walk away. The art of cheeking and staying put was Mr Walker's private delight. It ought also to be said that adversity has improved Mr Walker. He is unfortunate in a manner and accent which are profoundly off-putting, sounding more self-important than he wishes, and in the case of the accent just being wrong – a sort of thirties actor's la-di-dah, suitable for the playing of ingenues in a Number Two touring company. When he was going to inherit the universe as well, a voice said to have been a model for that of Leslie Titmus in *Paradise Postponed*, and the manner of a man condescending to do us good on his way to the top, were not easy to take.

He always had, then and now, one single thing in common with Mrs Thatcher: he liked to manage the press and he was good at it. There have been many booster stories about Peter Walker, from that first plug from Canadian sources in 1960 to the latest insider running commentaries on his struggles with the dragon lady. The miners' strike was a running festival of wonderful Peter Walker, variously doing a superb job, winning the confidence of the miners, standing up to the miners, being tremendously firm and tremendously compassionate and generally tremendous throughout.

He also came jolly close to losing that strike single-handed. The concessions granted to NACODS were the foundation for an equivalent deal with the NUM. Such a deal, had Mr Scargill not been the thickheaded egomaniac he is, would have warranted a balcony speech from union headquarters telling the lads, 'We have eighty-five per cent of what we wanted, which in my book is a triumph for the workers over Thatcher' – a sentiment with which no one would have agreed more fervently than the 1922 Committee of Conservative backbenchers.

In fairness, if Walker was conceding too much and offering dangerous openings, this derived from his inability to share the Prime Minister's wish for gloating triumph and the smashing of all her enemies. As I said somewhere else, she failed magnanimity at 'O' level, while it has always been one of Walker's favourite subjects.

The tragedy of the pit strike, which he perhaps understood more in profound terms than political ones, was the wind-up of the coalfields which was happening anyway. And the Ezra strategy against which Mrs Thatcher railed would have taken three times as long to do gently and cost less money than what she did across a year, involving one murder, a scatter of suicides and more misery than you get short of a civil war. The pit strike was both a war of Thatcher's face and a hysterical reaction to the native hysteria of Arthur Scargill, a man in whom the Thatcher instinct for apocalyptic ping-pong for once met its equal. Walker has this naïve and civilised belief in doing things by negotiation. It might not have been possible with Scargill, reeling in a daze of vainglory, but it was a creditable instinct from a more attractive school of politics. Mounted police beating people with night sticks is closer to the style of the America Mrs Thatcher adores, even if she can't quite yet manage Pinkerton's detectives armed with revolvers. It is odd how Mrs Thatcher's worst qualities, like Scargill's, have nourished themselves and grown great on bogies, and how they accommodated each other with bogies on draught.

But of course Walker had been, as part of the Heath government, a party to Tory defeats by the miners in 1972 and 1974. That didn't make the historical downward curve of the miners any less certain once oil prices had righted themselves. But the mood among Tories after 1974 was rather like that in the US after the death of General Custer. It wanted revenge, but had a genuine anxiety about redskin power not warranted by the real strength of the people on the reservations. Perhaps, like the Americans, they will grow ashamed of the false heroics and vindictiveness attaching to a victory over tribesmen. Walker, for better or worse, finished up as the good white man, a sort of hand-wringing clergyman attached to the punitive force, urging moderation to the inattentive desert.

Walker's time in office under Edward Heath was a mixed affair. He is damned in some quarters, notably by obsessive correspondents of the *Spectator*, for the 'Heatho-Walkerian local government "reforms"'. It is indeed a matter of regret that we should have lost Huntingdon and Rutland and – most treasured of all – Westmorland, and an even greater tragedy that we received Humberside, Cleveland and Avon. But people who work themselves repetitiously into a froth about the subject ought to have been told by now that these sad deletions and accretions actually represented a minimalist course and were part of the resistance to Lord Redcliffe-Maude's desire to resurrect the heptarchy and call it by numbers. We are very lucky not to be living in Seven-A.

Muddlesome interference of that sort – regionalism, devolution, authorities put into place like slices of layer cake – is still modish in the political centre. It is that something which is done in response to the question, 'Why don't they do something?' A cynical Peter Walker, if one can imagine such a thing, might just have said, 'Look, local government reorganisation does no real harm; it makes for jobs and spreads money around and I get Green Shield stamps for compassion.' It is a matter of regret that conflict over interventionary policies ceased to be a reasoned debate. In the process important things, like repair of the infrastructure, have been slung out with the same bathwater as metropolitan boroughs or municipal elephantiasis. Walker, of course, is happy wih both: to call him a neo-Keynesian is to make uncalled-for use of the word 'neo'.

He won a measure of affection in Labour hearts by instituting the payment of extensive attendance fees and expenses to councillors in the early seventies, something which was greeted by at least one provincial newspaper with a monthly list of councillors' takings! He believed generally in spreading money around and inflated local authorities so that work once done by little and manageable urban district councils was, in the name of a spurious efficiency, done in larger authorities by two and a half times as many people. The Walker outlook owed a great deal to Mr Pickwick. It derived, like Walker himself, from the pre-accountancy days of the City, where he made money with great zest.

His outlook could have been described as a wish that other men should be as happy as he, a sort of soft-faced capitalism, conscious that every man had his price and hoping that it would be enough. It is totally unmalicious, even it if is by no means sound. But there was always something of the bubble company about Walker's thinking. Money tipped into a sort of Speenhamland system; paid councillors, more officials, more paper circulating, new civic centres to build and the rest of it, creates a local government which is inefficient, too big and deluded about its real place in the scheme of things.

Naturally Mrs Thatcher wishes to smash local government; smashing things is second nature to her. But a disillusionment with local government became quite general as, duped into a foolish vanity, it began to assert itself at the top of a delicious high for which Walker's department had paid. He was using local government as a distribution point in the general reflationary policy, mistaken in itself and disastrous in its application.

Walker would, of course, also claim his part in the Thatcher era. We are told by his press contacts that he was the brain behind selling the council houses. The sale, also attributed to John Stanley, was an incontestable hit and played a major part in the unpeeling of a key strip of the working-class vote from its allegiance, the sort of idea which produced among sensible Labour politicians like Jeff Rooker the thought, 'Why didn't we think of that?'

The style of Walker is an odd thing. He is not a good Commons speaker and knows it. The accent was learned too soon and speaks of the school he would have liked to have gone to and the university he might have chosen. It has a butter-cream quality more glutinous than pleasing, the same accent Gordon Reece got rid of in Mrs Thatcher. Yet he is of an age with Norman Tebbit – authentic North London plus serrated vowels. He would have been wise to let Minchinhampton and Hammersmith, scenes of his boyhood, be their natural selves.

Together with the voice goes a tendency to boast about himself which is left over from early huckstering but is frankly counter-productive and at odds with his soft-focus political image. But he is a nicer, more human person than this self-advertising pout from the promotional manual suggests. I had sight of him one summer in the late eighties on the terrace of the House, entertaining his youngest son Edward, who must have been all of nine, with three other little boys, friends of Edward, for whom he was fussily and affectionately buying soft drinks. It was, if he could know it, a more pleasing image than all the high gloss he ever inexpertly sprayed on himself in the days when he was on the market as an early line of Cecil Parkinson.

None of the externals would matter if the Walker drift of argument were more interesting, but there is something sadly repetitive about the recurring square chords 'one nation' and 'not solving problems by a single solution'. He is using almost the identical words to damn Mrs Thatcher now as he did in 1981. Consistency is fine, but a touch of verbal flair would have been welcome as well. Yet he has to be given credit for courage and a plodding singularity of purpose.

He featured once in an irritating book by Jonathan Aitken called *The Young Meteors*, which might have been subtitled *The Ghastly New Rich*. But the nice thing about Walker is the way – a somewhat older meteor now – he is ready to plod on in a good cause. There is a certain plough-and-burn attitude to Parliament among the ambitious, keen to be off if high-profile office fails to materialise or, as is sometimes the case, it de-materialises. (If the soil were not so naturally rich, one might fear the effects of an Oklahoma dustbowl.)

Walker has never been like that. His will to fight on far

outlasted Mrs Thatcher's wish for his presence. After major office in the Heath government, Ag and Fish was something of a hint, Energy a sharp nudge towards the door and Wales a poke in the eye with a burnt stick. Walker, however, is perhaps like Denis Healey, who passed up any number of out-of-House glories to stay and fight his corner when Labour was being silly and his own advancement was receding. This instinct was also castellated by Walker's decision, often talked about, to take the advice he heard from Fred Marquis, Viscount Woolton, at the start of his career: to make a sufficient fortune first as the means to politics and never be caught *in* politics and wanting money.

Nobody with experience of the City of London clings to Ministerial office for the salary, but there are plenty of politicians anxious to cut and run or give Parliament second place to late-life retrieval of depleted funds. The fact that a Minister is cool-headedly valuable to a company – as lobbyist, intelligence source and flourishable letterheading – adds a twist to public service. It has become the means to subsequent great wealth; and that project will increasingly influence the ambitions of Ministers.

Wales was clearly intended as the sort of insult which sends the uncherished one through the door of his own volition; not so much a poisoned chalice as one patronisingly filled with orangeade! In fact, he has turned the Principality into something of a laboratory for the Walker view and annoyingly, by an intelligent use of such financial discretion as he has (plus some EC goodwill), is able to boast a growth rate twice the national level.

Quite why he spoke out as he did when a cosy continuation of enlightened neo-Keynesianism in Cardiff looked likely is hard to say. Perhaps he knew more than we did, having wind of a coming reshuffle without the option, and in the manner of Cromwell's great Major General, Thomas Harrison, decided to box the hangman's ears before the drawing and quartering. (This is the episode which Pepys sweetly described thus: 'he looking as cheerful as any man could in his condition'.) Perhaps he would have been wiser to pick a full quarrel and resign. But to make it to the Blue Queen's jubilee and to go in creditable bad odour with her, never having eaten dirt, never having conceded her correct view of the universe and having become in the process a sort of clumsy conscience, is no small achievement.*

Yet it is Walker's misfortune to have spent his best years on the wrong side of the fashion. He will be replaced, one supposes, by Michael Howard, an intelligent third murderer willing to do what he is hired for, currently smothering babies in the Tower for Mrs Thatcher. There will be another day, if not for wets then for a species of post-Stalinism – more amiable, relaxed and liberal-minded than the present government in its longing to function as *régime*. Walker has too many nephews and heirs-at-law among the Ministers of State for Mrs Thatcher to be able to bilk the future, hence her passion for staying on; with the death of John Moore, there are no little Thatchers to inherit.

Walker will look like one of those interim figures, a Virgil to future Christians or perhaps more gloomily a John Redmond to the Irish Republic. But, paradoxically, he grew more useful (and attractive) in his later phase. There are young meteors to be seen in politics the way there are plums to buy in Pershore. And the Heath brand of enlightenment was dogmatic itself about the wisdom of buddying up to unions, spending public money and trusting the multiplier effect (in the way of Macaulay's account of James II and the Virgin Mary) to do everything.

Whatever comes after Thatcher will be more sensitive and less hysterically adversarial, but it will be quite different from the Heath and Walker combination of money on trees linked to panic. A synthesis of market economics and social response there will be, and Walker has kept a light burning for it.

---

*Not to go at all, as it worked out, was best of all.

# CHAPTER 33

## *Mr Speaker Bernard Weatherill*

An article appeared in the *Führertreu Daily Mail* complaining that, good fellow though he was, the Speaker of the Commons, Bernard Weatherill, wasn't up to the job. Too many hooligans were getting away with trouble, dignity wasn't what it was, the Speaker was answerable, the Speaker had to go.

It was a pretty half-hearted and shamefaced piece, as it had good reason to be. Information received states that the Editor had that morning received a call in the presence of a third party from some higher instructing source, not within the newspaper, calling for the City Editor, a former sketchwriter, to return to politics for the day and make a bespoke attack on the Speaker.

The involvement of Downing Street in all this is deeply suspected. On the retirement of George Thomas, Mrs Thatcher had made no secret about her wish firstly to have the handsome Humphrey Atkins (a man with most of the intellect of a pit prop) in the job, and her categorical revulsion to the deputy speaker Bernard Weatherill. At some point in the proceedings, a heroic person pointed out to Mrs Thatcher that the Commons, slight and navigable craft though it is given a large majority, does by convention make the choice of Speaker and that the Prime Minister, by convention, does not.

Latterly, Mr Weatherill had made decisions in the chair inconvenient to Ministers. In particular, he had authorised an emergency debate on Social Security after the review announced by John Major. In that debate, as pointed out elsewhere in this book, the government had suffered a sort of cameral Naseby with its case in flight from the field and its Lieutenant-General not expected to recover from his wounds. Now emergency debates are allowed or not on criteria of the seriousness and public relevance of such debates. Since there were to be bitter complaints from the entire House (both government *and* opposition MPs) at the effects of the changes, and since quite significant modifications were subsequently made to effect disqualifications as a result of the debate, the rationale of the government's anger is instructive. It says that an emergency debate ought not to be called as it would focus public discontent upon the government and allow private Members to pursue the interests of their constituents to the great trouble of Ministers; ought not to be called because it would inconvenience government; ought not to be called because a Ministerial spokesman might not be able to answer for and defend his actions.

It was never quite spelt out in such Samantha Fox terms but as naked intimations of a government above both people and debate go it does rather well. This is government by the government and for the government. What made everything ten times worse was that Norman Tebbit, as unofficial envoy, visited the Speaker and threatened that the dogs would be set on him. Overall Norman Tebbit is a very good thing, but he has moments as the Freddy Kruger of politics. This particular piece of intimidation led to his being angrily asked to leave Speaker's House.

As the Speaker of such residual assembly as it tolerated to live, the new politics implied by this episode would require a compound of corporal and under-butler. Such people exist on all hands and it is the administration's tragedy that it had enjoyed the services of just such a public servant (a 'treasure' as Victorian ladies would have called him) that prideless humbleton George Thomas. Thomas had a handsome tenor voice and a lilting, melliloquent Welsh accent, oh he was lovely. He was also a man, naturally abject, who had spent years seeking advancement through the Labour party, but who was pretty keen on advancement from anybody able to give it. Having been Jim Callaghan's little dog in Wales for years, he would bark for anyone else with a decent biscuit. He was also on bad terms with his party of origin, caressing and nurturing various resentments.

Thomas, who adored the Queen Mother, found that he adored Mrs Thatcher. The mark of his Speakership was its ready compliance with the government's wishes. For example, Private Notice Questions are a nuisance to governments and useful both to Oppositions and private Members: Private Notice Questions dropped from the rate of sixty a year under Weatherill's predecessor to single figures. For another, questions to government Ministers about Opposition acts and statements are not normally allowed since they are not the government's responsibility; questions to Ministers, especially the Prime Minister, about Opposition statements and acts were allowed.

Thomas also made a point of thundering at the left and in particular at the disruptive Dennis Skinner, whose contempt for him reached down towards New Zealand. All governments are hungry for obedience, the Tories more so because they are better fed with the commodity. They were not disappointed. In the way of servants, Thomas gave satisfaction.

Weatherill and Thomas had one thing in common. They were distanced from their respective parties. Officially of course all speakers give up their partisan ties, becoming at the hustings 'Mr Speaker seeking re-election'. But it is surprising how often Speakers have felt delightedly liberated from the trammels of the party and its dull certainties. Selwyn Lloyd, snubbed and patronised as a bourgeois for years by Macmillan in an oddly cruel way for such a soft-styled man – 'Where did you say you went to school again Lloyd, Fattus [Fettes] College was it?' – is said to have sat back in the chair and murmured, 'Thank God I don't have to pretend to be a Tory any more.'

That was very reasonable; so, equally, is Weatherill's instinct that a desperately struggling Opposition should be understood and treated well. But George Thomas's desire to join up with the new winning side and to score heavily off his own party as it slipped away from authority was appropriate in one who would achieve elevation to a hereditary peerage.

However Weatherill's differences with his former party,

despite his long-standing wet credentials, have nothing to do with political views. It is a matter of resisting the notion that the chair is an extension of the executive. He has brought the number of PNQs back, almost precisely, to where Selwyn Lloyd left it. And when a question about the Opposition was set up for the Prime Minister he directed that Mrs Thatcher should not answer it. With some trepidation but the abiding courage to keep to his resolution, he has made his own decisions on emergency debates.

He has failings as a Speaker but in essentials he has been magnificent. His little-seen and less-understood function has been to restore the damaged reputation of the Speakership for impartial service to the House of Commons and independence of the executive. In consequence, Norman Tebbit talks about the use of 'the dogs'. One of those was of course that former sketchwriter of the *Mail*. Interestingly, that particular attack did not refer to the offence committed – the calling of an emergency debate – or to the disregard of the sovereign convenience of Ministers. It concentrated, surprisingly, on the lack of discipline against rowdyism in the Commons: the Speaker, it announced, couldn't control the hooligans.

The short answer to this is that no one controls the noise from both sides, which creates a worse impression when transmitted by radio than when heard in the Gallery. (Though some of us there may have uncommonly high thresholds for noise.) But anyway, despite his background as a cavalry officer and deputy Chief Whip, Weatherill is not a disciplinarian. He has the wisdom, even though it works against him, to have deep respect for the convictions of people like Dennis Skinner and Dave Nellist. He is a reluctant expeller, understanding the perfect convictions which move them to do tiresome things. It is a fair point against him that when he does throw people out he should get on with it; he asks for a last concession too often.

But really this, like his occasional dithering over a name: 'Mr Fred Blenkinsop, that is, sorry, Mr Claud Wotherspoon', is the least and littlest of sins in the chair. Speakers are not judged for their talents as drill corporals. The House does not behave worse in this Parliament than it did before 1983. It behaves rather better than it did in the days when Ulster Unionists were throwing missiles at the head of Winston Churchill. No one would be complaining in the official gazette about indiscipline if the Speaker concerned was suppressing the emergency debates required of him.

Weatherill's Speakership is anyway an extension of his own personal balance of the conventional and unconventional. Service as a Bengal Lancer ought to have produced a standard cavalry colonel. In fact, Weatherill came out of the army preoccupied by the hunger he had seen. His vegetarianism is partly a side product of this, though he has been heard to quote Rupert Brooke's poem about fish safe beyond the reach of anglers.

Membership of a family firm of tailors in Windsor with a royal appointment ought to have produced a toady. As illustrated, it did not. (Though the lady whose jodhpurs Weatherills make will not have felt too tragically about inconveniences caused to the alternative monarch.) The abiding Weatherill quality is one of affectionate humanity laced with a touch of devilment.

Happily, in a serious Christian, he can hit interesting heights of profanity. The reference to Jonathan Aitken, someone he regards with particular affection, as 'that fucker', clean into a microphone, was a source of general delight, not least to Aitken. Despite the sweetness, he is not a prig. 'The job I had in the Whips' office,' he has observed, 'was the shits' Whip.' He must, mathematically, have done his share of bullying but that idea lacks conviction. He is genuinely kind and solicitous, not an unknown quality among Whips by the way, there being more ways than one of killing a cat: the machiavellian Garrel-Jones, drawing on the barbarous instincts of the mob he runs like hounds, the soft-spoken Peter Lloyd, the deeply reasonable David Hunt are all exemplars of the genus as much as the menacing Lightbown. And the half-suppressed hysteria of Douglas Hogg actually rendered him incapable of doing the job.

But the Speaker – unlike Whips, especially unlike Whips –

must function alone. If we take the job seriously at the high constitutional level, the Speaker can have no allies, no ordinary discourse outside the social level. He is cut off from the casual places of the House – smoking room, terrace and so on – remaking his contacts only on his own ground at Speaker's House.

Whips by contrast are an intensification of the party role. They are the sinews of its purpose. They function as a pack to make the party function as nearly together as it perfectly can. Life must, for a Whip, be taken by the elbow and offered a drink or disclosure of the name of its mistress. As for equity and balance, no Whip worth his salt would recognise them under a spotlight.

How is it, one wonders, that recurringly Whips are recruited to the Speaker's panel and how frequently they prove singular, independent and unwhiplike? A recent elevation, Norman Hogg, did precisely Weatherill's job (deputy Chief) on the Labour side. He failed to become Chief Whip by a single vote in a run against Neil Kinnock's lumpen crony, Derek Forster. Yet Hogg has the qualities to be a Speaker in the Weatherill style – mild, gentle and persuasive. Yet another former deputy Chief Whip is John Cope, who perhaps most of all has the qualities for a superb, but mild and soothing Speaker.

The point is that you may function best in the rough world of Whips by being so liked that people don't like to fight you and so reasonable that, against judgement, they go along.

A magisterial Speaker like Onslow, who put the whole thing together in the eighteenth century, is in a class of his own, and heavy oppressive martinets like FitzRoy would provoke serious trouble today. At present the Commons is a quieter place than it was when there were a hundred separatist Irish in the place, but more difficult than in the sleepy fifties. But the Chair's troubles are partly a therapeutic exploitation of the House's own powerlessness. It gets angry, fairly spontaneously for the Labour left, synthetically for Garrel-Jones's rowing-men's militia, precisely because it doesn't matter very much.

In the circumstances drill corporals are irrelevant. The House, feeling neglected, needs soothing and talking out of escapades more than it needs barking at. But with the executive ever more peremptory (and I doubt if Mr Kinnock riding high would be hesitant about clicking his fingers), the first duty of the Chair is to recall that its occupant is not a government appointment or functionary. A Speaker threatened and bullied by government in the third Parliament of a large majority for not obliging it is a Speaker getting it right.

In his quiet way, Jack Weatherill should be remembered for defending Parliament. The cult of personality will not last for ever. When governments in their arrogance talk through spokesmen of turning on the dogs, when hirelings are directed to destroy someone through a liveried press, something is grievously wrong. The assault on the Speaker was part of the same impulse that created the GCHQ ban, the Ponting and Tisdall trials, the Zircon raid on the BBC and so many more undertakings which hardly need a Speaker or his Parliament at all. Bernard Weatherill will be remembered, and highly, for a brave refusal of compliance.